Oliver Milner is a pseudonym. *Memory Stick* is typical of the type of conversations we've all had about ourselves at some time or other, "Some of the facts may be distorted by time," as Laurie Lee once wrote sagaciously.

The author was born in Yorkshire, but grew up in post Biafran War Nigeria and boarding schools in England.

His career started at the *Financial Times* but not too soon after he lost his Territorial Army commission in the Intelligence Corps, uncovered a spy, met Madonna, Mad Dog Adair, various Prime Ministers, a Nobel Peace Prize Laureate and an X-rated film director.

Today he lives near Epping Forest, in the UK. He is married and has two grown up daughters, a tortoise, a Labradoodle, two cats and some sickly-looking runner beans.

To my (as yet unborn) grandchildren. We may never meet. But at least you'll have an idea of who (I thought) I was. And so, in part, where you're from. With all my love.

Oliver Milner

MEMORY STICK

To Katherine,

Hope you enjoy it – a review
would be really appreciated!

Best wishes,
Oliver Milner
June 2022

AUSTIN MACAULEY PUBLISHERS™

LONDON • CAMBRIDGE • NEW YORK • SHARJAH

A CIP catalogue record for this title is available from the British Library.

ISBN 9781398427013 (Paperback)
ISBN 9781398427020 (ePub e-book)

www.austinmacauley.com

First Published 2022
Austin Macauley Publishers Ltd®
1 Canada Square
Canary Wharf
London
E14 5AA

I would like to thank the Covid-19 outbreak for giving me the focus and drive to do something whilst on furlough in 2020. This book, after all, has taken 30 years to create, but 30 days to write. Actually, the amazing free resource – Wiki History, provided all the footnotes, proving, as if any proof was needed, that everyone has a *Memory Stick* inside them. Thank you to the warriors on the internet for providing such a resource.

Thank you to the many driving forces behind this book, but in particular a clutch of particularly inspirational teachers, Sheffield Exham, Roger Beaufoy, Val Hague and Peter Heywood. If this is any good, it is largely down to them.

Finally, and above, all to my family who appear anonymised across these pages. Haven't you suffered enough?

1961, London. Harrogate, North Yorkshire, England

Sunday, January 1, Well Hello, At Last

I've always thought all of us born in a strobogrammatic year should stick together. As *MAD Magazine* pointed out on its cover for the March 1961 issue, this was the first *upside-up* year – i.e., one in which the numerals that form the year look the same as when the numerals are rotated upside down, a strobogrammatic number – since 1881. The next such year will be 6009.

I appreciate the likelihood of my meeting someone born in the next anniversary of a strobogrammatic year is…slim, but for this fact, I am indebted to Wikipedia. Most of the footnotes and links owe their origin to the free, extraordinary, online encyclopaedia. Which I always used to think must be infinite. Until you start writing a history of oneself, and then you realise, uh oh, what to include and what to exclude?

I might be here all day. Hopefully, so might you reading this. Or in the case of my wife and daughter who read faster than Concorde [see p. 166], then the next hour and a half.

So, what happened next?

1961 (MCMLXI) was a common year starting on Sunday of the Gregorian calendar, the 1961st year of the Common Era (CE) and *Anno Domini* (AD) designations, the 961st year of the 2nd millennium, the 61st year of the twentieth century, and the 2nd year of the 1960s decade.

The year doesn't start well.[1]

---

[1] January 3 – Cuba: nuclear Armageddon is threatened, off the coast of Florida: US President Dwight D. Eisenhower announces that the USA has severed diplomatic and consular relations with Cuba (Cuba/US relations are restored in 2015).

Wednesday, January 4, Nuclear Cats

Erwin Schrödinger, he of the famous cat, the Austrian physicist and Nobel Prize laureate (b. 1887), dies. But has he *really*? Schrödinger theorised that if you placed a cat, a flask of poison and a radioactive source in a sealed box, and if using a Geiger counter once the flask of poison was released killing the cat, the Copenhagen interpretation of quantum mechanics implies that after a while, the cat is *simultaneously* alive *and* dead. Yet when one looks in the box, one sees the cat *either* alive *or* dead, not both alive and dead. This poses the question of when exactly quantum superposition ends and reality collapses into one possibility or the other. Clearly.

As if impossibly complex theories weren't enough in the *physical* world, atomic bombs nearly went off. *By mistake…*

Friday, January 20, JFK, 101

John F. Kennedy is sworn in as the 35th president of the USA. Four days later, a B-52 Stratofortress, with two nuclear bombs, crashes near Goldsboro, North Carolina.

More interesting for younger people, *Disney's One Hundred and One Dalmatians* is released in cinemas five days later. So, bearing in mind, I found *101* absolutely terrifying when I saw it 10 years later, the old film's fared pretty well.

That's the beauty of cartoon villains; they age very slowly.

Television loomed large too in the early 1960s. There wasn't much else to do except sit in front of the box. Most households had a TV set, although the world was broadcast to us in black and white. When eventually colour was discovered to exist, we turned our back on such alchemy. It took a while to appreciate that cartoons might not be better in grey.

One of my favourite programmes – when I was old enough to be propped up and deposited in front of the TV – was *Pogles' Wood*.

The Pogles were tiny magical beings who lived in a hollow tree in a wood. The four principals were Mr and Mrs Pogle, their adopted son Pippin, and a squirrel-like creature named Tog, who was Pippin's playmate.

Obviously, I was Tog. The initial episode only had a single showing. The story centred on a dark and evil old shape-changing witch.

The overall tone was so sinister and disturbing the BBC declared it *too frightening* for its proposed inclusion in *Watch with Mother*,[2] which had a very young audience, and all future episodes revolve around more everyday countryside matters.

I thought Andy Pandy was rubbish. I also hated Bill and Ben, the Flower Pot Men – *flob a dob* – but I loved the *Wooden Tops*. Later that was followed by *Trumpton*.

Later still, I wanted to breathe for extended periods underwater with the use of oxygum, with my TV best friend Marine Boy. He had jet boots that propelled him underwater and an electric boomerang. But the best part – the childhood secret of every child born in the 1960s, the grownups don't seem to have noticed – his mermaid girlfriend Neptima, was *topless* (although her hair always covered her breasts.)

What a show.

No disrespect to my mother either, but the person I most wanted to be tucked up into bed by was *Blue Peter's* Valerie Singleton. She could make anything, so long as she never said the word *Sellotape* live on air, all was well with the world.

Sticky backed plastic held our world together.

---

[2] *Watch with Mother* was a cycle of children's programmes created by Freda Lingstrom and Maria Bird. Broadcast from 1952 until 1975, it was the first BBC television series aimed specifically at pre-school children, a development of BBC radio's equivalent *Listen with Mother*, which had begun two years earlier. In accordance with its intended target audience of pre-school children viewing with their mothers, *Watch with Mother* was initially broadcast between 3:45 pm and 4:00 pm, post-afternoon nap and before the older children came home from school. The choice of the title for the series was intended to deflect fears that television might become a nursemaid to children and encourage 'bad mothering'. *Trumpton's* fire brigade: Pugh, Pugh, Barney McGrew, Cuthbert, Dibble, and Grubb is perhaps *Trumpton's* most-recognised feature. Captain Flack's roll call voiced by Brian Cant was recited in all but one episode: puppeteer Gordon Murray has explained that Pugh and Pugh are twins you must understand – not Hugh, Pugh.

Thursday, February 9, FAB 4

The Beatles perform for the first time at The Cavern Club. For all the fuss, the Fab Four formulate, I much prefer Prince[3], however, the Beatles' impact on social history is so profound they'll make several appearances later on.

Even Prince's girlfriend appears later too (see p. 197).

Monday, March 6, Turned out Nice Again

Bad start to the week: sadly it *didn't* turn out nice again today, for him; George Formby, British singer, comedian and actor (b. 1904), dies. One of the first singles I later bought was *When I'm Cleaning Windows*. From memory, the B-side was *Mr Wu's a Window Cleaner Now*.

Today, it's hard to see why the BBC banned him for gentle innuendo.

Three cheers to the Wigan Ukulele Society for keeping it up. And his memory alive.

Sunday, April 9, Zog

King Zog I of Albania (b. 1895) dies. He was also the 11th prime minister of Albania, and its 7th president. Clearly, a busy man.

Who knew there was a King Zog?

Wednesday, April 12, Hero #1

No respecter of the passing of King Zog, the USSR celebrates an event to which world history owes it a whole page.

Taking off in Vostok 1, Soviet cosmonaut Yuri Gagarin becomes the first human in space, orbiting the Earth once before parachuting to the ground.

Monday, April 17, Pigs, Invade

The Bay of Pigs Invasion of Cuba begins; it fails by April 19.

---

[3] American musician Prince Rogers Nelson (better known as Prince, aka Symbol for a mad few years) was born June 7, 1958 – died April 21, 2016. As a writer and performer, I think, he and Mozart would have been soul mates, mutually admiring the other's talent. What I would pay for a gig to see them perform together. Especially as The Beatles, The Rolling Stones, Kate Bush and ACDC are the warm up acts…

The day after Fidel Castro announces that the Bay of Pigs Invasion has been defeated. Classic.

Well done, America!

Monday, May 5, Hero #2

Not to be outdone by the USSR, the American's space programme finally makes headlines: total legend Alan Shepard becomes the first American in space, aboard Mercury-Redstone 3.

Well done, America, but you were second. "The first man gets the oyster, the second man gets the shell," as Andrew Carnegie might have added.

Thursday, May 25, the Other Things

This isn't a diary about space travel, I promise. But this *was* a big speech: President Kennedy announces, before a special joint session of Congress, his goal to put a man on the Moon before the end of the decade.

The Apollo programme has begun, which would delight this little boy all his life. You could jump forward to the Moon landing (see p. 65), but wait, I've not been born yet.

In fact the famous *Moon speech* occurred 18 months later, four days after my first birthday, in which JFK said: "We choose to go to the moon in this decade and do the other things, not because they are easy, but because they are hard, because that goal will serve to organise and measure the best of our energies and skills, because that challenge is one that we are willing to accept, one we are unwilling to postpone, and one which we intend to win, and the others, too."

The bit I always find amusing is, *And do the other things*, as if there was a list of other things he thought, nah, this speech is good enough with the moon bit.

He was right of course.

Sunday, July 2, Bang

Another celebrity death: Ernest Hemingway, American writer, Nobel Prize laureate (b. 1899), committed suicide. Have you actually tried reading his masterpiece *The Old Man and the Sea?* It's like *Waiting for Godot*, only with less action.

Sunday, August 6, Hero #3

Here, just because no one ever remembers his name – who was it that said "history is only ever written by the victors"?[4] Vostok 2 fires Soviet cosmonaut Gherman Titov into space and he becomes the second human to orbit the Earth, and the first to be in outer space for more than one day. And lands successfully the following day.

Thursday, September 7, Cartoons

Tom and Jerry make a return with their first episode since 1958, *Switchin' Kitten*. The new creator, Gene Deitch, makes 12 more Tom and Jerry episodes over the next twelve months.

Saturday, September 9, Ta Da

At 04:20 hrs (GMT) I am born. In Harrogate General Hospital, England. I am almost a month older than Meg Ryan and Nadia Comaneci.

Saturday, September 30, Politics, a Dirty Business, Funny Too

The Organisation for Economic Co-operation and Development (OECD) is formed. Thankfully. At last.

Replacing the Organisation for European Economic Co-operation (OEEC). Hurrah. What a difference a vowel makes. And everyone laughed at Monty Python's *Judean Popular People's Front*, in 1977.

Politics is bonkers. Or as my dad said, "Show me a politician and I'll show you a crook." It didn't stop him from helping me when I decided to run for Parliament. Although I think, he thought I'd dodged a bullet when I came second on election night in 2005.

That wonderful scene from *Life of Brian*:

> REG: Listen. The only people we hate more than the Romans are the f*****g Judean People's Front.
> P.F.J.: Yeah…
> JUDITH: Splitters.

---

[4] Winston Churchill, apparently, paraphrasing Hermann Goering.

FRANCIS: And the Judean Popular People's Front.

P.F.J.: Yeah. Oh, yeah. Splitters. Splitters…

LORETTA: And the People's Front of Judea.

P.F.J.: Yeah. Splitters…

REG: What?

LORETTA: The People's Front of Judea. Splitters.

REG: We're the People's Front of Judea!

LORETTA: Oh. I thought we were the Popular Front?

REG: People's Front! C-huh.

FRANCIS: Whatever happened to the Popular Front, Reg?

REG: He's over there[5].

Sunday, December 31, Wheezing Away

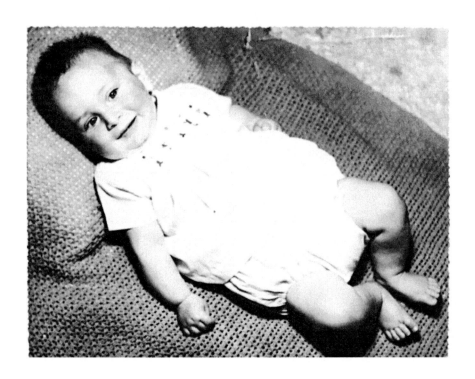

---

[5] Back in the autumn of 1961, three wonderful artistic endeavours happen:

October 18 – *West Side Story* is released as a film in the United States.

October 19 – The first edition of *Private Eye*, the British satirical magazine, is published.

November 10 – *Catch-22* by Joseph Heller is first published.

My First New Year's Eve! How Exciting. Well, Hardly

Like all babies, on family photos I look just like every other baby; trussed up in a babygrow and swathed in woollen baby blankets on a feather pillow. And of course, the photos are in black and white, printed on matt paper and protected in a leatherette photo album.

Assuming the chill of a North Yorkshire winter was bad for my feeble asthmatic lungs, my mother kept me warm, indoors. I rarely saw the sun and had the skin to prove it. Meanwhile, my little lungs did their best not to inflate and my anxious parents were in an out of Leeds General Infirmary (faster than something very fast, angry clackers?). What was wrong? There was nothing wrong, with me.

The consultant blamed the weather.

So my parents resolved to leave grey Great Britain, on the cusp of exploding as the centre of the Swinging Sixties, and settled in civil war-ravaged Nigeria.

Into the sunlight and back a century. A great choice.

Turns out the wool and the goose feathers were making it hard for me to breath. A heaf test years later reveals I'm also allergic to grass pollen, horsehair, cat faeces, buttons, goose feathers and wool.

I know what you're thinking. Just avoid cantering across a cricket pitch on a horse covered in cat shit? I've avoided it so far.

The buttons? I'll explain, later.

But we're jumping ahead. Asthma wasn't a global thing until I was five, the year when England wins the Football World Cup on Saturday, July 30, 1966. The match was contested against West Germany, with England winning 4–2 after extra time to claim the Jules Rimet Trophy.

1962 Leeds, West Yorkshire, Northern England

Earth continues its journey through space at 1.3 million miles per hour, revolving around the Sun at 67,000 miles per hour and turning on its axis at 1,000 miles an hour approximately.

My second year on earth came and went.

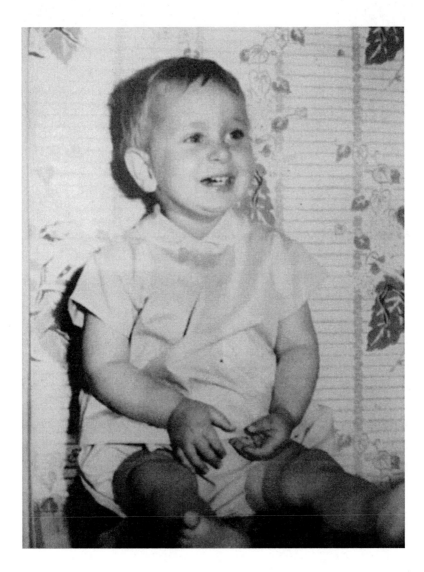

Happy and smiling now, but moments later the terror of Manston Crescent as I plucked out all the feathers from Auntie Joan's wedding hat. Well, who left it on the bed anyway whilst they were waiting for the wedding cars?
(Note the wallpaper – from a distance don't those look like lungs, rather than bugloss leaves?)

1963, Leeds. Harrogate, North Yorkshire, Northern England

In 1963, the world stood still and remembered where it was – except me, I was only two years old – when they heard that John FitzGerald Kennedy, the 35th president of the United States, was assassinated on November 22, 1963, at 12:30 p.m. Central Standard Time in Dallas.

See also Grassy Knoll.

Also this year, Ndabaningi Sithole founded the Zimbabwe African National Union, a militant organisation that opposed the government of Rhodesia, in July 1963. A member of the Ndau ethnic group, he also worked as a Methodist minister. He spent 10 years in prison after the government banned ZANU. And my later ability to pronounce his name when I was at Malsis means that Mr Sithole is an early front-runner on my *Names to Cherish* list (see p. 75).

The Reverend Canaan Banana (and Cardinal Sin) also makes the *Names to Cherish* list, (ibid.). But for different reasons.[6]

---

[6] Canaan Sodindo Banana (5 March 1936 – 10 November 2003) was a Zimbabwean Methodist minister, theologian, and politician who served as the first president of Zimbabwe from 1980 to 1987. He was Zimbabwe's first head of state after the Lancaster House Agreement that led to the country's independence. In 1997, Banana was arrested in Zimbabwe on charges of sodomy, following accusations made during the murder trial of his former bodyguard, Jefta Dube. Dube, a policeman, had shot dead Patrick Mashiri, an officer who had taunted him about being Banana's homosexual wife. He split [geddit] to South Africa whilst released on bail before he could be imprisoned, apparently believing Mugabe was planning his death. He returned to Zimbabwe in December 1998, after a meeting with Nelson Mandela, who convinced him to face the ruling. Banana was sentenced to ten years in jail; nine years suspended, and was also defrocked. Banana died of cancer in 2003.

Cardinal Sin was also the 30th Roman Catholic Archbishop of Manila instrumental in the 1986 People Power Revolution, which toppled the regime of President Ferdinand

1964, Harrogate

Quiet, again. Not much of note for me. Be fair, I am just three years old.

"The boy who is waiting for something to turn up might start on his shirt sleeves."[7]

This is also a Winter Olympics year, (Innsbruck, Austria), and it follows a pattern through my life of being totally disinterested in anything performed in the cold or in ice and snow. Give me a beach holiday any day.

That said, Torvill and Dean, John Curry, Robin Cousins, Amy Williams, Lizzy Yarnold and of course Eddy the Eagle, do capture my imagination during their few weeks of fame.

Saturday, February 1, No 1

Just so, we're keeping track of the Fab Four's progress: The Beatles vault to the #1 spot on the US singles charts for the first time, with *I Want to Hold Your Hand*.

Saturday, April 25, Introducing: Leeds United

And if I wasn't just three and a half years old, this would be my best news of the year.

PROMOTED! Leeds United football club win the 1963/64 Second Division title, thanks to the stewardship of manager Don Revie. Hold on to your scarves and rattles. It's going to get exciting, for Leeds' fans.

Meanwhile some other stuff happened in 1964.[8]

Marcos and installed Corazon Aquino as his successor. He died peacefully on 21 June 2005 and is buried in the Philippines.

[7] Attributed to Gareth Heinrichs.

[8] February 25 – Cassius Clay (later Muhammad Ali) beats Sonny Liston in Miami Beach, Florida, and is crowned the heavyweight champion of the world.

February 27 – The Italian government asks for help to keep the Leaning Tower of Pisa from toppling over.

March 15 – Richard Burton and Elizabeth Taylor marry (for the first time) in Montreal.

June 16 – Keith Bennett, 12, is abducted by Myra Hindley and Ian Brady in the north of England. His body has never been found.

June 19 – Boris Johnson born. See also 24 July 2019, becomes the prime minister of UK.

1965, Harrogate

Saturday, January 30: Hats Off, Hats On

The cranes along the Thames all bowed in respect as the body of Britain's most famous and surely favourite statesmen wended its way through London. My life has been peppered by Churchill aphorisms, quoted by teachers or friends. Possibly, the most notorious is his exchange with Bessie Braddock: "Winston, you're drunk!"

"Bessie, you're ugly. But tomorrow I shall be sober."

Often confused with his exchange to Nancy Astor: "Winston, I were your wife I'd put poison in your coffee."

"If I were your husband, I'd drink it."

This being the day of his funeral, these words ring true, and could only be his: "I am ready to meet my Maker. Whether my Maker is ready for the ordeal of meeting me is another matter."

The state funeral of Sir Winston Churchill was broadcast live on the BBC and seen around the world. It was the first state funeral of a politician in the century and the biggest national event since the Coronation of 1953. I have seen the footage of the ceremony so many times it's etched in my mind. Could I have been there? Was I?

No. We lived in a small terraced house in Manston Crescent, Leeds.

My parents: Jerry Milner m. Mary Agnew, March 1961. He was a trainee bank clerk in London, making ends meet by 1965 for his young family by also cleaning buses at night to bring in some extra money, and at the weekends going

---

August 27 – Walt Disney's Mary Poppins has its world premiere in Los Angeles. It will go on to win five Academy Awards, including a Best Actress for Julie Andrews. It is the first Disney film to be nominated for Best Picture.

October 10–24 – The 1964 Summer Olympics are held in Tokyo, Japan, the first in an Asian country.

on Territorial Army training with the Royal Parachute Regiment. Prior to meeting Mum, he had joined the regiment during his National Service. Unlucky for many, 1965 was the last year when National Service for all men aged 18 was scrapped, but it was one of the highlights of my father's career. He qualified for the SAS and saw active service in Aden and Cyprus. Sometime in 1960, he contracted what was later diagnosed as malaria and woke up in the Royal Free Hospital, London, on the tropical diseases ward. In the care of Nurse Agnew. How he survived that is even more impressive than his prowess in hand-to-hand combat.

Mother: was a nurse (as above).

Incredibly, Dad recovered and asked Mary out.

It was a major dent in both their futures that their one night of passion resulted in my conception one January evening. They married in March 1961. With a baby on the way, the race was on to find a home, which they did eventually in Leeds where Auntie Joan, Mum's spinster sister and 13 years her senior, was a health visitor and their mum, a housekeeper/cook. Another sister, Harriet, 12 years older than Mum, quickly escaped the Agnews and married quickly.

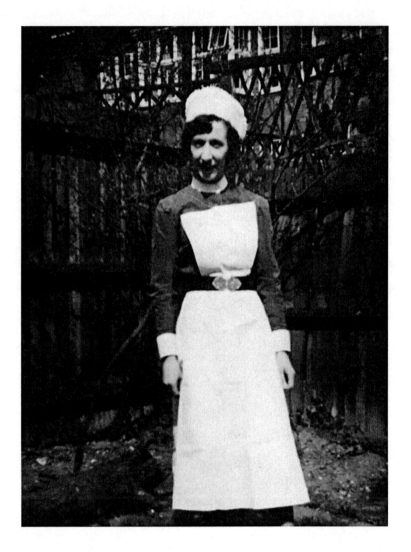

London, 1960: Another nurse in the family. This one is my scary Auntie Joan, who preceded my mother and cousin Julia who both trained and qualified at the Royal Free Hospital, Hampstead.

Their mother Margaret had four names. Joan and Harriet called her 'Mother'; my mother called her 'Mummy' and we children called her 'Nana'.

Their father Arthur, deceased, 1961, had been for most of his life a professional observer of equine fitness and stamina.

Sadly for his family, his professional investments at the turf accountants and bookmakers rarely turned the hoped for profit and Margaret fought beak and claws during and for fifteen years after the war to ward off the bailiffs and keep her three girls in school uniforms, spam, dripping and corned beef.

Completing the character line up at this time was my favourite uncle. Uncle Desmond was a spectacular hypochondriac but also the kindest and gentlest person I ever met. And he loved me. Which was just as well because my young mother, she was only in her early twenties herself, found me a real handful.

Perhaps because she was insecure around me, I played up all the time, and when I wasn't being naughty, I was being ill. At times, frightened out of my wits – and hers – as I struggled to breathe for no apparent reason, childhood asthmas in the 1960s were poorly understood and my wheezing seemed as fickle as my moods.

Harrogate 1961: A major dent in their futures. Mr and Mrs Milner, my parents.

23

Uncle Desmond (always *Des*) invariably behaved as if he had walked off a page of Jeeves and Wooster. *By jingo's*, *Heavens to Betsy, gosh, by George*, and *cripes* were antiquated phrases even in Wodehouse's day, but Des clung on. Similarly, he hung on to his rounded collars and floral ties long after kaftans and flares had come and made their exit on the British fashion scene.

He was great fun.

His wife Joan, on the other hand, frightened me and I always found her spikey and easy to take offence. It took particularly deft peacekeeping from Des and my mum to stop Joan from walking out forever when I called her a whiskered witch.

I'd be eight or nine. She was tending my chicken pox with calamine lotion at the time – Mum must have been at work – and in spite of being a health visitor, she was really clumsy. It was unfair to call her a witch. But she did have fur on her face like a peach, and never sought to remove it.

But Des and Joan were loyal to us. They'd married late in life, both of them believing, I imagine that, they would be single forever. In my eyes, they were perpetually sixty. They had no children of their own. In the years that followed when my parents were in Nigeria, they acted as in loco parentis. Taking me and my trunk in the back of their green DAF 33 to boarding school. And attending every school concert and play, picking me up for half terms and taking me to the airport when it was time to fly to Nigeria for the holidays.

They were a very odd couple indeed but loved each other deeply in their other worldly fashion.

But of life in Leeds, then, I have little memory. Other than in my parents' bedroom, they appeared to have wallpaper with a repeat pattern of lungs, bronchus and trachea attached. The family photo album bears out some justification for this. The leaves of the Siberian bugloss plant, which was the actual decoration on the wallpaper, do look like human lungs.

The rest of the year is a terrific one for the three of us.
West Africa beckons.[9]

---

[9] Also in 1965:

January 4 – T. S. Eliot, American-British poet, Nobel Prize laureate (b. 1888), dies.

February 6 – English footballer Sir Stanley Matthews plays his final First Division game, at the record age of 50 years and 5 days

February 15 – Nat King Cole, American singer and musician (b. 1919), dies.

1966, Apapa, West Lagos, Nigeria

Sunday, January 10, Splott

The Commonwealth Prime Ministers' Conference convenes in Lagos, Nigeria.

So we'd left the Milners in Leeds. What happens next is really quite remarkable.

Whilst my dad was still a paratrooper (heavy drop), the prospect of him and my mother becoming parents made her persuade him to give up life as an action man and wear a suit and tie, as a trainee bank clerk for Lloyds Bank in London.

Within four years, Mum and Dad had saved sufficient money for a deposit on a three-bedroom house, 9 Oval View in Harrogate, cost £6,000. And within four and a half years, my father answered a call from Standard and Chartered Bank of West Africa for bank staff with four plus years' banking experience and a willingness to travel abroad to be a deputy financial controller of the Standard Chartered branch in Apapa, Lagos, Nigeria.

March 2 – Vietnam War: Operation Rolling Thunder – The United States Air Force 2nd Air Division, United States Navy and South Vietnamese Air Force begin a 3½-year aerial bombardment campaign against North Vietnam. The film *The Sound of Music* premieres in New York.

April 23 – The Pennine Way officially opens.

May 1 – FA Cup Final, Liverpool 2, Leeds 1. Fluke.

July 27 – Edward Heath becomes leader of the British Conservative Party.

August 1 – Cigarette advertising is banned on British television.

October 29 – Moors murders: Ian Brady and Myra Hindley appear in court, charged with the murders of Edward Evans (17), Lesley Ann Downey (10), and John Kilbride (12) from Manchester.

November 7 – The Pillsbury Company's mascot, the Pillsbury Doughboy, is created in the USA. David Lean's film *Doctor Zhivago*, starring Omar Sharif and Julie Christie, is released.

For a lad from Splott, with only half his banking qualifications, the old man did exceptionally well for his family. For the next decade, he and my mother enjoyed the last throes of the British Empire. Then one day, his job at the bank was Nigerianised, and he escaped with his life, just.

He subsequently jumped at the chance to work in a gentler regime – the Middle East – but we're leaping ahead. Growing up in Wales, I think my father was keen to leave as soon as he could. A bit like Dylan Thomas: "Wales is the land of my fathers. And my fathers can have it."

Nineteen sixty-nine was about to become a very busy one for any political studies student of Nigeria's history.

Friday, January 15, Mayhem

A bloody military *coup* is staged in Nigeria, deposing the civilian government and resulting in the death of Prime Minister Abubakar Tafawa Balewa.

Samuel Akintola, Nigerian premier of the Western region and Aare Ona Kakanfo XIII of the Yoruba (b. 1910) are assassinated as well as Abubakar Tafawa Balewa, Nigerian politician, first prime minister of Nigeria (assassinated) (b. 1912) and Ahmadu Bello, Nigerian premier of the Northern region (assassinated) (b. 1910).

Sunday, January 17, Mayhem and Vietnam

The Nigerian coup is overturned by another faction of the military, leaving a military government in power. This is the beginning of a long period of military rule.

Over in Asia – a world away – the globe's attention is watching with mounting concern about 8,000 US soldiers landing in South Vietnam; US troops now total 190,000. Nigeria, the ex-British colony, barely ranks a footnote in the morning papers.

Friday, January 22, More Mayhem

The military government of Nigeria announces that ex-prime minister Abubakar Tafawa Balewa was killed during the coup.

So perhaps it wasn't so strange that the young man from Splott, who had the same amount of experience in the paras as he had as a cashier, was chosen for a potentially dangerous role in West Africa. He knew how to handle himself.

Like most married couples, Mum and Dad were forever bickering, not on the scale of Burton and Taylor (see p. 11) but there was much to be said for absence making the heart grow fonder. Quite peculiarly, whenever my father was away for several months on his return to the UK, my mother would sneeze for several days afterwards. It didn't seem to happen when we went out to visit him, but I'm sure she was allergic to him in some way.

Back to 1966: he flew on ahead to Lagos, Nigeria's largest city on its Atlantic coast.

Mum and I were to follow later, by ship on the SS Accra, with our crockery, some furniture and personal affects wrapped in paper, stuffed in empty tea boxes, and three trunks each filled with our clothes.

Nana moved in to 9 Oval View to make sure the water didn't freeze in the pipes whilst we were away. Bless him; my father essentially bought her a house. At last, now she could stop moving from temporary cleaning job to temporary cleaning job.

If his intention had been that she was just a temporary lodger, as the family were told, it didn't work out like that. She lived there with us for twelve years.

Meanwhile England, but London in particular, was getting ready for a general election and the Football World Cup.[10]

---

[10] February 28 – British Prime Minister Harold Wilson calls a general election in the UK, to be held on March 31.

March 1 – The British Government announces plans for the decimalisation of the pound sterling (hitherto denominated in 20 shillings and 240 pence to the £) to come into force in February 1971 (Decimal Day).

March 10 – *The Frost Report*, which launched the television careers of John Cleese, Ronnie Barker and Ronnie Corbett and also the careers of other writers and performers, is first broadcast on BBC.

March 31 – The British Labour Party led by Harold Wilson wins the general election, gaining a 96-seat majority (compared with a single seat majority when the election was called on February 28).

Friday, March 4, Imagine

In an interview with *Evening Standard* reporter Maureen Cleave, John Lennon of The Beatles states that they are "more popular than Jesus now".

Sunday, March 20, My Legend

Football's Jules Rimet Trophy is stolen while on exhibition in London; it is found seven days later by a mongrel dog named Pickles and his owner David Corbett, wrapped in newspaper in a south London garden.

Leeds United's Norman Hunter is selected for the England 1966 squad but was forever on the subs bench waiting for Bobby Moore or Jack Charlton to make way. Neither did, and so in spite of being in the squad, Hunter never even picked up a World Cup winner's medal, which at the time were only given to the 11 players on the pitch at full time.

Perhaps that's why he became the Leeds player I idolised. Brilliant, but not yet the household name he deserved to become.

Thursday, April 21, Child Killing

Although I was young, I was sufficiently receptive to pick up when the grown-ups were sad. Especially so about this story which dominated the TV news. Ian Brady and Myra Hindley went on trial at Chester Crown Court for the murders of three children who vanished between November 1963 and October 1965.

The trial ended early the next month with Ian Brady being found guilty on all three counts of murder and sentenced to three concurrent terms of life imprisonment.

Myra Hindley was convicted on two counts of murder and of being an accessory in the third murder committed by Brady, and received two concurrent terms of life imprisonment and a seven-year fixed term for being an accessory.

It's a story that has haunted my generation for over fifty years. Both my Nana and Mum would shed a tear for the mothers not being able to bury their children whenever the story was reported on the TV. Over the years, the search for the missing children took place from time to time with the two murderers extending the families' grief as they toyed with the police's efforts to find the remains, buried somewhere in the vast Saddleworth Moor, in Lancashire.

I was sat watching the TV with my mother decades later when Hindley's death was announced.

"Those poor mothers," she said, and dabbed her eyes.

Saturday, April 30, On a Cushion of Air

Another icon of the age started life this month.

Regular hovercraft service begins over the English Channel (discontinued in 2000 due to the Channel Tunnel). I liked travelling on the British Rail hovercraft to Calais. It was possible to go on a day trip and many of us did, just so we could say we'd been on one. The sensation was much more like flying than sailing with the exception that there were more seats across the body of the cabin than in an aircraft. Presumably, although they appeared big, the number of people each hovercraft could carry was probably no more than several carriage loads on a train.[11]

You could see why the Channel Tunnel won out – bigger economies of scale. However, the Swinging Sixties were still about to catch a wave.

Monday, May 16, Surfing, Sailing

The legendary album *Pet Sounds* by The Beach Boys is released.

Back on the SS Apapa, Mum is having a lovely time entertaining any bachelors who were, like my father, on their way to Nigeria to make their fortunes. Companies like Barclays, Lever Brothers, Cadbury and Guinness see in English speaking Nigeria, newly independent from the UK, a ready market for their products and services from an aspirational middle class.

We'd set sail from Liverpool, without a Beatle in sight.

The SS Apapa was also a mail and cargo vessel, so whilst the travelling passengers were reasonably well accommodated in their sea view cabins, it took an age to arrive into Lagos.

By the time we got there, Mum had acquired an all over, deep chestnut tan. Apparently, none of the young officers had noticed the young women sunbathing on the forward deck of the ship. Neither did the African waiters readily supplying the women G&Ts notice any *nubility*.

---

[11] April 1 – *The Flintstones* aired its series finale on the ABC network.

April 8 – *Time* magazine cover story asks, "Is God Dead?"

April 13 – United States' magazine Time's cover story is London: The Swinging City.

I noticed nothing. Other than I was the first to spot my daddy on the quayside, weeks later. With an excited wave, I waited an agonised half-hour as we docked and then joined seemingly endless queues to have this form and then that form stamped and handed on to yet another next desk.

Suddenly, we heard a roar across the customs hall.

"Hey, you man. Stop. Stop right now. This be my wife!" My father, flanked by officials with caps, and braid, hurried us through the throng.

"Ah, he be big man. This be big woman. Sorry, sorry, sah!" said another official.

"What was all that about?" asked my mother giving him a kiss.

"It's the bank, really. Out here, we're VIPs. I'm the chief cashier now. The government needs our cash, so we don't have to dash. At least not very much."

"What's dash?" I asked.

"Oh, you'll learn soon enough. You'll have dash at breakfast, lunch and dinner. Essentially, a Nigerian will do whatever a white person asks so long as they are encouraged to do so, with a dash. You could say it's a tip. Other people would call it a bribe."

"I dashed the head of customs to walk you through customs. I dashed the gateman to let me park here. And I dashed the port master to get our cases and trunks off the ship first. Look here they are."

We looked up, and high above us a huge crane was lifting a huge net sack containing all our tea chests and trunks. We could tell they were ours as Milner was written boldly in white on the side of each case.

From that height, the sack looked no bigger than an ordinary bag of shopping.

Suddenly, the sack started to swing wildly and the tear in its side grew larger and larger. With every swing, one of our tea chests would tumble and smash onto the quayside.

Crash. "There goes the crockery!"

Crash. "Oh, no, not my dressing table!"

Crash. "There go his toys!"

Crash. "Oh, not all our clothes too!"

We stood in silence looking up for a moment at the empty sack and pandemonium began to spread on the quayside below it. Nigeria's smell, pervasive wherever you were in the country, of dusty road dust (laterite), wood smoke from the open cooking pots and the miles of stagnant drains began to fill our nostrils.

"Looks like you didn't dash him enough, Daddy."

The queue of porters who had been due to carry our belongings to the truck that my father had hired disappeared like mist. Nigeria's noises of the constantly rumbling traffic and its car horns, of the chatter from the markets and the shout of a matriarch admonishing a husband filled our ears.

"Welcome to Lagos, darling. C'mon, let's see if we can salvage anything."

Tuesday, May 24, Political Mayhem

News flash: The Nigerian government forbids all political activity in the country until January 17, 1969.

Tuesday, June 14, Censorship

The Vatican abolishes the *Index Librorum Prohibitorum.*

Today I have a shelf of books, which would have been banned had the Pope not inconveniently abolished this list of prohibited books on this day.

My shelf contains titles including: *Lolita; Spycatcher; 120 days of Sodom; Lady Chatterley's Lover; To Kill A Mockingbird; Brave New World; The Satanic Verses; Animal Farm; The Grapes of Wrath; Catch 22; The Canterbury Tales; The Catcher in the Rye; Ulysses.*

Friday, July 29: Gunfire

News flash, and multiple gunfire, a military counter coup has taken place in Nigeria. Army officers from the north of the country execute head of state General Aguiyi-Ironsi and install General Yakubu Gowon.

Mum is at the hairdressers with me, as shots are heard across Lagos. As the shopkeeper boards up the front of her shop, we all flee to the roof and watch in shock and awe as below us, protestors are herded up – some shot – and men in uniform loyal to General Gowon retake the country.

By lunchtime, it is all silent, and the hairdresser calls my father at the bank to confirm we are safe and well. Dad picked us up and our route takes up the Presidential Palace, smoke coming from its chimney.

As we approach a crossroads, our path is halted, somewhat to my parents' consternation, to make way for a line of military vehicles escorting an open topped Land Rover. I give General Gowon a wave as he enters the presidential gates.

General Gowon smiled. And waved back.

Friday, September 9, Speed Junkie

I am five. And receive from Mum and Dad a bright yellow go-cart, with pedals and red trimmed wheels. It is the best present, of all time, ever given to a little boy. And it can shift!

I have goggles and wear a hanky to keep out the dust. I look like Stirling Moss. I am almost as fast.

I share my birthday with NATO's decision to move SHAPE (Supreme Headquarters Allied Powers Europe) to Belgium (see also p. 213).

Thursday, December 15, Bear Necessities

Walt Disney dies while producing *The Jungle Book*, the last animated feature under his personal supervision.

Sunday, December 25, F.A.B.

Thunderbirds airs its final episode on ITV with a Christmas special.[12]

---

[12] May 27 – Heston Blumenthal, British chef is born.

July 11 – The 1966 FIFA World Cup begins in England.

July 30 – England 4 West Germany after extra time, to win the 1966 FIFA World Cup at Wembley.

September 8 – *Star Trek*, one of the most influential science fiction television series, debuts on NBC in the United States with its first episode, titled The Man Trap.

September 19 – Scotland Yard arrests Buster Edwards, suspected of involvement in the Great Train Robbery.

October 4 – Israel applies for membership in the EEC.

October 9 – David Cameron, former prime minister of the United Kingdom is born.

October 21 – The Aberfan disaster occurs in South Wales, United Kingdom.

October 29 – TV viewers' first sight of a regeneration in *Doctor Who* as William Hartnell's features morph into those of the Second Doctor, Patrick Troughton.

November 24 – The Beatles begin recording sessions for their *Sgt Pepper's Lonely Hearts Club Band* album.

On board the SS Apapa, sailing out to Nigeria. Obviously, fancy dress night for the kids. There's possibly an eye patch involved, taken off obviously so I could focus on the chips. I like the pirate's pencilled in moustache, sideburns and headscarf but why am I wearing a hat?

1967, Kano, North West Nigeria

Over the next few months[13], a pattern of life emerges into which my mother and I quickly assimilate. The dry weather of the north suits my health and the daily sun suits my mother who deepens her chestnut tan every day by the pool of the Kano British Club.

I play with lion ants at the bottom of their cone traps in the sand, and my new friend Gaddo, who is my age and our steward Musa's eldest son. The steward and his family were assigned to the bank's villa, which my father had been posted to after 12 months in Apapa. All the Brits' houses came equipped with a steward whose job description was that of a butler. He was also in charge of the cook, the gardener, a *houseboy* who did the ironing, but not the cleaner; there were two of them, night watchman and a driver.

Musa and my father were of similar age and realising his new master was new to Nigeria, Musa took him under his wing. They remained friends even after we left Nigeria. The bank granted my father a special dispensation in allowing Musa and his huge family; he had eight children and two wives, to follow him around Nigeria. In return, Musa was fiercely loyal and scrupulous in his efforts that we were never taken advantage of. He tried to teach me my tables and Hausa, his family's language, and he taught my mother how to supervise a household employing ten staff.

---

[13] January 23 – Milton Keynes is founded as a new town by Order in Council, with a planning brief to become a city of 250,000 people. Its initial designated area enclosed three existing towns and twenty-one villages. The area to be developed was largely farmland, with evidence of permanent settlement from the Bronze Age.

January 18 – Jeremy Thorpe becomes leader of the UK's Liberal Party.

January 26 – The Parliament of the United Kingdom decides to nationalise 90% of the nation's steel industry.

March 1 – The Queen Elizabeth Hall is opened in London.

Occasionally, there would be an abrupt change of personnel. Musa would apologise and then introduce Danjuma, he who is born on a Friday, the new houseboy. "What was wrong with Tanimu (he who is born on a Monday)?" my mother asked.

"He be tiefman, madam," Musa would say. They were invariably *thief men* according to Musa. Just occasionally, a former employee would seek some financial compensation for their summary dismissal and possibly a reference. In return, Tanimu brought back some of the cutlery he had stolen.

My father delighted him by providing him a glowing reference.

"I can thoroughly commend Tanimu to you. He works very hard and is extremely light fingered. Indeed, I can highlight that as being the key reason he is looking for a new employer so he can refine his skills elsewhere."

Another characteristic of the staff that Musa would employ was that they were always from the north of Nigeria, where Hausa was spoken, rather than the south, which was predominantly Igbo and Yoruba.

Several years later, he did employ a Yoruba, but Buba who also spoke Hausa as well as English. He was essentially Jeeves, without the waistcoat. It was an appointment born out of sadness though.

Musa was going blind.

Fearing he'd lose his livelihood, he did everything he could to avoid my parents finding out. At first, he stopped reading to me at night, which was a special treat whenever my parents had an evening engagement and left him to put me to bed.

Then he began putting creased shirts back into my father's wardrobe. The cleaners who needed supervising at the best of times to keep the house clean started to miss smears on the windows, or sand in the bathrooms if we'd gone to the beach.

The climax came one evening during Ramadan when the cook was away. Musa served my parents the sheep's head with all the trimmings, rather than the leg of lamb, which had been in a similar pot on the stove.

Rather than sack him – which would have been the accepted practice – my father paid for him to see a consultant. Sadly, their verdict was that Musa's sight could not be saved.

In the meantime, my parents confirmed that if he could find and work with an under steward, training him to run our household as his deputy, then Musa and his family would be most welcome to stay in my father's employment.

Looking back, this act of generosity would not have cost my parents a great deal of money, but it was a creative solution to a difficult problem.

The hiring of Buba had another advantage. The Nigerian civil war fought mainly in Biafra was a vicious affair with each side slaughtering whole families with machetes.[14] Although there was peace now across West Africa, memories ran deep. Being back in the south with Buba, a Yoruba and a Muslim, was a much safer bet than it had been with Musa, a Hausa Christian supervising our household in the north.

For good measure, Buba also added a sentry for the gate during the day, and an extra night watchman an Igbo clansman – to check on the first night watchman.

When we left Nigeria, Musa's eldest son Gaddo (the inheritor) continued being my pen pal and a best mate. As we grew older not surprisingly the frequency of our letters stretched until today we exchange Christmas cards and pick up where we left off.

Gaddo today, just like his dad, has a first wife and second wife and enough children to fill a minibus. But for now, at least both he and I are resisting Musa's best efforts to teach us our tables, and to read and write.

----

[14] The Nigerian-Biafran War was a civil war fought between the government of Nigeria and the secessionist state of Biafra from 6 July 1967 to 15 January 1970. Biafra represented nationalist aspirations of the Igbo people, whose leadership felt they could no longer coexist with the Northern-dominated federal government. The conflict resulted from political, economic, ethnic, cultural and religious tensions, which preceded Nigerian's independence from British rule in 1960. Within a year, federal government troops surrounded Biafra, capturing coastal oil facilities and the city of Port Harcourt. The blockade imposed during the ensuing stalemate led to mass starvation. During the two and half years of the war, there were about 100,000 overall military casualties, while between 500,000 and 3 million Biafran civilians died of starvation.

In mid-1968, images of malnourished and starving Biafran children saturated the mass media of Western countries. The plight of the starving Biafrans became a cause célèbre in foreign countries, enabling a significant rise in the funding and prominence of international non-governmental organisations (NGOs). The UK and the Soviet Union were the main supporters of the Nigerian government while France, Israel and some other countries supported Biafra.

It will be a while before I have pen pal.

At present, I can't spell, let alone read my name yet.

Thursday, March 16, Nursery

The five days a week when Dad was working were full of boredom; life only came alive at the weekends. He taught me how to swim in the pool in the Brit club and took us for picnics in the jungle or the desert, depending where he was stationed at the time.

To keep me occupied for some of the time, Mum did after all have sunbathing to do; they sent me to school.[15]

Corona Trust School, Kano, Nigeria

School Report
Name: Oliver Milner
Class: I
Age: 5 years 9 months
Spoken English: Good. Often contributes to class news.
Reading and Writing Abilities: Oliver tries hard and writing is improving with constant practice. Likes to copy the writing in his new book, which is encouraging. Has begun Janet and John series *Here we go* and reads matching cards on the walls of the classroom.
Number (*sic*): Beginning to recognise numbers and their symbols and to use them in simple addition sums.
He is a Friendly, happy child.
Signed: *Ms Rowena Marjoribanks.*

Musa is doing his best, trying to teach me to read when it's time for my bedtime story, but I can easily undermine his efforts by distracting him with descriptions of life in Britain whenever I am bored.

He is fascinated by Mrs Queen, and thinks it's absolutely hilarious that the British Empire is run by a lady, nor can he understand why most men only have one wife. Clearly, I don't have the intellectual firepower to engage in a rational debate about the merits of either.

---

[15] "Nothing comes from doing nothing." – Shakespeare.

However, whenever we get to repeating the letters of the alphabet, we never get much past *G* because Musa is so eager to learn about Yorkshire vs. Lancashire, or football vs. rugby, so for most of my life I've always favoured words beginning with letters A–M, and always felt rather sorry for the N–Zs.

I blame Musa; bless him.

Saturday, March 18, Oil and More Oil

One of my more vivid memories of Britain this year, albeit in black and white, presumably broadcast on Nigeria TV News because of its proprietor's British interests is the news footage of the super oil tanker SS Torrey Canyon running aground between Land's End and the Scilly Isles off the coast of Britain.

Pictures of the raging sea and driving rain were rather smugly observed from the air-conditioned splendour of Dad's Nigeria villa. However, the images of oil drenched cormorants had a profound effect on us all, and one I'm pleased to say in later life have driven me towards a career objective helping to bring to book the company directors who let such preventable disasters happen.

Wednesday, March 29, Boom

Torrey Canyon oil spill: British Fleet Air Arm and Royal Air Force aircraft bomb and sink the grounded super tanker SS *Torrey Canyon*.

Now that was exciting to watch, even aged nearly six.

Saturday, April 8, Soundtracks

Puppet on a String by Sandie Shaw (music and lyrics by Bill Martin and Phil Coulter) wins the Eurovision Song Contest 1967 for the United Kingdom.

The Soundtrack to the Summer of Love passed Nigeria by.

Neither of my parents was particularly interested in The Beatles, but they did have a huge collection of LPs. This in itself was a miracle because in the summer the heat was capable of melting the steering wheel of our VW Beetle into Dali shapes. So how the soundtrack to *My Fair Lady* and Lonnie Donegan's Greatest Hits survived is a mystery. Particularly, in my clumsy six-year-old hands.

At the end of spring, The Beatles release *Sgt Pepper's Lonely Hearts Club Band*, nicknamed *The Soundtrack of the Summer of Love*; it will be number one on the albums charts throughout the summer of 1967.

Monday, June 5, War and the Holy Lands

The soldier, and now politician with an eye patch, Moshe Dayan becomes Israel's minister of defence and thus begins the Six-Day War. Israel launched Operation Focus, an attack on Egyptian Air Force airfields. The allied armies of Egypt, Syria, Iraq, and Jordan invaded Israel. The Battle of Ammunition Hill starts off the Jordanian campaign.

Two days later, the Israelis captured East Jerusalem in a battle conducted by their forces without the use of artillery in order to avoid damage to the Holy City. I mention these facts because in 1974 as part of an Educational Preparatory Schools Holiday – which I won as a scholarship prize – one of the places we visited was Israel.

Even as a twelve-year-old on a schools' trip, the Holy Land was fascinating. We saw the three places in Bethlehem where Jesus Christ himself was *certain* to have been born. The Garden of Gethsemane – sponsored by Coca Cola, I think – is a real place. And the Wailing Wall is enormous and filled with prayers written on tiny pieces of paper wedged between the brickwork. It reminded me years later of the way tilers keep their tiles apart to make sure the grouting stays regular.

Ever mindful of our safety and comfort, the tour guides took us for a swim in the Sea of Galilee. We hoped for a miracle, of course, but the afternoon picnic was curtailed when suddenly above us on the Golan Heights we saw an Israeli Air Force jet shoot down a Palestinian MiG fighter.

Talk about exciting.

The SS Uganda in which we were touring the Mediterranean was that night berthed in Haifa docks before we were due to set sail to Crete. Our berths were adjacent to the Plimsoll line on the ship, so prior to setting off, our portholes in our cabin were under the water, and as the ship sailed on and grew lighter and lighter, the horizon suddenly hove into view.

That night hunkered down, below the water line, at around 2 am, there was an almighty boom and the ship jerked violently upward. One of the Palestinian Special Forces mini subs had collided with and detonated an Israeli mine.

No one would believe me when I wrote this up my school trip project in 1974.

In 1982, the SS Uganda set sail for the Falkland Islands converted into a floating hospital, her true intended purpose. "Hey, I've been on that ship," I said to my university friends.

No one believed me then, either.[16]

Saturday, June 10, Fighting

Moshe Dayan won. The Six-Day War ended and Israel and Syria agree to a United Nations-mediated cease-fire. Typical of the Israelis to have a war that lasted less than a week compared to us Brits who had a Hundred Years' War.[17]

Asking my dad which side were we on in the Six-Day War, he explained, "Neither."

"But why is Israel usually at war with someone?" I asked.

"Well, two reasons, really. Firstly, they always like to win. Secondly, given half a chance they'd pick a fight with themselves if they weren't fighting someone else."

I suspect his views on nationalism would have been coloured by the same forces that Dylan Thomas experienced, they were Welsh, and similar ages, after all. When asked his opinion of Welsh nationalism, Mr Thomas replied in three words, two of which were *Welsh nationalism.*

Another Dylanism my father would certainly have recognised is: "An alcoholic is someone you don't like who drinks as much as you do." He didn't always keep out of trouble either when he'd had a drink. Just most of the time.

Friday, June 16, Neat

Corona Trust School, Kano, Nigeria

School Report
Name: Oliver Milner.
Class: I.
Age: 5 years 9 months.

---

[16] SS Uganda was built in 1952 as a passenger liner, and successively served as a cruise ship, hospital ship, troop ship and stores ship. She was laid up in 1985 and scrapped in 1992.

[17] The Hundred Years' War was a series of conflicts from 1337 to 1453, waged between the House of Plantagenet, rulers of England and the French House of Valois, over the right to rule the Kingdom of France. Each side drew many allies into the war.

Spoken English: Very good. Oliver thoroughly enjoys contributing to class *news*.

Writing Abilities: Greatly improved. Oliver now forms his letters well and copy writes very neatly for his age.

Reading: Improving. Has just finished *Here we go* in Janet and John series and has started *Off to play*.

Number (sic): Tries very hard. Can now do + and – sums up to 10 with the use of counters and has experience in simple shopping sums.

Progress: Good. Oliver needs to feel that the teacher is interested in him, and with encouragement tries very hard. His behaviour is always very good and he has enjoyed learning about *Other lands* in Geography.

Signed: *Mrs Rowena Philips.*

Saturday, July 1, Harriet and Laurence

The first UK colour television broadcasts begin on BBC2. The first one is from the Wimbledon tennis championships. A full colour service begins on BBC2 on December 2.

Auntie Harriet was always exceptionally turned out. She would think nothing of spending three hours in the bathroom. ("She must be taking a bloody big shit," my father would grumble whenever she came to stay.) Even when she in her nineties, Harriet looked immaculate.

Uncle Laurence was also immaculately turned out. He was smooth, a bit like Jason King, without the moustache and sideburns. He drove a Jensen Interceptor and he wasn't our uncle.

He wasn't even Auntie Harriet's husband. All this I had yet to learn.

For a brief episode, Uncle Laurence was also my nana's saviour.

Against everyone's better judgement, she bought herself a sausage dog (which, unusually, she always pronounced sew-sage) and it hated her, growling and baring its teeth whenever she came near.

On the other hand, it lusted after my mother and any time Toby came near her, he would flip himself on his back and his enormous penis would unsheathe like a bright red lipstick.

When we wasn't gnashing his teeth or flashing, Toby would make a beeline for gaps in the hedge, and being so short was forever wriggling free. Neighbours were forever ringing Nana up to say, "There's a sausage dog at the bottom of our garden and he's, aww no! He's exposing himself."

Uncle Laurence came to the rescue. His parents wanted a dachshund, but none was available in Derby. So Nana gave him away.

They gave Toby a better name and from them on he was as good as gold.

Tuesday, July 4, About time

The British Parliament decriminalises homosexuality. Finally.[18]

Monday, August 14, Poliomyelitis

The whole of the summer holidays in Nigeria stretch out in front of us. Whilst Dad's at work during the day, we spend all of our time in the company of other white families in the British Club, in a leafy suburb of Kano.

Mum is always to be found at the side of the pool, working on her deep chestnut tan. I am a restless little creature and rarely settle, so the weekend drive to go shopping into the centre of Kano is a much-welcomed distraction and treat.

However, before you can step into the air-conditioned splendour of Kingsway's, a massive department store selling everything from fresh fish, baked beans, toys, knickers, curtain hooks and furniture, you have to step through a writhing carpet of deformed limbs.

As Dad pulls off the road and into Kingsway's car park, his way is blocked by pitifully deformed people, some little more than heads on stumps, propelled by makeshift platforms on roller skates. This is the signal for the security staff to literally beat a path for us through the throng and into a reserved parking space near the doors of the store.

Then, still beating at the mass of beggars with a huge stave the security – bodyguard – escorts my mum through the entrance doors, who carrying me rushes into the store with me in her arms, crying, "Don't look, don't look."

Desperately, the beggars continue to hold out battered tin cans moaning, "Dash, sah, dash, dash."

As soon as we're safely in the shop, out of sight, they gather and swarm around the next car coming into the compound and the scene repeats again.

It's an appalling, heart-rending sight.

---

[18] October 12 – *The Naked Ape* by Desmond Morris is published.

At the time, the sight of the dislocated feet, withered arms and twisted spines terrified me. The effect on the bodies of these poor people who the worldwide vaccination against the poliovirus had not yet reached is beyond the worst nightmare. With open sewers and contaminated drinking water, the virus had an easy route into the bodies of the poor in the high-density Kano slums.

For those with the disease, there was no cure. There was no social security, no healthcare system to care and tend for the victims of the slowly progressive muscle weakness and bone deterioration.

Despicably, we just pushed through them, so we could go shopping.

At its peak in the middle of the twentieth century, the disease killed half a million people every year. In 1988, when the World Health Organisation launched the eradication programme, there were more than 350,000 cases in 125 polio-endemic countries. Since then, cases of wild poliovirus have decreased by over 99%, according to WHO, to fewer than 100 this year.

In the two countries where the type 1 virus is still endemic, Pakistan and Afghanistan, ongoing political conflicts continue to challenge the eradication efforts.

The push to eradicate polio has been a huge global health success.

Tuesday, September 5, Moving Stairs

It's not my birthday but as Mum and I are flying back to the UK in a few days' time, it won't be possible to have my birthday party in Kano with Dad. As a treat, we're going to Kingsway's where there are two treats in store.

Not only does Kingsway's have an ice-cream maker, imported from America – it's the talk of the British Club – they have also had installed Nigeria's first escalator.

In fact, escalators were still really rare, and I certainly hadn't been on one in Harrogate.

So we went to Kingsway's to ride on the escalator. As you might imagine, there was quite a queue when we got there, but I was soon on it, carefully holding Dad's hand. Suddenly, I realised there was a choice. You could go up, and down on the one next to it.

What a blast. "Again, again, again!"

Eventually, my parents tired of the free entertainment and went in search of my birthday present, and also the ice-cream treat. Leaving me to it, all they asked was that I stay next to the escalator and not to walk off, so they could find me easily.

There was no danger of me straying. This was AMAZING. Look the rubber handrail disappears into the floor...

Suddenly, my parents heard my ear-splitting screams. Fascinated at the movement of the handrail as it disappeared into the floor, I hadn't let go and my hand and arm were being neatly flayed of skin as the escalator continued to rotate.

Someone pushed the emergency stop button. My parents rushed through the crowd to see the skin on my right arm neatly ruched up to my elbow, like a sleeve. Mum fainted, she usually does at the sight of her children's extreme distress, but for my part, I have next to no recollection of what happened next.

I woke up at home in bed, with an impressive bandage from my hand to my shoulder. This would be great to show my friends when I went back to school.

All I can remember asking was, "Did we get any ice-cream?"

Monday, October 9, Celebs

Che Guevara, Argentine communist revolutionary (b. 1928), dies.[19]

I'm not becoming especially maudlin here but aren't these four deaths all within six weeks together absolutely extraordinary? All of them seem to belong to a totally different age. Sassoon was a war poet I mistakenly thought had died in 1918. Sir Malcolm Sargent and Clement Attlee seemed to me to belong to the period shortly after WWII and as for Che Guevara, I thought he was a 1970s kind of guy.

Well, they all died the year after England won the World Cup. So now, you know.

------

[19] September 1 – Siegfried Sassoon, British poet (b. 1886), dies

October 3 – Sir Malcolm Sargent, English conductor (b. 1895), dies.

October 8 – Clement Attlee, British politician, 60th prime minister of the United Kingdom (b. 1883), dies.

September 30 – In the United Kingdom, BBC Radio completely restructures its national programming: the Light Programme is split between new national pop station Radio 1 (modelled on the successful pirate station Radio London) and Radio 2; the cultural Third Programme is rebranded as Radio 3; and the primarily talk Home Service becomes Radio 4.

Sunday, December 3, Lub Dub

Christiaan Barnard carries out the world's first heart transplant at Groote Schuur Hospital in Cape Town, South Africa.

Ten years later, I was privileged to shake the hand of the first Englishman to survive a heart transplant for over five years. Keith Castle was a small kindly man in his late fifties I imagine. He was invited to address the school assembly and afterwards joined us in classes talking about the ethics of taking a dead person's heart.

We asked all sorts of dumb questions which he patiently dignified with an answer. "No, I don't want to drink wine now, rather than beer." "Yes, I think a lot about the donor's family and how they must wish he hadn't died." "No, I don't think I'll be given another heart if this one conks out."

He was a tremendous ambassador to the organ donor transplant service.

I'm so lucky throughout my career to have shaken the hands of a Nobel laureate, three prime ministers, an astronaut, the captains of the England's football and cricket teams, Madonna, the Emir of Bahrain and best of all Keith Castle. I'm very blessed. [20]

I couldn't wait to sign up as an organ donor. It's something we should all do. It makes you very happy, and can save lives.

Saturday, December 16, West End

Whatever it was that we were being taught at the Corona School in Kano, it wasn't enough. My first report from Preparatory School in England indicates I struggled to count to ten, let alone write my name.

It might have been of course that I missed Africa and my little Nigerian friends.

It might have been that I didn't much like sleeping in the same bedroom as my grandmother.

One fateful night, I went to take a sip of water and accidentally drank from the glass her dentures were in, soaking in Steradent.

---

[20] Not many Nobel laureates also competed in the Olympics. He was a remarkable human: Philip Noel Baker https://www.nobelprize.org/prizes/peace/1959/noel-baker/bio graphical/. I've also met British prime ministers: Sir John Major, Baroness Margaret Thatcher and David Cameron. Astronaut: Michael Foulds. England sporting captains: Alan Shearer (football) and Graham Gooch.

It might have been that I was just thick.

It might have been that Mrs Sproule's goitre on her neck, which was the size of a melon, fascinated and horrified me. Did she not notice it was there? Did it wobble when she went up the stairs? Did she sleep on it? Was it full of puss? I was so frightened it was, and that it might burst, I always edged up to her non-goitre side.

She terrified and horrified us.

She knew.

West End Kindergarten and Preparatory School Harrogate, England

Name: Oliver Milner

Christmas Term 1967

Form: 1

General Remarks on Term's Work

Oliver has found settling down extremely difficult and finding even basis classroom tasks hard. He has very little confidence in simple number work and his written work does not seem to progress. He is interested in listening to stories and is then more attentive in class. He joins in readily in games and activities and takes a keen interest in stories. His inclination to walk around in his bare feet was alarming at first, but the colder weather has persuaded him shoes and socks are a benefit.

Next term commences: January 16 when an Extras Form must be returned by each child.

Signed: *E Sproule*, Form Mistress and *D M W Gray*, Principal.

Back to Kano for Christmas.

Uncle Des and Auntie Joan and the lad from Splott – Dad – looking as if he's walked off the set of Reservoir Dogs. I wonder, where they were going. As she's not in the picture, I assume the photo was taken by Mum. It's a shame the photo's in black and white or we could enjoy the Kermit Green Daff 33 in all its splendour. Note the second rear view mirror; Des did all Joan's driving for her, although he was never behind the steering wheel himself. His side seat driving used to send us up the wall.

Sunday, December 31, He Soars

All little boys had an Evel Knievel action figure. It was the law. He looked just like Elvis, riding a motorbike. He was clad in an all-white jump suit and had the stars and stripes on the side of his white helmet.

The real sized one was undoubtedly immensely brave, but he was also error prone. As per today.

Motorcycle daredevil Evel Knievel attempts to jump 141 feet over the Caesars Palace Fountains on the Las Vegas Strip. Knievel crashes on landing and the accident is caught on film.

It was almost as if Henry James' words were written especially for him. "Until you try, you don't know what you can't do."[21]

Just because you can't see any knives and pistols doesn't mean they're not there. Living close to the Sahara Desert in northern Nigeria, which in later years infamously became a stronghold of Boka Haram, we lived a charmed life never to have been seriously threatened by angry mobs. But we never were, in spite of decades of white imperialism, which ended formally in 1960 with Nigeria's independence.

---

[21] "Courage is doing what you're afraid to do. There can be no courage unless you're scared." – Eddie Rickenbacker.

1968, Harrogate, Kano

Sunday, January 8, Smoke That

British Labour Prime Minister Harold Wilson, the non-smoking pipe smoker, endorses the *I'm Backing Britain* campaign for working an additional half-hour each day without pay.

Wednesday, February 1, Vietnam

A Viet Cong officer named Nguyễn Văn Lém is executed by Nguyễn Ngọc Loan, a South Vietnamese police chief.

The event is photographed by Eddie Adams. The photo makes headlines around the world, eventually winning the 1969 Pulitzer Prize, and sways US public opinion against the war.

Thursday, March 2, Marching on Together

Amidst the madness of the Vietnam War, and the crumbling of the economy (not that I noticed either) *this* was news.

WINNERS! The 1968 League Cup Final Arsenal 0 Leeds United 1. I am more than vaguely aware that *my* team is the best in the country.

Monday, March 27, End of Term

Yuri Gagarin, Soviet cosmonaut, first human in space (b. 1934) dies. A tragedy for the world. And a tragedy for his loved ones that he should die so young, aged 33.

My career at West End School is not going well.

It is the start of the Easter holidays.[22]

Peace has broken out between my parents and Auntie Joan and Uncle Des drive us to Yeadon airport, near Leeds. We catch the plane to Heathrow and then on the BOAC VC 10 to Kano.

Dad will be waiting to pick us up and take us to his new residence in Jos. Jos sits on the top of a plateau in central Nigeria. The climate will be dry, rather than humid.

West End Kindergarten and Preparatory School, Harrogate, England

Name: Oliver Milner

Easter Term 1967

Form: I

General Remarks on Term's Work

Oliver only occasionally tries when it pleases him but has made a little progress in Reading and Writing. His handwriting is neat but immature for his age. Whilst he has worked well sometimes this term the progress he has made in Elementary French and Arithmetic has been towards the lower end of the class. He really is less able than children two years below him. He has a disturbing habit of lowering his eyes whenever I approach but seems less ill at ease with the other teachers.

He is now sitting at the front of the class where it is hoped he will be less of a disruptive influence on others next term. He can be really naughty unless a close eye is kept on him. I do hope he will try harder next term. We are judged by our actions – not our intentions. One may have a heart of gold, but so does a boiled egg.

Next term commences: May 7 when an Extras Form MUST be returned by each child.

Signed: *Gertrude Sproule, Form Mistress and D M W Gray*, Principal.

I think I'm going to be on the goitre side. I could tell them now that next term is going to be a catastrophe. Why don't I just stay in Nigeria?[23]

---

[22] March 17 – A demonstration in London's Grosvenor Square against US involvement in the Vietnam War leads to violence; 91 people are injured, 200 demonstrators arrested.

[23] April 2 – The film *2001: A Space Odyssey* premieres in Washington, D.C.

Saturday, April 20, Koumpounophobia

English politician Enoch Powell makes his controversial *Rivers of Blood* speech.

It's about this time that I ought to articulate my irrational phobia. I did then, and still do, hate buttons. Nothing on earth could persuade me to put my hand in a jar of the things. I would sooner put my hand in a jar of wasps.

I associate buttons with a particular kind of person. Enoch Powell being a good example of the particular type. Tidy, smart buttoned up. Invariably wearing a waistcoat. In women of the same ilk, they are invariably wearing a twinset, and a dreaded cardigan.

I absolutely loathe cardigans. It took my mother some time to realise that a babygrow that fastened with buttons would make me fractious and I'd continue to cry, until she put me in one with press-studs or Velcro.

I used to think the aversion stemmed from Nana. My grandmother always wore a cardigan – even in summer – and invariably it would have some egg yolk, fag ash or remnants of last week's supper buried in it.

I couldn't – can't still – bear to be cuddled by anyone wearing buttons.

When I'm putting on a shirt, it can only be done if I close my eyes and try not to gag.

My sister's the same. So we buy each other presents of hoodies, zip tops and T-shirts.

Less you think us totally mad, we're in good company, Steve Jobs was also a koumpounophobic. Without his hatred of buttons on a mobile phone keyboard, we'd never have had the iPhone.

Wednesday, April 3 – Martin Luther King Jr delivers his *I've Been to the Mountaintop* speech in Memphis.

Thursday, April 4 – Martin Luther King Jr is shot dead at the Lorraine Motel in Memphis, Tennessee. Riots erupt in major American cities, lasting for several days afterwards. On the same day, the Apollo-Saturn mission 502 (Apollo 6) is launched, as the second and last unmanned test-flight of the Saturn V launch vehicle.

Saturday, April 7 – British racing driver Jim Clark is killed in a Formula 2 race at Hockenheim.

Thursday, April 18 – John Rennie's 1831 New London Bridge is sold to Arizona entrepreneur Robert P. McCulloch and is rebuilt in Lake Havasu City, Arizona, reopening on October 5, 1971.

Back to grannies, generally, Nana is a big force in my life because so often she is the one I come home to in Harrogate when Mum and Dad are abroad.

Once or twice a week, she used to let me run along to the tuck shop on my own giving me half a crown to buy her cigarettes. This used to entail crossing two busy main roads and trying to pronounce Peter Stuyvesant. I didn't mind the dangerous roads but was frightened I'd not remember how to pronounce the name of her favourite packet of twenty.

Another treat was being allowed to stick the Green Shield and Co-op stamps into their stamp books. A hangover from the war, and a generation conditioned to ration books, it was a way of earning a discount on your shopping.

I liked the taste of the glue and sense of achievement in completing a page.

Peculiarly, for one of her generation, she absolutely loathed Frank Sinatra. But when Elvis Presley died, she blubbered all day. I never once heard her play or sing any of his records.

My father's family live in Cardiff, so I see them no more than half a dozen times, but Nana is always there, at 9 Oval View.

Ten years on, one Sunday a sixth form friend, Philippe Peters and I decide to cycle from Bootham to 9 Oval View for Sunday lunch and then cycle back to school.

Philippe's exoticism, he's from Chile, has Nana transfixed. And Philippe falls for my Nana, calling her a beautiful woman, and an amazing cook. They are flirting with each other.

It's all rather sickening and uniquely I'm quite glad when it's time to cycle back to school.

My Nana – and my children's granny (also called Nana) – are best captured in Jenny Joseph's poem, *Warning*.

For copyright reasons you'll just have to look it up yourself, (see the footnote below). Having been ordered, dependable and thoroughly reliable throughout her life Jenny Jones' heroine, old now and devil may care, decides, she'll wear purple. If she chooses.[24]

---

[24] *Selected Poems* (Bloodaxe, 1992) © Jenny Joseph, reproduced with permission of Johnson & Alcock Ltd.

May 13 – Manchester City wins the 1967–68 Football League First Division by two clear points, over club rivals Manchester United.

I don't know at what age a woman regards herself as old, but in my experience most grannies' characters become richer and possibly more esoteric over time.

Saturday, May 18, The Need for Speed

Mattel's *Hot Wheels* toy cars are introduced. It's off to Collinson's toyshop in Harrogate to buy my first strip of orange strips of track and the loop the loop attachment.

The problem with the loop the loop is that if the speed of entry is too fast the cars spin off the loop.

Terminal velocity can best be attained for a spectacular leap by positioning the track down the stairs. Next weekend, I will have to go to Collinson's to buy more tracks. I need another eight strips I think to include all of the stairs. At present, I am having to start from about two-thirds up.

The arrangement looks a bit like a bright orange ski jump for miniature cars.

Sunday, May 19, Power Cuts

Nigerian forces capture Port Harcourt and form a ring around the Biafrans. This contributes to a humanitarian disaster as the surrounded population already suffers from hunger and starvation.

This is one of the darkest days in all of Africa's history.

Some 2.5 million Biafrans died, many of them children, due to starvation as well as slaughter from the blockade that the Nigerian republican army established.

It goes dark a lot in Nigeria. Often just as Musa is about to serve us dinner or putting down the mosquito netting. Frequent power cuts are endemic. The electricity power grid is ancient, poorly maintained, or if the dash for the next consignment of oil to drive the turbines hasn't been big enough, they simply won't turn.

Sometimes the power cuts go on for days. This results in us having to go to bed by candlelight, which is a bit spooky. It also terrifies my mother who's afraid the mosquito netting over our beds will catch light and burn us in our sleep.

_____

May 14 – The Beatles announce the creation of Apple Records in a New York press conference.

One of the benefits of a power cut is that we have to eat the contents of the freezer at high speed. This results in brain freeze as I binge on ice pops before they melt. To this day, if the lights go out unexpectedly, I associate them with ice pop brain freeze.

One of the disadvantages of the extended power cut is the air conditioning – which is on all the time – goes off and we swelter in the heat. In the north where the air is very dry, it's uncomfortable. But in the humid south, it's almost unbearable.

Not all our houses had air conditioning. The next house Dad moved to in Zaria just had ceiling fans. They were great for disturbing the dust around a room, but pretty useless as a means of cooling the house down. They were extremely good though to launch Action Man, in his spacesuit outfit, across the room and into infinity. By placing him on one of the blades and then slowly increasing the speed of the fan, not only could you give him vital centrifuge training, to withstand the massive G Forces when Saturn V took off, you could launch him through the window and into the garden. Through my bedroom window upstairs, he would literally fly through space. About 30 yards, on a good launch.

Saturday, May 25 The Need for Speed, Contd.[25]

Bought more strips of *Hot Wheels* track. When I have more pocket money, I will buy more suitable cars. At the moment, the Batmobile is racing an ice cream van...

Friday, July 12, More Sproule

West End Kindergarten and Preparatory School, Harrogate, England

Name: Oliver Milner

Summer Term 1968

Form: I

General Remarks on Term's Work

Little improvement has been shown this term. His hand control in Writing is rather weak. His Composition is reasonable when he puts his mind to it, which is rarely, I'm afraid. His Spelling is only fair. Arithmetic causes the greatest concern he really must learn his tables if he is to advance up the school. Much more effort needs to be put into all his work.

His lack of ability in the classroom would be compensated for if only he were less disruptive in the classroom. He appears a most unhappy child and apt to settle most disagreements with his fists.

---

[25] May 29 – Manchester United win the European Cup Final, becoming the first English team to do so.

June 3 – Radical feminist Valerie Solanas shoots Andy Warhol at his New York City studio, The Factory; he survives after a 5-hour operation.

June 5 – US presidential candidate Robert F. Kennedy is shot at the Ambassador Hotel in Los Angeles. Sirhan is arrested. Kennedy dies the next day.

July 31 – BBC television sitcom *Dad's Army* is broadcast for the first time in the UK.

August 11– The last, main network timetabled, passenger steam train service runs in Britain. A selection of British Railways steam locomotives make the 120-mile journey from Liverpool to Carlisle and return to Liverpool on the Fifteen Guinea Special.

September 8 – Virginia Wade wins the US Open Women's singles tennis title.

Arthur Ashe wins the US Open Men's Final, also becoming the first black male to capture the title.

October 5 – Police baton civil rights demonstrators in Derry, Northern Ireland, marking the beginning of The Troubles.

Next term commences: September 24 when an Extras Form MUST PLEASE be returned by each child.

Signed: *Geraldine Sproule*, Form Mistress and *D M W Gray*, Principal.

September 7, Amazing

I have a sister! I knew I was going to have a sibling, given all the recent fuss attended to Mum and her interesting shape. But a sister? How unexpected.

I am extremely proud, and probably a little too zealously proprietorial. I turn out to be a brilliant nappy changer and bottle feeder.

Slightly disappointed that she didn't squeeze out two days later, then we could share our birthdays. Disappointment will turn to sadness later on. She is not a Leeds United supporter.

How could this be?

Saturday, October 12 – Sunday, October 27, Higher, Faster, Longer[26]

The Olympic Games begin in Mexico City. The high altitude was unusual but our black and white TV recorded some extraordinary highlights. Dick Fosbury introduced the Fosbury Flop to the high jump by jumping over backwards, whereas the previous methods involved jumping forwards or sideways.

The World Record was broken in the Men's Triple Jump five times by three athletes, including the final jump of the event.

---

[26] October 20 – Former US First Lady Jacqueline Kennedy marries Greek shipping tycoon Aristotle Onassis on the Greek island of Skorpios.

October 20 – Bud Flanagan, British entertainer and comedian (b. 1896)

October 25 – Led Zeppelin makes their first live performance, at Surrey University in England

October 31 – Vietnam War: Citing progress in the Paris peace talks, US President Lyndon B. Johnson announces to the nation that he has ordered a complete cessation of all air, naval, and artillery bombardment of North Vietnam effective November 1.

November 5 – 1968 US presidential election: Republican candidate Richard Nixon defeats the Democratic candidate, Vice President Hubert Humphrey, and American Independent George C. Wallace.

November 14 – Yale University announces it is going to admit women.

The top five finishers all beat the previous world record. It was a unique event.

Friday, October 18, Beamon

In particular, Dad (still in Nigeria) and I exchange letters about this remarkable World Record.

US athlete Bob Beamon broke the Long Jump world record by 55 cm / 21¾ inches at the Olympics in Mexico City. In actual distance, it's further than the length of our drive.

I realise it's exciting, but Dad is truly amazed, and with good reason. Beamon's record stands for 23 years, and is still the second longest jump in history.

Friday, November 22, Snog

Plato's Stepchildren, 12th episode of *Star Trek* 3rd season is aired, featuring the first-ever interracial kiss on US national television between Lieutenant Uhura and Captain James T. Kirk.

Friday, December 6, Honky Tonk

The Rolling Stones release *Beggars Banquet*, which contains the classic song *Sympathy for the Devil*.

I was too young at the time to pick this up properly. But *Sympathy for the Devil*, or possibly *Honky Tonk Woman*, would most likely feature in my final eight Desert Island discs.

"She blew my nose, and then she blew my mind." Could there ever be a better lyric for a rock and roll song?

Wednesday, December 11, Where Is Love

Going to the pictures in Nigeria was always a treat. Firstly, because the cinemas were outside and we watched the film once it was dark, from the car and secondly, because the journey home always meant that it was late to bed.

The film *Oliver!*, based on the hit London and Broadway musical, goes on general release in cinemas. It goes on to win the Academy Award for Best Picture.

Lionel Bart's musical score for the stage musical has stood the test of time too. The hits just roll on and on. ("Please, sir, can I have some more?")

However, Bill Sykes' character terrified me, for months.

Friday, December 13, Strange Men

Christmas Eve is even better than Christmas Day in my opinion. The excitement of what Father Christmas will bring. Has he got my list? Will he know to deliver the presents in Kano, rather than Harrogate?

Well, no he didn't. Or least on this Christmas Day, he got his geography a little awry. For some strange reason, all my presents were lying at the end of my parents' bed, on my father's side. Father Christmas must have got the bedrooms muddled up…

The next year, I actually thought I saw Father Christmas at the end of my bed. I must have been mistaken though as it looked like my dad.

A few months later, when I was back at school, there was another case of mistaken identity.

The house was all locked up for the night. My father was away up country for a few days, and was back in the morning. My mother had gone to bed and Musa and the houseboy had locked up the house and locked the windows and doors.

Except *that* night seeing that my father's car wasn't in the drive, three intruders crept into the house thinking it was empty. Lights were turned on and Mum heard a chattering in the hall. Thinking my father had arrived home early, she turned over and carried on snoozing.

Then the light went on in the bedroom, and there, at the end of her bed was a man dressed in a black tunic and turban carrying an enormous machete.

"Ahhh," they both screamed, seeing each other unexpectedly.

My mum, dressed in very little, dashed for the security of the en suite bathroom, where she locked the door. "Take whatever you want and go," she called through the door.

And there she would have stayed until my father came home.

Musa and the night watchmen, seeing lights on in the house and then hearing screams rushed to see what was going on. The night watchmen fierce at the best of times ran after the thieves laden down with our TV and a drinks cabinet, and lashed out with their machetes, exercising summary justice on the intruders.

There was a knock on the bathroom door.

"Madam, it is me, Musa. I have the baby, here. She is safe."

In her terror, my mother had forgotten my sister.

Tuesday, December 24, Dawn

What a Christmas Eve, all televised too, before Father Christmas arrives.

The manned US spacecraft Apollo 8 enters orbit around the Moon. Astronauts Frank Borman, Jim Lovell and William A. Anders become the first humans to see the far side of the Moon and planet Earth as a whole, as well as having travelled further away from Earth than any people in history.

Anders' photographs *Earthrise*.

The crew also reads from Genesis.

Happy Christmas.[27]

Dad's pad, in Zaria, Nigeria. No wonder Father Christmas didn't find my room; the place was the size of a palace.

---

[27] "Don't be afraid to take big steps. You can't cross a chasm in two small jumps." – David Lloyd George.

1969, Kano. Harrogate

Thursday, January 30, Less Than Fab[28]

The Beatles give their last public performance, of several tracks on the roof of Apple Records, later featured in the film *Let it Be.* (Which Dad also later took me to.)

They must have been really cold. It's still the middle of winter.

Sunday, February 9, Biggest

The Boeing 747 Jumbo Jet is flown for the first time, taking off from the Boeing airfield at Everett, Washington.

---

[28] January 2 – Australian media baron Rupert Murdoch purchases the largest-selling British Sunday newspaper, *The News of the World.*

January 12 – *Led Zeppelin*, the first Led Zeppelin album, is released in the United States.

January 14 – The Soviet Union launches Soyuz 4.

January 15 – The Soviet Union launches Soyuz 5, which docks with Soyuz 4 for a transfer of crew.

January 16 – Two cosmonauts transfer from Soyuz 5 to Soyuz 4 via a spacewalk while the two craft are docked together, the first time such a transfer takes place. They then undock and return to Earth successfully.

January 26 – Elvis Presley steps into American Studios in Memphis, Tennessee, recording *Long Black Limousine*, thus beginning the recording of what becomes his landmark comeback sessions for the albums From Elvis in Memphis and Back in Memphis. The sessions yield the popular and critically acclaimed singles *Suspicious Minds*, *In the Ghetto*, and *Kentucky Rain*.

February 2 – Boris Karloff, British actor (b. 1887), dies.

February 4 – In Cairo, Yasser Arafat is elected Palestine Liberation Organization leader at the Palestinian National Congress.

March 17 – Golda Meir becomes the first female prime minister of Israel.

Sunday, March 2, Fastest

In Toulouse, France, the first Concorde test flight is conducted.

Sunk: the Longhope life-boat is lost after answering a mayday call during severe storms in the Pentland Firth between Orkney and the northern tip of Scotland; the entire crew of eight die.

Wednesday, March 19, Sledging

A 385 metres (1,263 ft.) tall TV mast at Emley Moor, England, collapses due to ice build-up. It *was* a really cold winter. Before Christmas, Dad had bought me my first and only sledge.

It wasn't as fast as *Hot Wheels*, because the incline down 9 Oval View is only about 10 degrees. But it's a tick, so far as counting as another form of transport taken.

Thursday, March 20, Ono

John Lennon and Yoko Ono are married in Gibraltar, and proceed to their honeymoon *Bed-In* for peace in Amsterdam.

One hundred of the 105 passengers and crew on a United Arab Airlines flight, most of them Muslim pilgrims returning to Aswan from Mecca, are killed when the Ilyushin-18 turboprop crashes during a sandstorm.

Friday, March 21, Travelling Backwards

WEST END KINDERGARTEN and PREPARATORY SCHOOL, HARROGATE, ENGLAND

Name: Oliver Milner.
Spring Term 1969
Form: II S
General Remarks on Term's Work
Arithmetic – remains weak.
Reading – some progress.
Writing – fairly good.
Composition – improved written work.

General remarks – Oliver must try much harder with all his work, as he is below the standard required. The poor standards set in Nigeria have put him behind his peer group by at least 18 months in my view. He is always full of ideas, but ideas are funny things, they don't work unless you do.

Next term commences: April 24, an Extras Form MUST PLEASE be returned by each child.

Signed: *Daphne Wilkinson, Form Mistress* and *D M W Gray,* Principal.

I think Mrs Sproule died, sometime during half term. I don't remember Ms Wilkinson. I imagine she'd also think it a good idea to see the back of me too.

Tuesday, April 1, Jump Jet

Obviously, it didn't bother the Ministry of Defence that April Fool's Day was a risky date to unveil one of the most innovative aircraft/weapons of all time.

Coolest: the Hawker Siddeley Harrier enters service with the Royal Air Force. Television news is very excited. This eight-year-old is very excited. It can take off and land vertically! And it's only 1969. How cool is that? #VTOL. It's very exciting.

Hopefully, there will be an Airfix model of a jump jet amongst my birthday presents in September. I wonder if I can wait that long?

Tuesday, April 22, Gypsy Moth

Robin Knox-Johnston becomes the first person to sail around the world solo without stopping. For some reason, RK-J always reminded me of Bill Oddy, from The Goodies. And Sir Francis Chichester – the other sailor of our childhood – of Graeme Garden, the tall one from The Goodies. I'd like to take this opportunity to apologise to the four of you for this misrepresentation. But there it is. History should be about facts. And dates. Obvs.

Monday, April 28, Premier League

WINNERS! Leeds United win the 1968/69 First Division title after a 0–0 draw vs. Liverpool, at Anfield. My team is the best.

What a squad: David Harvey; Gary Sprake; Jack Charlton; Terry Cooper; Nigel Davey; Norman Hunter; Paul Madeley; Paul Reaney; Mick Bates; Johnny Giles; Terry Hibbitt; Jimmy Lumsden; Terry Yorath; Rod Belfitt; Eddie Gray;

Albert Johanneson; Mick Jones; Peter Lorimer; Michael O'Grady; Willie Waddell and Don Revie.

Thursday, May 22, So Close

Apollo 10's lunar module flies to within 15,000 m of the Moon's surface (Gene Cernan, Tom Stafford, John Young). I am so excited on hearing this I nearly wee.

So close, and yet so far.

Tuesday, June 17, Checkmates[29]

After a 23-game match, Boris Spassky defeats Tigran Petrosian to become the World Chess Champion in Moscow.

I thought I was quite good at chess. Dad taught me reasonably well and without being the best at it, chess club became one of my things. The top two or three players in the school could always beat me, but on the way through Inter House tournaments, I could pick up quite a few house points for Lund.

Nowadays playing against my iPhone I never get beyond level 7 of 20. I'm not all that good after all.

Saturday, June 28, Stonewalled

The Stonewall riots in New York mark the start of the modern LGBTQ+ gay rights movement across the world.

The Stonewall Inn, an LGBT nightclub was the place where the Stonewall riots occurred, a situation in which members of the LGBTQ community rioted against police who had raided the nightclub.

Tuesday, July 1, Rooms

HRH Charles, Prince of Wales, is invested with his title at Caernarfon. I watched it in black and white on the TV with Nana. For some reason, the TV is temporarily in our dining room – I wonder if the living room was being redecorated? Possibly.

---

[29] June 22 – Judy Garland dies of a drug overdose in her London home.
July 3 – Brian Jones, musician and founder of The Rolling Stones, drowns in his swimming pool at his home in Sussex, England.

Nine years later Nana dies in that dining room, which is doubling as her bedroom, downstairs, as she lies dying of cancer.

The sun lounge then becomes the dining room.

Once she dies, the dining room is then rented out to Pat, a lodger who Mum works with as dental nurse in Dr Dykes' surgery.

I just thought I should clear the room issues up.

History will judge whether HRH Prince Charles was an adequate Prince of Wales.

Monday, July 14, Immature

WEST END KINDERGARTEN and PREPARATORY SCHOOL, HARROGATE, ENGLAND

Name: Oliver Milner.
Age: 8 years 10 months
Summer Term 1969
Form: II S
No. in Form: 25
Average age: 7 years 5 months
General Remarks on Term's Work
Oliver's work is immature and below the level for his age group in both English and Arithmetic. He has made some progress this term and he always tries. Oliver finds Arithmetic especially difficult as was reflected in his exam result where his position was 24[th.] But he is trying to understand. In the non-examined subjects Divinity, Nature Study, Speech and Drama, PE and Handwork his work is towards the top of his class, and appropriate for his age.
Next term commences: September 23 when it is ESSENTIAL that an Extras be returned by each child.
Signed: *Edith Salisbury, Form Mistress and D M W Gray,* Principal.
Who cares what Ms Salisbury thinks? One of the most exciting six days in history is about to begin.
And then we're off to see Daddy in August.

Wednesday, July 16, Buzz

Apollo 11 (Buzz Aldrin, Neil Armstrong, Michael Collins) lifts off from Cape Kennedy in Florida towards the first manned landing on the Moon.

I am so excited it's all I can do not to wee myself.

Saturday, July 19, Rickety Bridge

US Senator Edward M. Kennedy drives off a bridge into a tidal pond after leaving a party on Chappaquiddick Island, Massachusetts, killing Mary Jo Kopechne.

Kennedy does not report the accident for nine or ten hours. Because of the Moon landing, the TV is on most of the time.

I remember this TV news clip and thinking at the time how could such a rickety wooden lathe bridge hold up the weight of a whole car. But I am only nine, and the TV is in black and white. Perhaps the bridge is stronger in colour.

John Fairfax lands in Hollywood Beach, Florida near Miami and becomes the first person to row across an ocean solo, after 180 days spent at sea on board 25 ft ocean rowboat *Britannia* (left Gran Canaria on January 20, 1969). Why? Just why bother?

Just look up at the Moon…

Sunday, July 20, Mankind's Giant Leap

The most exciting day of my life so far? Surely? Yes.

At 02:56 GMT Apollo 11's lunar module *Eagle* lands on the Moon's surface.

An estimated 500 million people worldwide, the largest television audience for a live broadcast at this time, watch in awe as Neil Armstrong takes his first historic steps on the surface.

Where to begin, well…Nana has her brandy and soda. She and I are both in our dressing gowns, but as it's very late and the fire in the grate has been let to go out. But it's summer, and the central heating is still on. So we're fine.

I think my mum's asleep in bed.

Meanwhile Neil Armstrong is walking about on the surface of the Moon at a temperature of 120 C, and we can see the Moon between the curtains of the sun lounge window. AMAZING!

Today Eddy Merckx wins the Tour de France for the first time. A total legend, but who cares? Two men are asleep in the Lunar Module ON THE MOON tonight.[30]

Thursday, July 24, Lunar Germs

The Apollo 11 returns from the first successful Moon landing and the astronauts are placed in biological isolation for several days in case they may have brought back lunar germs. The airless lunar environment is later determined to rule out microscopic life.

I am so excited, I can't even wee.

Thursday, July 31, ½p

Juxtaposed between the rest of this month's space age news, this seems so Dickensian: the old halfpenny ceases to be legal tender in the UK today.

There was total mayhem and uproar on the day in 1971. *Decimalisation Day*, when the old money was replaced with decimal currency.

Anyone born before 1990 will refuse to accept that the government ideally wanted a mile to convert neatly into 1,500 km in order to fit in with the metric system, rather than be exactly 1.60934 km. What the government tried to do in the 1970s was to pretend 12 was the new 10 and no one would notice.

Anyway, what do I care. The day after tomorrow, I'll be knocking mangoes out of a tree with a long stick with my best friend Gaddo in Nigeria.

Friday, August 8, Walking Working

The Beatles have photographer Iain Macmillan take their photo on a zebra crossing on Abbey Road.

Saturday, August 9, Moved Sideways

The Haunted Mansion attraction opens at Disneyland in Anaheim, California. Later versions open in Florida, Tokyo and Paris.

I've been on the Haunted Mansion in Florida. Best attraction, ever. If you can survive Florida's humidity in summer, and enjoy thunderstorms, go immediately. You'll be pleased you did.

---

[30] "Great ideas need landing gear as well as wings." – C D Jackson.

Sunday, August 10, Hot, Hot, Hot

Back in Nigeria during the summer holidays, Dad takes us to Ikeja where a rugby sevens tournament is taking place. It's not Mum's thing at all, but there's a festival atmosphere and for two of the matches Dad is asked to *run the line* as a linesman. A benefit I suspect of having been the one to authorise Standard Chartered Bank's part-sponsorship of the tournament.

Naturally, we went to support Dad, when his matches were on, and fortunately, nothing of major controversy occurred while he was a linesman. Then one of the most controversial family situations occurred that to this day perhaps you are best placed to adjudicate who was most to blame.

After the sumptuous curry buffet – these were always amazing in West Africa – the afternoon settled down to a pattern of seven minutes each way, match after match after match.

Having run out of things to do and friends to play with, and both my parents engrossed in conversations with friends from other British Clubs, I bet my Dad – for one Naira (the equivalent of £1 at the time, £485 today, that's inflation for you in a corrupt nation state) – that I couldn't run around the racetrack.[31]

My father assumed I was talking about the running track around the main rugby pitch. I on the other hand set out to complete a course of the horseracing track, which was adjacent to the rugby pitches, and some three miles and three furlongs in diameter.

Sometime later, I returned, to claim my one Naira. "I'll make it 10 Naira for ten circuits," my dad said casually, not really paying much attention.

The tournament was winding up, and cars were beginning to depart when my parents became aware neither of them had seen me for several hours.

The search party fanned out to look for me. When eventually a motorcade finally caught up with me two miles along the racetrack, I was on lap seven still determined to finish but delirious with heatstroke, exhaustion and dangerously dehydrated.

My parents, with some skill, did all their military and nursing training had taught them to do and saved my life.

Later I woke up at home in a bath full of ice.

---

[31] "What matters in not the size of dog in the fight but the size of the fight in the dog." – Coach Bear Bryant.

"Your parents do very bad 'ting," said Musa, gently dabbing my face with a cold flannel, sitting by the bath. "Very bad."

"I no cook for them tonight. I tell them, they be very bad peoples. I stay here. Look after the little boy."

Nobody was fed that night. There wasn't time, what with the shouting at each other that carried on between my parents, pretty much for the rest of the holidays, and Musa tut-tutting and shaking his head.

In the morning, I woke up bright and breezy as usual. The house was beginning to wake up as normal. Musa was ordering the houseboy about. Cook was clattering in the kitchen. Mum was asleep in bed. Dad's car wasn't in the drive, so he must have gone to work.

And on my bedside was another glass of water with a note from my dad saying, *drink this*. And underneath the glass was a crisp 10 Naira note, and a 1 Naira coin.

Tuesday, August 12, All Change[32]

Later that summer, there is an intervention. It is decided – in my absence – by my parents that I will not go back to West End School. I am immature for my years and my academic progress is virtually non-existent. Instead, I am to go to Malsis School, one of the most highly regarded preparatory schools of its day, nestled on the edge of the beautiful Pennine Way, in West Yorkshire.

It was a boarding school for boys aged 7–12. It seems terribly cruel to send a little boy away but it was standard procedure for expatriate young professionals at that time. The bank paid a substantial contribution for my massive school fees and paid for my air travel to and from England.

Meanwhile I was blissfully unaware of my fate.

We were blissfully unaware of the Woodstock Festival too, in northern Nigeria.

---

[32] August 12 – The Troubles: violence erupts after the Apprentice Boys of Derry march in Derry, resulting in a three-day communal riot known as the Battle of the Bogside, and violence elsewhere in Northern Ireland. Two days later British troops are deployed in Northern Ireland to restore order following three days of political and sectarian violence, marking the beginning of the 37-year Operation Banner.

Friday, August 15 – Monday, August 18, Films

The Woodstock Festival is held near White Lake, New York, featuring some of the top rock musicians of the era. Completely passed the Milner family by.

Whilst life in the local British clubs were mostly all intravenous bottles of Star beer for the men, cocktails for the ladies and Fanta or Coke for the kids by the pool, culturally life was pretty sparse.

Once a week, the Film club would rig up a sheet between two flagpoles and play three reels of film that came over in the diplomatic pouch. The choices could be pretty eclectic, but young and old never missed a Western, musical or horror film on Friday film night.

War stories and Bond movies were the favourite. The spectre of the Cold War between the USSR and the USA was very far removed from the cinema goers in 1960s Nigeria.

Of Nigerian culture, we knew hardly anything. The international affirmation of West African music and Nollywood was at least 25 years away. The only Nigerians we met in the club were waiters.

Monday, September 1, Shopping

The days before it was time to go to my new school were counting down.

Diagonally across the Saharan desert from us, a bloodless coup in Libya ousted King Idris and brings Colonel Muammar Gaddafi to power. Gaddafi was someone else's headache. Nigerians had problems of their own. And so did I. We were going shopping for my school list, *on my birthday.*

Tuesday, September 9, More Shopping

We seemed to spend hour upon hours in Allen's in the centre of Harrogate, queuing first for the red blazer, then four grey shirts, new shoes, new rugger boots – Mum – bought me the wrong make and style. I looked like Stanley Matthews in my huge boots, red Malsis rugby top and white shorts.

But the worst of the look was the school trousers. Grey corduroy. Shorts.

Only seniors (12-year-olds) wore long trousers. For the next four years, I would run around scuffing my knees and getting stung – we all did.

And because she was like a fish out of water herself, Mum had left school at 16, prequalified as a nurse and then became an SRN; she had no idea of the calamity, which was not having any name tapes. Every single item of clothing or possession HAD to have a sewn name. My mum had assumed the school somehow named our possessions.

The supercilious git in Allen's told my mother yes, name tapes with my name on could be ordered. They usually took two weeks to deliver. I was due to go to Malsis on Saturday.

I was the only boy in the school's history ever to arrive with my name absent on any of my clothes. The calamity was rectified in time, but I remained nameless till half term. In the meantime, as Sister Westmuckett sensibly pointed out, logically any item without a nametape could only have been mine.

I'm pleased to report Allen's is no longer the school outfitters of choice in Harrogate. It went broke.

Saturday, September 13, Alone

My mother never recovered her social poise with any parent or teacher at Malsis, least of all Gerald Watts, the headmaster[33] who stood now commanding the vestibule, and greeting all the new parents and boys.

"Mrs Milner," he boomed, "delighted to see you, and meet little Olly here. Run along young man and one of the older boys will show you where they're taking your trunk."

"I see you've got the meter running Mrs Milner." We'd come by taxi as we didn't have a car in the UK and Mum didn't drive. "Do you have time to join the other parents in my study for sherry?"

---

[33] Former Commonwealth Games pentathlete for the Isle of Man 1962 (Silver medallist); Coldstream Guards, DSO Aden 1958; MCCC 1960 – 1969; Cambridge MA (Greats), arrived Malsis 1965. As the *Daily Telegraph* recorded in their obituary for him: 'He was known by boys as "The BFG". Watts was a tall, impressive figure, but not always friendly, being an old-fashioned disciplinarian, and a stickler for courtesy, kindness and correct form and dress – he even polished the soles of his shoes. Yet, as his nickname from Roald Dahl's book suggests, he was tremendously popular – not least with parents. When he retired from teaching in 1990, Watts was invited to become the Secretary of Royal St George's golf club at Sandwich in Kent, with responsibility for organising the Open in 1993. Before the tournament he gave assurances that discipline would be strict. "Golfers and schoolboys are exactly the same," he said. "If schoolboys don't behave you rap their knuckles or smack their bottoms. With golfers you have other sanctions." He continued in the post until 2001. He died in 2003.'

When I'd found my dorm, I ran back to the balustrade where the cars were parked to say goodbye to my mum.

But when I got back, there were no cars. She'd gone.

The school believed in tough love. Tearful goodbyes just weren't permitted.

The first few nights at boarding school must be terrible for homesick little boys – and their parents – but I don't remember my first week at Malsis. Presumably, I blanked them out.

My mother cried for a fortnight, apparently.

And then for a week, after our first Sunday exeat (when you could go home for a Sunday) three weeks into term; and then for the night, after I went back after half term.

And then probably not much at all after that.

Monday, September 22, Cross Country

The world divides in two between people who love physical education (although we called PE *Games*) and those who detest it.

In my first two years at Malsis, I was in the second category; I hated Games. The reason was because none of the sports we juniors participated in played to my skills.

I was also rubbish at gymnastics.

I loved football, but we played rugby. Although virtually, all of us were Leeds United fans, it was the nearest First Division team to the school.

Then there was swimming. Every weekday morning when the Rising Bell was rung by 06:30 hrs by the Prefect on Duty (PoD), the school tradition was for all of us to run down to the swimming pool in our pyjamas, strip off and naked, swim one length of the pool. As a strong swimmer, I didn't mind the swimming necessarily, it was the drying in the cold and draughty changing room that I really detested.

We all went to breakfast with wet hair dripping into our cereal. In the winter months, everyone had a semi-permanent cold, if not full blown flu.

I detested cross-country running. Nationally, the school had a reputation for nurturing runners of potentially international class, with several competing at international level. My bête noir however were the long and middle distance runs that the whole school had to do every Monday after lessons at 4 pm, to the cannonball.

The route followed the edge of the moors and along the roads on a one or a three-mile circuit to the gates of a large mansion house just within sight of the school. Outside the gate was a bronze cannon alongside which was a pyramid of cannon balls, the top one of which was highly polished. You had to touch the cannonball – hence the gleam – and make sure you weren't the last one back, or you'd be sent around to do the run again.

It was impossible to cheat because – we were told – the lady of the manor had a clipboard and was watching us from one of the bedroom windows, checking that we'd all touched the cannonball. It never occurred to us – even as seniors – that the lady of the manor probably had better things to do with her Monday afternoons.

On more than a dozen occasions in my first year, I was still running when it got dark.

Our PE instructor was a young, hard as nails ex royal marine called Jack Barrow. He was a magnificent specimen of man, with rippling pecs and tight iron buns. The physical life suited him as much as it did the string of assistant matrons whom he would daily take out after classes on the back of his beloved Norton motorbike.

There was a long queue of women, young and old, hoping for a ride.

Like most of the men at the school, Jack had of course been a National Serviceman and had stayed on and typically served with tremendous distinction. As indeed had Dosh and Mr Watts each having received DSOs in Aden. What tales of derring-do Jack had committed we never learned, but one day we did learn how stoic he was.

Quite by accident in the changing room in between lessons, one of the boys slammed a heavy locker door on Jack's hand severing his middle finger.

He picked the finger up and drove on his motorbike to Airedale Hospital and came back three hours later to take his table at lunch. To prove that his finger had been reattached, he scraped the two pins that stuck through his bandages onto any boy rude enough to gawp at the wound.

My mother, who cared very little for the goings on at the school, was always interested to learn how many girlfriends Mr Barrow had on the go.

During the school holidays, towards the end of my time at Malsis, tragedy struck.

Coming back to school late one night on his Norton, the bike had a mechanical fault. The wheels locked and Jack was thrown under the wheels of on oncoming lorry. Rumour soon spread around the school parents.

His body had not been immediately possible to identify, only that it was his Norton involved in the accident. Even Gerald Watts, asked to identify the body, was shocked.

The school had lost one of the rocks on which its reputation in the 1970s had grown.

Wednesday, September 24, Doubles

I have always liked Wednesdays and I think it's because very early on in my career at Malsis, I began to worship at the desk of Dosh.

DSE, or Dosh as we also called David English, taught us for double geography in the morning on Wednesdays and then for double history after lunch. And he was a terrific teacher. But quite apart from fostering a lifelong love of geography and history, Dosh's classes were unusual in that Peter his border collie would always sit under his desk.

Wherever Dosh went, Peter would follow.

Man and dog were one of the first to our knowledge who hiked along the length of the newly described Pennine Way. Peter was the most immaculately trained and behaved dog I've ever met. He would sit in the passenger seat of Dosh's half-timbered Morris Minor Estate and would accompany him to the Dog & Gun every night where Dosh would drink all night until he was carried home.

As a bachelor Dosh's other major love, after Peter and Theakston's Old Peculier, was classical music on BBC Radio 3. His small transistor radio would blare out wherever Dosh was. The only time he turned it off in front of us was during exams. Otherwise, we learned all about Canadian timber production or the wars of Charles V, to the sound of Bach or Beethoven. The Brandenburg Concerto was his particular favourite; he would ask us to stop what we were doing and LISTEN.

In class if he wanted your attention – or wanted us to desist doing something that displeased him – he would hurl the blackboard rubber at the miscreant. Which Peter would then leap to his feet and retrieve.

Many a dull winter afternoon in class were deliberately naughty so as to put Peter through his paces. He was a lovely old dog.

They both were.

Sunday, September 28, Silly Willy[34]

I remember this but only for the hilarious comedic value. I thought at the time that one of the world's most important men was called *Willy*. I considered changing my name to Dicky.

In the 1969 West German federal elections, the Social Democrats led by Vice Chancellor Willy Brandt, and the Free Democrats led by Walter Scheel formed a coalition government with Brandt as Chancellor, after the Social Democrats severed their relationship with Chancellor Kurt Georg Kiesinger's Christian Democratic Union.

On the subject of rude words and their double meanings, my mother, who rarely laid a hand on me, gave me the most almighty wallop during half term, across the back of my legs, for calling her *a twat*. It took a long time for my sense of outrage to subside and I snot-cried for a good hour, face down in my pillow upstairs.

We had been cleaning out Goldie the goldfish's bowl during which time I had affectionately called my mother *a twat*, she was at the time pregnant with my soon to be born brother.

A twat is of course a pregnant goldfish. I thought everyone knew this.

My mother did not.

It is of course also vulgar slang and a coarse word. I did not know that.

Whilst words can get you into more trouble than a slap amongst two of my most cherished possessions are the *1982 Viz Profanosaurus* and *Mrs Byrne's Dictionary of Unusual, Obscure and Preposterous Words.* It's impossible to take either off the shelf and not laugh out loud before closing either book up.

For example: galactophagist *noun* a milk drinker; koomkie *noun* a trained female elephant used to decoy wild males; rhabdomancy *noun* fortune telling by sticks or wands, not to be confused with rhapsodomancy *noun* fortune telling with poetry.

And then again, there are names.

Ever since my wife mentioned the name of a former lecturer at her university, I have been collecting *Names to Cherish*. I apologise if I find humour in your names on the next page, but really Mr and Mrs Sprout (bad enough) did you really have to call your son Russell?

---

[34] September 26 – The Beatles release their *Abbey Road* album, which is an enormous commercial success, and although receiving mixed reviews at this time, comes to be viewed by many as the group's best.

Fresh entries are always welcome. The only caveat is that some form of proof is needed to verify they aren't made up. But then why make a name up when the originals are as daft as these. Actually, Douglas Daft is there, at number 11. Below Chuck Fruit and Wayne Carr (another teacher).

At one time or another, each of these entries has made me cry laughing. There's also a certain poetry in Delroy Corinaldo, Mimmu Mannermaa or Usman Dandifodio.

But the names I most enjoy are the ones that are complete statements in themselves: Mustapha Kunt; Hans Frei, Henrietta Titcombe, Go Lik Kok and of course – still my favourite – Chris Peacock.

And before you reach for your red pen, dear editor, check out LinkedIn, they're all to be found online.[35]

---

[35] *Names to Cherish*
1. Russell Sprout; 2. Harsh Sanklesha; 3.Wayne Carr; 4. Ana De Jesus; 5. Karl Marx Parrimalam; 6. Titiya Plucksataporn; 7. Chuck Fruit; 8. Dick Bush; 9. Dick Willey; 10. Aviva Bola Suiton; 11. Douglas Daft; 12. Nipper Reed (of the 'Yard); 13. Chainsaw Al Dunlap; 14. Delroy Corinaldo; 15. Mike Griesgraber; 16. Dearbail Jordon (Dervil); 17. My Chung; 18. Ad Neefs; 19. Oral Roberts; 20. Bonko Chan; 21. Randy Mann; 22. Begonia Arce; 23. Klaus Zumwinkel; 24. Ralph Pecker; 25. Roisin Woolnaugh; 26. Siobham Romp; 27. Cherie Wanka; 28. Mish De Schmidt; 29. Julie Pielsticker; 30. Babak Khakpour; 31. Kylee Dickey; 32. Theresa Zimmer; 33. Thomas Wanker; 34. Stefan Kuntz; 35. Randy Slack; 36. Tinne Teugels; 37. Josef Bugavitz; 38. Ram Ramachander; 39. Randy Mott; 40. Randy Baumgardner; 41. Dina Medina and Stephanie Storm; 42. Caramel Quin; 43. Mr Kermode and Mr Perfect; 44. Mark Etting; 45. Rupert Tinkler; 46. Dan Jelinek; 47. Gaye Hooker; 48. Philip Reckless; 49. Dick Brown; 50. Herr Koch; 51. Fevzi Turkalp; 52. Dilip Mistry; 53. Crispin Plaskitt; 54. Mimmu Mannermaa; 55. Fred Slezak; 56. Cardinal Sinn; 57. Charlie Haddock; 58. Randy Barber; 59. Grover Righter; 60. Dick Pound; 61. Mike Pigg; 62. The Reverend Cannan Banana; 63. Ndabaningi Sitole; 64. Rick Bacon & David Pie; 65. Dewald Pretorius; 66. Monde Zondeki; 67. Gael Meadows; 68. Melanie Chesters; 69. Andrea Moorhead; 70. John Thomas; 71. Thaddeus P Kubis; 72. Otis Spunkmeyer; 73. Melinda Melons; 74. Dick Search; 75. Nichola Hornblower; 76. Mark Etting; 77. Beth Laalaa; 78. Rama Velaramanathanputhu; 79. Jane Arscott; 80. Angus de Watteville; 81. Geoff Wenker; 82. Bruce Chism; 83. Liz Clinkenbeard; 84. Chris Peacock; 85. Randy Rapehole; 86. Dick Gigante; 87. Colin Raper; 88. Simon Shorthose; 89. Geoff Tittensor; 90. Go Lik Kok; 91. Dr Willy Dick; 92. Esther Lynchmuff; 93. Louisa Pnginbid; 94. Randy Bishop; 95. Gordon Mycock; 96. Ophelia Dickie; 97. Tony Banano; 98. Usman Dandifodio; 99. Mandy Dicks; 100. Lettice Leif; 101. Robin Banks; 102. Ewan Kerr; 103. Henrietta

Sunday, October 5, Pod At Last

Monty Python's Flying Circus first airs on BBC One. It's not until my last and fifth year at Malsis that as a PoD (Prefect on Duty) I'm allowed to watch *MPFS*. From memory, it airs at 9:00 pm and lasts half an hour. *The seniors* all watch it in front of the TV in the hall, in our dressing gowns. Why we had a TV in the entrance to the school who can say. But they were the best of nights. Full of laughs and silliness.[36]

Friday, November 14, The After Party

NASA launches Apollo 12 (Pete Conrad, Richard Gordon, Alan Bean), the second manned mission to the Moon.

Whilst I'm excited about this on the day, it's a shame to admit it these Apollo missions now come too thick and fast for my pocket money and a schoolboy's interest to maintain attention. Firstly, why not wait till the school holidays, NASA, when we can give this our full focus? Secondly, I haven't yet finished building my Airfix Lunar Module – the legs and satellite arrays are a bit fiddly.

Strange to say whilst I coveted Airfix's Saturn V rocket model, the biggest they ever manufactured, the sheer scale and number of pieces were too daunting. Or perhaps I didn't drop sufficient hints to Father Christmas? Or perhaps he couldn't afford it.

Mann; 104. Mike Ock; 105. Emma Dale; 106. Reverend Phil McCraken; 107. Dordi Norby; 108. Sebastian Schweinsteiger; 109. Mustafa Diker; 110. Sir Keith O'Nions; 111. Musta Diker; 112. Bent Wesslass; 113. Kuntal Thakutra; 114. Mr Fukada; 115. DJ Reacord; 116. Klaus Titz; 117. Klaus Wanke; 118. Sally Styles; 119. Rory Borealis; 120. Perri 6; 121. Ben Pink Dandelion; 122. Ajax Scott; 123. Lulu Grimes; 124. Klaus Wanke; 125. Jesus Prat; 126. Mario Twittenhoff; 127. Rolf Bender; 128. K Ichinose; 129. Klaus Kochs; 130. Trevor Earwicker; 131. AM Titov; 132. Bob Sleigh; 133. Reinhold Willi; 134. Roman Flunt.

[36] October 22 – Led Zeppelin release *Led Zeppelin II* to critical acclaim and commercial success. Passed me by at the time. I discovered it 10 years later in the first year of sixth form (Year 12).

November 7 – Pink Floyd release their *Ummagumma* album. Ditto, Oct 22. Once again, I discovered it 10 years later in the first year of sixth form.

November 10 – *Sesame Street* airs its first episode on America. Passed us by in the UK at the time. But it was must watch Saturday night viewing later on for years and years.

Either way, I never made the Saturn V model. (Something for the bucket list, perhaps?) But I did make the Lunar Rover later when it came out. And painted the wheels grey (I think?) but felt a bit cheated that the rest of it was already white.

Sunday, November 15, About Bullies

Interesting to learn that events like this actually occurred. I don't think it made the *6 O'clock* News: The Soviet submarine K-19 collides with the American submarine USS *Gato* in the Barents Sea.

Whilst I am trying to avoid Martin Bennett, the bully from the Form 6, NATO is trying to avoid a nuclear tit for tat between America and the USSR.

As a Prefect on Duty, Bennett was able to command me to do certain chores, such as sweeping floors, keeping roll calls, and checking all the lights were out in the schoolroom corridor. This had a particular terror because it meant having to walk back some 200 yards in the dark.

He could also deliberately get me into trouble. He threw a glass of water over Peter, and blamed me. He set fire to a waste paper basket, and blamed me – although having matches was a serious offence I would have never dreamed of.

In the changing room, he and his friends would invariably flick me with wet towels. He'd report me for talking after lights out. He once made me get into the big basket where the cricket kit was kept and locked the lid. Luckily for me, a friend was on hand to let me out but not until he was out of sight.

Quite possibly, he was a psychopath to everyone, but it seemed to me that he singled me out for special attention.

Tuesday, November 19, *J'ai Connais Pas*

Apollo 12 astronauts Charles Conrad and Alan Bean land at Oceanus Procell-arum (Ocean of Storms), becoming the third and fourth humans to walk on the Moon. Only eight more men who walked on the Moon still to name…All Americans, to date.

Today as well, professional footballer Pelé scores his 1,000[th] goal. I would have probably raved about this but for the fact Malsis played rugby, and TV during term time at least was only viewed during French classes to improve our comprehension. I comprehended nothing, and still struggle with French today, much to my angst. I half understand what's being said or written. But usually the wrong half.

Tuesday, November 25, Imagine

John Lennon returns his MBE medal to protest the British government's involvement in the Biafran War in Nigeria. An easy gesture from a difficult man, but a timely one: 2.5 million were slaughtered in the Biafran War, a conflict that hardly anyone knows about, still.

Friday, December 12, Tears Before Break Time

Everyone is super excited to be going home for the Christmas holidays. As is the custom, Mrs Rose (Mabel) reads out our letters from home aloud to the class before lessons start.

I've no idea why we did this. But it was a school practice based on the assumption perhaps that parents' handwriting was too difficult for Year 1s to read. I can only assume they were read aloud to compensate for those children who didn't receive a weekly letter. Then Mrs Rose read out a letter that would change my worldview, and that of all of Form 2 forever.

Tom Shreve's mother dropped the bombshell, reminding Tom that little Nichola had not yet learned the truth behind Father Christmas. The silence lay heavy in the room. Then the questions burst out to the front of the room like an angry press conference.

"Mrs Rose, Mrs Rose, what does this mean?" we cried as one. Some of us later just cried, quietly, through lesson 1 with Mrs Hollingsworth. This history is not sufficiently informed to record what conversations may have subsequently taken place between Mrs Rose and Mrs Shreve. But we can be sure there were words.

'Grief is just live with nowhere to go,' I've heard it said.

Another sentiment, envy of bereavement is often felt whilst compatriots become the centre of the ultimate unspeakable announcement. This didn't happen to me until 2007 when my own father died. By then I'd grown old enough to know how to feel. Numb. And grief stricken.

The poet Edward Lucie-Smith captures exactly the turmoil we all have when a father dies. You're never trained to expect it.

His poem *The Lesson* is brilliant. But brace yourself when you look it up. And find a hanky.[37]

Monday, December 15, Rather Weak

Malsis School, Cross Hills, Keighley, England

School Report for: Milner, O.

Age: 8.3

Christmas Term 1969.

Form: 1. Number of boys in form: 15

Average Age of Form: 8.4

Height this term: 4' 2"

Weight this term: 3st 9lb 8oz

Subject reports

Mathematics: Very erratic. He must try to put more consistent effort into his classwork. He does not yet know his tables. Exam position 14/15.

English: He enjoys listening to the stories attentively and with obvious interest. He joins in practical work with zest and usually carries out his ideas successfully. Exam position 14/15.

French: After a slow start he began to improve steadily to make more oral contribution.

Music: A fair start.

Headmaster's report: We find Oliver rather weak in the classroom and help in the holidays with his *tables* and spelling would be very much appreciated. At times he has been inclined to fool about excessively and in many ways he is rather immature when compared with other boys of his age.

Boys who try to do something and fail are infinitely better off than those who try to do nothing and succeed. He really does need all your encouragement to participate in more school activities from next term.

---

[37] Commenting on this verse, written in the 1950s, the poet said the poem is about the difference between what one is supposed to feel and what one actually does feel, when faced by some shaping event.

He has stuck to it well on the games field.

G E Watts.
Next term begins on Thursday, January 8, 1970.[38]

Tuesday, December 16, Cheers

LETTER

From the study of the Headmaster, Malsis School
Dear Mr and Mrs Milner,
Just a brief line on Oliver written in my official capacity as his
Housemaster.
In fact, there is very little I can add to this report as the younger chaps
have little opportunity to make much contribution to house activities as
such. However he has collected his share of Star points and in this report
has done quite well.
His work is not really up to standard at the moment and any help you are
able to give him during the holidays should be much to his benefit next
term.
In my experience boys can be divided into three groups: those who make
things happen, those who watch things happen, and those who wonder
what happened. Rest assured it is not our intention to allow Oliver the
luxury of settling into either the second or third of these camps however
tempted he may be at present.
The bottle of sherry which you so kindly left after the Carol Service was
greatly appreciated: I am so sorry I did not have the opportunity to see you
myself.
Anne joins me in extending Christmas greetings.

Yours sincerely,
Gerald Watts

---

[38] December 2 – The Boeing 747 jumbo jet makes its first passenger flight. It carries 191 people, most of them reporters and photographers, from Seattle to New York City.

1970, Cross Hills, Keighley, West Yorkshire, Northern England

Thursday, January 8, Taking Stick

Back to Malsis for the Easter term.

This term is difficult. One of the reasons is that Martin Bennett has decided to lie in wait for me during breaks and taunt me till I cry.

The other reason is that I get caned, for the first time.

It was my misfortunate that Martin Bennett's father was a senior heart consultant at the private hospital where my mother occasionally worked as a relief night sister. One day realising both their children were at the same school, Dr Bennett offered to take me back with Martin every time we both had the same Sunday exeats.

This was fine for my mother, as it meant she didn't have to rely on Joan and Des to take me back to school from Harrogate, a 90-minute round trip, but it was a disaster for me. It meant saying goodbye at 5:30 pm on a Sunday at home, instead of 6:15 pm when we arrived at school.

But much worse was to come.

The first time Dr and Mrs Bennett picked me up, they arrived in their beautiful powder blue Daimler. Sitting apart from Martin who just glowered at me on the enormous back seat was easy enough. But the winding roads across the West Yorkshire moors and the up and down motion of the car and the effects of its soft suspension were too much.

I had never been car sick before, but I knew I was going to throw up now. Desperately, I searched for something to vomit into. Martin's kit bag for Games was the nearest thing to hand. I tried and tried not to puke, but it exploded out of my nose, onto my clothes, onto their beautiful leather upholstery and even in my hair.

I looked a mess. The car reeked, and Martin's retching stopped just in time as the gates of the school came into view.

Having taken any opportunity as a prefect to make my life as a junior hell, I suppose puking on his sports kit was revenge of some sort. Martin backed away from me after this most of the time, but his friends would call me Vom Milner when they were the Prefects on Duty.

I knew he would be gone in the summer. But until they did, I tried to avoid Bennett whenever I could. His parents were most gracious about the carsickness incident and Mrs Bennett drove us back to school for the rest of the year in her Mini, in which I was much better suited.

Wednesday, January 14, Gowon's Day

In the library, during reading, my status as a frequent flyer to Nigeria gives me some minor status when the vicious fighting in Nigeria makes the front pages of the English newspapers.

Today Biafra capitulates, ending Nigeria's civil war. The next day, after a 32-month fight for independence from Nigeria, Biafran Forces under Philip Effiong formally surrendered to General Yakubu Gowon.

He has won, at last. Living up to his Hausa name, which means *rainmaker*.[39]

Monday, January 26, Three of the Worst

Mick Jagger is fined £200 for possession of cannabis.[40] Fitting too that I should get caned today. For shouting the words, "Fuck, NO!" Just as Milligan was about to throw a darts board's dart straight at Shreve's head.

Who should walk in before the scripture class began than Mr Watts.

"Who said that? Milner? My study, now. We do *not* use language like that!" (Like hell…) "Three strokes."

It was the ignominy of having to bend over the headmaster's highly polished desk and the suspense, whilst he administered justice, that made me cry. He was a powerful man but had no intention of wounding the young, poor scrap of humanity in front of him.

---

[39] Tuesday, January 20 – The Greater London Council announces its plans for the Thames Barrier at Woolwich to prevent flooding in London (the barrier opens in 1981).
[40] One of the best comments ever made about Jagger comes from the sadly late lamented, Joan Rivers: "With lips like those Mick Jagger could French kiss a moose."

I would get caned three times whilst I was at preparatory school.

Wednesday, March 25, Jinxed

Alf Ramsey picked Norman Hunter for the England squad for the World Cup in Mexico. But the international jinx never left Norman really and he only played as a late substitute. We lost 3–2 against who else but West Germany and that knocked us out of the competition.

Saturday, April 11, Lucky 13

Apollo 13 (Jim Lovell, Fred Haise, Jack Swigert) is launched toward the Moon. Two days later, an oxygen tank in the spacecraft explodes, forcing the crew to abort the mission and return in four days.

Thursday, April 16, The Scariest Man on TV

The Rev Ian Paisley wins a by-election to gain a seat in the House of Commons.

Friday, April 17, Survived

Apollo 13 splashes down safely in the Pacific.

The story of that mishap and how Mission Control saved the three astronauts' lives remains an even bigger achievement in my opinion than Apollo 11's successful landing. The Tom Hanks film still makes me cry too. Who doesn't love a happy ending?

Friday, May 8, Let It Be

The Beatles release their 12th and final album, *Let It Be*.

Sunday, May 10, The Best Day

The headmaster advances towards me after Sunday service. "Now, young man, I know you're not on Sunday exeat today, but a special treat awaits you. Your father has flown in from Nigeria, and he's going to take you out for the day."

I am speechless, and nearly burst into tears.

"Now, young Milner, enough of that. I suggest you put the school flag on the flagpole [a unique privilege, much sought after], so he knows we're in. And wait for your old man on the balustrade. He should be here soon, I expect." It was a beautiful, hot, cloudless day.

I waited. And waited. 11 am came and went.

I waited. Noon chimed on the chapel clock.

And waited.

I heard the bell go for lunch, but still waited.

Through the heat haze at the end of the drive, a speck appeared. Gradually, the speck turned into a man and then grew larger as the man came jogging up the drive.

It was my dad. His suit jacket over his arm. His white shirt glistening in the sun. We ran to each other and he swept me up. His shirt dripping with sweat.

"Hello, Jerry, I see you've made it. Nice to meet you, at last," said the headmaster, emerging from his study. "Let me get you a sherry. Or perhaps a beer, as it's such a warm day?"

"Good to meet you, Headmaster. I'm sorry I'm so late. My taxi broke down, just outside Keighley so I jogged the rest of the way."

"Good God, man, that's twenty miles away!"

"Yes, well, needs must. It's a shame I'm so late. We've missed lunch and we won't have a whole day in Skipton now."

"You can bring Olly back whenever you like, Mr Milner. I think he can skip Evensong for one night. I'll tell the Master on Duty he'll be late back."

And so began the best day of my life up until then, with my daddy.

We had pork pie, strawberries and cream while we watched a cricket match on the green in Skipton.

We hired a canal boat for an hour and pootled on the water. We had a cream team as we floated along and looked at the fish in the reeds.

Then we bought the biggest box of chocolates Whitakers had in their window and ate them as we went around the chilly stone rooms of Skipton Castle.

Just as the sun was beginning to set, The Castle Inn's doors opened. Dad ordered himself a Theakstons and half a pint of shandy for me.

"What'd you like to do next? How about Chinese?"

I'd never had a Chinese meal.

Was that even possible?

"C'mon, sup up. I've a table for two booked at the Lychee Cantonese Restaurant. It's supposed to be the best."

For three hours, we ate like kings. I prattled away about linseed oil, Fleabag, trumpet practice, Thor Heyerdahl, Leeds Utd and the tuck shop. Dad filled me in on Musa's newest wife, his new car (Opal Record Estate) and where the bank were moving him to after Kano.

That evening, the walk back up the school drive was done with leaden boots.

At some stage, my father picked me up and I fell asleep in his arms. Gentle arms put me to bed.

The next I knew, the bell was ringing. It was 06:30, and time for morning swim.

It was the one and only occasion Dad ever visited me at school.

Sunday, May 17, Thor

One of the leading adventurer/explorers of the day Thor Heyerdahl casts off from Morocco on the papyrus boat *Ra II*, to sail the Atlantic Ocean.

For us who had been mesmerised at Thor Heyerdahl's earlier achievement of sailing the *Kon Tiki* made of balsa wood logs, across the whole of the Pacific ocean, sailing just across the Atlantic in a paper boat didn't seem as romantic, or sensible.

He arrived in Barbados on July 12. But by then, it was nearly the end of term, and didn't he know there was a World Cup on.

We weren't really bothered.

Monday, May 25, Science

"Please, sir, will the Russians end up in New Zealand eventually?"

The scientific drilling of the Kola Superdeep Borehole began in the USSR today. It was a legitimate question, but not one we thought appropriate to ask Dosh in geography. In the wrong mood, he would think this frivolous and aim for your head with the board rubber.

It was fair game to ask Chris Wright our new science teacher. It was kind of a sciencey question. Mr Wright struggled to convince us that the core of the centre of the Earth couldn't technically be bored through. That gravity and magnetic forces would make this a technical accomplishment beyond modern engineering.

However, he had axolotls in a tank, so it didn't matter. If you've never seen an axolotl, they're the amphibious alternative to a platypus. They look as if they're several different animals welded together.

This was much more interesting than the Superdeep Borehole.

Science suffered during the summer. If the weather permitted, Mr Wright would tell us all to don wetsuits and we'd go canoeing. He was an accomplished canoeist, and before long, we were all pretty good for our age too. Capable easily of shooting the weirs near Skipton.

Occasionally, we'd get out the Bunsen burners, which meant only one thing. When he wasn't looking, we'd crumble the fire mat they were stood on over the head of the boy on the bench in front. It was great, if you were really lucky, the material which was really friable and dry, grey powder would shower down in a fine dust like talc.

The fine material was asbestos.

Science was also notable for the most excruciating 45 minutes in a classroom of all time. "These are the sexual organs of the female and these the male," said Mr Wright.

It was the pubic hair that made us burst out laughing. It was everywhere.

"And what are these?"

"They're the balls, sir." More laughing.

"I think you'll find they're the ovaries, on a woman."

"I'd like you all to carefully learn the names of these parts, there'll be a question on them in the exams."

It was a measure of my prudery at the time that I *deliberately* marked up my two diagrams in the exam incorrectly, as I didn't want Mr Wright to know I had carnal knowledge.

I know my balls from my ovaries, at least.

Tuesday, June 2, Amateur
CERTIFICATE

Amateur Swimming Association and English Schools' Swimming
Association
Joint National Swimming Award
Stage 1
Oliver Milner,

The committee of the Amateur Swimming Association and the English Schools' Swimming Association wish to congratulate you upon your achievement in gaining the above award, and are pleased to present you with this badge which you are now entitled to wear.
We wish you every success with your swimming in the future.
Signed: *Miss L V Cook,* Organiser

Thursday, June 18, Mourning Cloud

1970 United Kingdom General Election: the Conservative Party wins and Edward Heath becomes prime minister, ousting the Labour government of Harold Wilson after nearly six years in power.

The election result is something of a surprise, as most of the opinion polls had predicted a third successive Labour win.

Friday, June 19, Nubiles

Westmuckett, Spickett and Evans was not a firm of solicitors but the successive names of the matrons who looked after the 160 of us boarders.

Sister Westmuckett was close to retiring when I arrived at Malsis. She looked and acted like she ran field hospital in the Crimea. She was even scarier than Gerald Watts. Apparently, she'd served in the Congo during the war. None of our childhood complaints registered as illnesses with her, unless you were bleeding from the eyes. The cure was always to make better use of your handkerchief and blow your nose, or stuff your head under a towel and breathe in menthol vapour from a device that looked like a potty with a spout.

Sister Evans was sandwiched in between the two other matrons and I guess must have only been an interim. She was a real pushover. Or possibly also enjoyed us cuddling in her massive bosom when we complained of homesickness. She was the sort of person who would insist that when we had our vaccinations against polio vaccine, they were served on a sugar lump.

Sister Spickett never dispensed sugar lumps, but discipline, yes.

This must have broken the hearts of the young bachelors in the staffroom especially because she banned all interaction between the termly au pairs, who were hired to put the Junior school to bed and ensure we wore our jumpers the right way around when we got up.

The *assistant nurses* were all extremely nubile, wore practically nothing and the school must have had a contract with a Scandinavian recruitment agency because all the young women were blond, and willowy and had names like Agnetha, Dinny, Elsa and Maya.

Sister Spickett soon put a stop to all that.

When we came back for the Christmas term, all the new assistant nurses were in uniform. Most had warts on their noses or at least one tuft of bristles sprouting from their chins.

Saturday, June 21, Imagination Is More Important than Knowledge[41]

What I might have lacked in academic ability in my early years, I made up for in guile and knowing just how far to push the nursing staff to admit me into the Sanatorium for a few days away from classes and prep. Free to watch colour TV and eat whatever I fancied. Avoiding mince and semolina on a Monday lunchtime altogether if I wanted to.

Today was one such day. Agnetha and I stay side by side in my bed watching Brazil defeat Italy 4–1 to win the 1970 FIFA World Cup in Mexico.

Being in the San was also the best way to keep up with Wimbledon. It was the era of Ilie Nastase, Vitas Gerulaitis and Bjorn Borg.

Whenever Borg was playing, the au pairs would be certain to be lounged in front of the colour TV cheering him on. "I was once a ball boy at Wimbledon," I lied to Agnetha.

"Wow, that's fantastic," said Agnetha. "I thought the ball boys all came from a school for orphans? Aww, you poor thing. Come here," she cooed and gave me a huge hug, clasping me close.

It became quite wearing trying to maintain the lie outside the earshot of any other boy or teacher. But eventually, Agnetha must have said something one day in the staff room because for days afterwards every teacher would make a sly reference to Oliver, or the poor house, or orphans whenever I was near. They knew.

That didn't stop me lying to Maya one day that I had a bad case of Gerulaitis. She wasn't in the ward of the San, so I knocked on the door to her room, where the assistant matrons all slept. She had no idea what Gerulaitis was but gave me a cuddle all the same.

---

[41] Attributed to Albert Einstein.

On her bedside table was a big bowl of strawberries, which she caught me looking at out of the corner of her eye. Whilst she went to get a bowl to put some in for me I noticed there was also a torch, or at least something that looked like a torch on the table, too.

"Maya, this torch doesn't seem to have a light? What's it for?"

"Oh, that's for helping me get to sleep," she said taking it off me and putting it smartly into a nearby drawer. "Here, have these strawberries, but don't tell anyone, or everyone will want some."

As a distraction technique, there was none better.

I haven't thought about that torch, that wasn't a torch, for over fifty years.

Monday, July 13, A Good Ear

MALSIS SCHOOL, CROSS HILLS, KEIGHLEY, ENGLAND

School Report for: Milner, O
Age: 8.10
Summer Term 1970
Form: 1. Number of boys in form: 15
Average Age of Form: 8.8
Height this term: 4' 3.5"
Weight this term: 3st 12lb 9oz
Subject reports
French: Much improved, he has taken a great interest and had much to offer in all the oral work.
Mathematics: Oliver still does not know his tables well and must revise them in the holidays. His class work has shown some improvement this term and his examination was good. Exam position: 11/15.
English: Good all-round progress has been made. He now settles more quickly to his work. He has approached these subjects with an independent spirit that has been pleasing. Exam position: 6/11.
Music: He is making some headway now. At first, he did not find it at all easy, but now there are more hopeful signs. He has a good ear.
Headmaster's report: We find Oliver a great deal more confident now. He shows more initiative and good sense than he showed in his early days and his work is improving steadily, too. *G E Watts.*

Next term begins on Monday, September 14, 1970.

I was indeed *a good deal more confident*. And it was entirely down to Musa's encouragement. He'd realised in the Easter holidays that pretending to be right-handed was holding me back. The real reason I'd been struggling in the classroom to write anything was because I could barely hold a pen in my right hand.

For five years at three different schools none of the teachers had realised I was left-handed.

Initially, Musa had been coaching me the only way he knew how too. In his family, anyone who was a leftie must have been possessed by a juju. But as I grew older, he realised how foolish that was and his encouragement was all I needed to be myself.

Re-reading this school report, it's hard to fathom that no one thought to mention I was now using my left hand to write with, parting my hair left to right, and picking up a spoon in my left hand this term.

Perhaps they thought them minor details.

Thank you, Musa.

Wednesday, July 29, Lowering the Baton

Sir John Barbirolli, English conductor (b. 1899), dies. Mum's second favourite conductor. After Sir Malcolm Sargent.

Thursday, July 30, Thalidomide's Legacy

Damages totalling £485,528 are awarded to 28 Thalidomide victims. By today's standards, less than half a million doesn't sound a lot, but they were huge damages at the time.

Thalidomide was given to pregnant mothers in the early sixties to alleviate morning sickness. Fortunately for me, when my mother took it pregnant with me, it made her feel even worse. So she stopped taking it.

The drug damaged foetuses in the womb preventing the proper formation of limbs. Tragically, the drug was not withdrawn quickly enough although the causal effects were beginning to be known by those in authority to do something about it.

Lucky for me.

Wednesday, August 26, Lip-Smacking

The Isle of Wight Festival 1970 begins on East Afton Farm off the coast of England. Some 600,000 people attend the largest rock festival of all time. Artists include Jimi Hendrix, The Who, The Doors, Chicago, Joan Baez, Emerson, Lake & Palmer, The Moody Blues and Jethro Tull.

Meanwhile in Kaduna, Nigeria, I am practicing the trumpet in readiness for Grade II next term.

Music at Malsis is led by Baggy West and later Baggy Turner. Both attempted to teach me the violin, but being left-handed, I refused to play it properly, right-handed.

The trumpet and singing were much easier, and as my report indicated, I was better than average. I also really liked the choirmaster and my trumpet teacher. It pained the poor man who played in one of the world's leading brass bands that we strangled any ensemble piece he was brave enough to try and teach us.

One day, I got him into terrible trouble. Mr Hassle suggested during a trumpet lesson that my cracked lips could be softened by the application of a small dab of urine. For whatever reason, I later queried this with Sister Spickett who hit the roof. She stormed into the headmaster's study, demanding Mr Hassle's immediate removal.

Gerald Watts DSO had seen off almost as fearsome foes in Aden, but Mr Hassle only just kept his job.

Inevitably, thenceforth the school of course called him Mr Piss. What with that and pressure from Sister S in the staff common room, the poor man decided to make a fresh start elsewhere, and after the next term, we had a new teacher for brass, and not nearly as good. Milner's fault.

Wednesday, September 9, 9

Nine years old on the 09/09/70. Well, I thought it was neat.

Oh, suit yourself.

Today seems as good as any to marvel that is the wonder of the toilet roll holder. Imagine you've never seen one reloaded, how on earth can they work? The magical mysteries were revealed to me for the first time today. How can the sides move out, if they're screwed to the wall?

It's a magic trick in everyone's toilet. Don't look at me like that, pleading. I'm not revealing the trick.

Absolutely not.

Thursday, September 17, A Cheerful Start

Why my parents received this when I'd already been at the school for two terms, I'm not sure. Unless they were already thinking I should be kept back a year, although my age militated against that. I'm not doing well, but anything was an improvement on West End.

I'm pleased to report that West End was soon to be converted into a block of luxury apartments. And then knocked down in the late 1990s and then redeveloped, as another block of even more luxurious apartments.

Headmaster's Interim Report for New Boys 1970

During his first few days at Malsis, a boy is given tests, which include Reading, Spelling and Mathematics and these tests are also taken by boys in the lowest form.

This helps us to compare the standard of the new boys with those already in the school. As a new boy may not be at his best because of the strangeness of his surroundings, and because of home sickness, the results of the tests are always considered in relation to the report I obtained from a boy's previous school.

The results of the tests this term are as follows and form placings are shown. Oliver achieved only two correct answers out of 60 in Spelling, 8 correct answers out of a maximum of 50 in Arithmetic but scored a reasonable 11 out of 20 for his Reading.

General remarks

Rather weak and it appears that quite a struggle may lie ahead. I must say now that we will certainly need some help with his spelling in the Christmas Holidays, please. Quite a cheerful start.

Signed: G E Watts.

Saturday, September 19, Glasto[42]

The first Glastonbury Festival is held at a farm belonging to Michael Eavis.[43]

---

[42] September 18 – Jimi Hendrix dies at age 27 from an overdose of sleeping pills. October 4 – American singer Janis Joplin dies at age 27 from an overdose of drugs. Jochen Rindt becomes Formula One World Driving Champion, first to earn the honour posthumously.

[43] Add to bucket list: Go to the Glastonbury Festival.

Friday, November 20, the Angry Brigade

The Miss World 1970 beauty pageant hosted by Bob Hope at the Royal Albert Hall is disrupted by Women's Liberation protesters. Earlier on the same evening, a bomb is placed under a BBC outside broadcast vehicle by The Angry Brigade, in protest at the entry of separate black and white contestants by South Africa.

Tuesday, December 16, Go Slow

LETTER

From the study of the Headmaster, Malsis School
Dear Mr and Mrs Milner,
By the time you receive this, Oliver will doubtless have given you all the news of the term, embellished with problems which resulted from the go slow by the electricity workers in this country. What he may not have told you is that next term now begins on Tuesday January the 12th, two days earlier than previously arranged.
I guess you will have already made the necessary arrangements for Oliver's return via his grandparent. If this new date does not tie in with those arrangements, please do not go to the trouble of endeavouring to rearrange things.
At the moment Oliver is something of a wanderer and I would very much like to see him engaged in something profitable.
All good wishes for Christmas.

Yours sincerely,
Gerald Watts

Tuesday, December 22, Olive?

Every year the British Club committees – much as Rotary Clubs do in the UK – operate a charity Christmas party for the children. In Kaduna, in North West Nigeria, where Dad is now posted, it is no exception.

At the appointed hour, all the younger children gather around the poolside and divide into two groups, little girls on the left and little boys on the right.

At the appointed hour, a man dressed as Santa Claus – although it is clearly the president of the club, just dressed up arrives in the scoop of a bright yellow JCB. Lowered slightly so that he can delve into the boys' and girls' sacks and handing out his presents, he calls out each child's name written on each present and bought by their parents who have bought their child something appropriate and wrapped it up so that Santa Claus might delight them.

A boy and girl's name is called out alternately. "Olive Milner," ho hos Santa Claus.

No response. No one comes forward.

"Olive Milner?"

"Olive Milner?" And then it dawns on me, that Santa Claus thinks I'm a girl. "No, Olive Milner? What a shame, she must have gone." And Santa Claus continues to call out the remaining children's names.

"Why on earth didn't you go up?" hisses my mother later.

"Because everyone would laugh at me if I went to collect a girl's present."

"But it's a boy's present. I know what it is," said my mother.

"Yes, but he called out a girl's name. Olive, not Oliver. I'm not going up."

My mother wasn't very impressed. "Stupid child."

I never did find out what the present was. I never collected it.

Wednesday, December 23, Topped Out

The North Tower of the World Trade Centre in New York City is topped out at 1,368 feet (417 m), making it the tallest building in the world.

1971, Kano. Cross Hills, West Yorkshire, England

Tuesday, January 12, School Starts[44]

As Gerald had predicted, my air ticket had been booked in advance. So as term started, I was just boarding the VC10 at Kano.

Travelling as a UM (an unaccompanied minor) *and* a member of the BOAC Junior Jet Club was, I imagine, as close to being the child to the prince and princess of Monaco. On regular scheduled services, we children were treated like royalty – I imagine the airline was terrified we'd be abducted so we were pretty much chaperoned from arrival at our departure airport to the arrivals lounge at the other end by a gloriously glamorous bevvy of young trainee air stewardesses.

What heaven it was to actually be recognised on a flight by one of the regular air stewardess! That alone was worth an invitation to the cockpit to exchange weather and flight information with the captain and co-pilot. On one occasion, the co-pilot actually gave up his seat for me for ten minutes and the captain let me bank the VC10 to the right, and then correct our course.

The Lollipop Specials, which were semi-chartered flights ferrying expatriate families' children to and from their schools in the UK were hateful affairs. Discipline was lax and the cabin crew gave up any pretence of keeping us in order. I liked my travel five-star, and travelling with other children was anything but.

None of this luxury was available on the Nigerian Airways flights.

On one occasion, it was reported that a flight was downed because a family unfamiliar with air travel lit a fire under the family cooking pot in the toilets in

---

[44] January 3 – The Open University begins in the United Kingdom.

January 5 – The first ever One Day International cricket match is played between Australia and England at the Melbourne Cricket Ground.

the back of one of their old Tri-Stars, depressurising the cabin, with the total loss of the plane.

Even as a child, it never seemed right to board a plane through its anus, but that's how you boarded a Nigerian TriStar in cattle class. It was never great news to learn the bank had booked me on a NA flight.

Thursday, January 14, Arrive Back

Classes are underway but immediately on my arrival, I am put into the library to complete the School Christmas Quiz. A tradition started when the school began. A hundred fiendish questions are sent home in the boys' luggage at Christmas with a view to involving the parents in some quasi-educational pursuit connected to the school.

I forget all the answers my parents had a look at, and the Milners do really badly. The shame is exacerbated because of course our positions in the quiz are circulated when Gerald Watts posts out the answers.

In the future, my dad bases the British Club Christmas Quiz, exclusively on the Malsis quiz, and for the next three years, the Milners do much better. Resulting in us winning in my final Christmas term.

Sunday, February 15, 10 x 10 = 82

Decimal day; the United Kingdom and Ireland both switch to decimal currency.

At the Wednesday tuck shop that the school ran for us, we handed over our 6D shilling, which was converted into 5p. Historically, twelve old halfpennies = 6D, or a shilling, bought you 12 Black Jacks. But the new 5p divided into ten half ps only bought you 10 Black Jacks.

I always thought decimalisation was a swizz. Still do.

Saturday, February 28, Rocket Man

Evel Knievel sets a world record and jumps 19 cars in Ontario, California. All the more remarkable as the next leap year is not till 1972…[I'll get my coat.]

Wednesday, March 25, Not Entirely Satisfactory

MALSIS SCHOOL, CROSS HILLS, KEIGHLEY, ENGLAND

Malsis School Report
Name:
Age: 9.6
Easter Term 1970.
Form: Junior C. Number of boys in form: 19.
Average Age of Form: 9.3
Position at the end of term: 16.
Subject reports
English: Oliver's work is not entirely satisfactory: he must try and work consistently well. He needs to concentrate fully, listen carefully to instructions and carry them out. While not curtailing a lively and imaginative approach to creative writing he should try to make his stories realistic. Exam position: 15/19.
Mathematics: Oliver has worked much more steadily this term and has produced some really good results. His second examination paper was especially pleasing, as it required a good deal of thought. If you could only put this effort into his class work the results might start us all. I'm sure that he has the ability to do better. Exam position: 13/19.
Discovery: During the discovery lessons which incorporate French, History, Geography, Nature Study, Scripture and the educational television programs, Oliver is still apt to draw attention to himself by asking irrelevant questions. He must try to develop a more mature attitude to life here.
Music: He is now making much more rapid progress.
Housemaster's report: Oliver remains a cheerful young man about the school and is delighted with himself for coming 43rd out of 70 in the Junior running competition, a great improvement on last year. He still lacks hobbies and interests. Oliver has not had a single day in sick bay this term, which is a great improvement. He is eating better and I hope that one day the scales will be surprised.
Headmaster's report: The overall standard in this form is high and I am sure that Oliver has the ability to keep pace with the others. All too often,

however, he shows a lack of determination with new work and he seems to find it difficult to sustain his effort for any length of time. *G E Watts.*

Next term begins on Tuesday, April 27, 1971.

Thursday, June 3, The Finest Margins

It's a great day to be alive. For a Leeds United fan.

WINNERS! 1971 Fairs Cup Final (the precursor to the Europa League Cup). Leeds United win on away goals having drawn 2–2 vs. Juventus in Turin and then holding them to a 1–1 draw at Eland Road.

Somewhere in the attic, I still have the pennant of that day.

Friday, June 16, Hello Brother[45]

Sports day. I am entered in the House team for Triple Jump, where I come 4th out of 45. Long Jump, where I come 4th out of 50.

---

[45] June 30, death in space – after a successful mission aboard Salyut 1, the world's first manned space station, the crew of the Soyuz 11 spacecraft die after their air supply leaks out through a faulty valve.

The classical musical fantasy family film *Willy Wonka & the Chocolate Factory*, based on the novel *Charlie & the Chocolate Factory* and starring Gene Wilder and Jack Albertson is released today.

In the 100 yards sprint, second left, I dip for the line moments later Jack Barrow's tannoy commentary wafts across in our direction…"And there goes Olly Milner dashing to the line so he can see his younger brother. News has just reached us his new brother was born this morning at 11 o'clock…"

I slow down to digest this information. I have a brother.

Saturday, July 24, Not Strong

MALSIS SCHOOL, CROSS HILLS, KEIGHLEY, ENGLAND

Malsis School Report
Name: Oliver Milner.
Age: 9.7
Summer Term 1971.
Form: Junior C. Number of boys in form: 19.
Average Age of Form: 9.4
Position at the end of term: 18.

Subject reports [46]

English: He has found the standard of work difficult to maintain. Exam position: 12/19.

French: Not strong, but keen in a rather disorganised sort of way. His work is not yet neat, but he has made an effort to put that right. Exam position: 18/19.

Mathematics: Oliver is still not giving his mind fully to his work. When he does get on the results are quite satisfactory but he does lose ground when he is daydreaming. Exam position 19/19.

Trumpet: A very good start has been made. Works hard, knows the fingering of notes and has a very pleasant tone. Very pleased with standard of playing up to date.

Housemaster's report: Rather better. Oliver has made more effort to involve himself in the various activities here. He did well to pass his ASA swimming bronze award for personal survival and he seems to enjoy his carpentry and trumpet lessons.

Headmaster's report: Although not especially strong in the classroom, Oliver has made sufficient headway to justify promotion through to the middle school in September. *G E Watts.*

Next term begins on Wednesday, September 15, 1971.

Monday, July 26, Zaria

Apollo 15 is launched. A few days later, astronauts David Scott and James Irwin become the first to ride in the Lunar Roving Vehicle, a day after landing on the Moon.

I fly, as an unaccompanied minor, on the Lollipop Special BOAC VC10 to Zaria Airport, via Kano. It's a little bit dodgy after Kano, as I have to transfer to the inland Nigeria Airways flight. I must have made it okay, as we had a lovely holiday in Zaria. Dad had yet another new big house. Mum had the baby and my three-year-old sister to look after so I had a lovely time, pretty much on my own during the daytime weekdays.

Although still quite far north the landscape around Zaria was much more lush, and at the end of the compound, which we shared with another expatriate family's house, the tropical jungle started. Millipedes became my favourite

---

[46] "If you do what you've always done, you'll get what you've always got." – Anon

playmates for a time. Then Fiona Whitaker. Then back to millipedes when her family returned to the UK.

On their last night in Zaria, we threw a big party for the family. After dinner, I ran back to our house to pick up a present we'd forgotten to bring with us. In the dark, I missed the gap that separated our two houses and ran full tilt into the rusty barbed wire fence.

As I thrashed about to get it off me, it wound around me tighter and tighter. Realising something was wrong the search party soon founded me guided by my howling. I imagine I must have brought the party to an end. I don't recall being especially ill, but the threat of tetanus, at least, must have been a worry to my mother.

Fifty years later, I still have two small nicks on temple and on my ankle where the barbed wire left its mark.

Tuesday, August 10, Small, Orange and with Very Long Arms

Mr. Tickle, the first book in the *Mr. Men* series is published.

Sunday, October 31, Into London[47]

A bomb planted by the IRA explodes at the top of the Post Office Tower in London.

Friday, December 17, At Long Last

MALSIS SCHOOL, CROSS HILLS, KEIGHLEY, ENGLAND

Malsis School Report
Name: Oliver Milner

---

[47] October 1 – Walt Disney World opens in Orlando, Florida.

October 30 – Rev Ian Paisley's Democratic Unionist Party is founded in Northern Ireland.

December 4 – The Montreux Casino burns down during a Frank Zappa concert, memorialised in the Deep Purple song *Smoke on the Water*. It's the law that every first borne child must learn how to pluck the opening four bars of Smoke on the Water on any stringed instrument. Preferably, a guitar.

Age: 10.3

Christmas Term 1971.

Form: III C. Number of boys in form: 12.

Average Age of Form: 9.10

Position at the end of term: 5.

Subject reports

English: An enthusiastic member of the class who has produced some lively work. He is always ready to contribute in discussions and can generally be said to be making the best use of his opportunities. Exam position: 2/12.

French: Oliver works at great speed and with plenty of enthusiasm, but he is neither accurate nor neat enough to do himself justice. A steady approach would be beneficial. Exam position: 8/12.

Mathematics: Oliver has worked very well this term and must be congratulated on his progress. He's appeared more mature and is willing to tackle his own problems, a thing which he has not done in the mathematics lessons since he came. Well done! Exam position: 9/12.

Trumpet: I am very pleased with the progress Oliver has made this term. He tries hard and practises well all the work given to him he should be ready for more advanced work next term. Exam position 1/12.

Housemaster's report: Oliver's main failing in the classroom would seem to be over enthusiasm and this is certainly a fault in the right direction. But I hope that he will try very hard to restrain his impetuosity next term as his performance during the second half of term was rather disappointing. Oliver contributes to House activities in every way that he can. He swam in our victorious Junior Relay team, and also reached the semi-final of the Under 10 Draughts competition. Typical of his enthusiasm was his decision to enter the Open Chess competition and he did very well to win his first two matches.

Headmaster's report: It is good to see Oliver in the top half of a form at long last. It is the first time he has been in this position since he came here. He has worked quite well throughout the term, although age is not on his side and he will need to redouble his efforts if he is to reach a reasonable Common Entrance standard in three years' time. We find him a cheerful young man and he certainly appears to enjoy his days here. *G E Watts*.

Next term begins on Tuesday, January 11, 1972.

Sunday, December 19, Cinny

The controversial dystopian crime film *A Clockwork Orange*, directed by Stanley Kubrick is released in New York City. The other film that Malcolm McDowell famously starred in was the first pornographic film that I ever remember seeing. Caligula came out in 1979 and I saw it in one of the seedy downstairs cinemas off Leicester Square a few months later.

All the stars who appeared in it – John Gielgud even makes an appearance – have subsequently disowned it. But it looked to me as if they were all having great fun. I did.[48]

---

[48] Also worth noting this month: December 20 – Two groups of French doctors involved in humanitarian aid merge to form Médecins Sans Frontières.

December 30 – The first McDonald's in Australia opens in Yagoona, Sydney. That's progress I guess. Of a sort. About time, Australia should experience fine dining, for them.

1972, Cross Hills, West Yorkshire. Maiduguri, Northern Nigeria

Tuesday, January 11, Grow Up

Back to Malsis for the Easter term.

Friday, January 14, Wash bag

Letter Writing. Lesson 3

Hi Dad,

It's a bit sad to be back at Malsis after such a good holiday, but the BOAC flight was brilliant. I've now got 44,134 miles in my Junior Jet Club book and the Captain of the flight, Charles Wainwright let me go in the cockpit (VC10) as we were crossing the Atlas mountains. (I reckon only Gascoigne in 5th Year has more air mileage than me, as they live in Singapore AND he's nearly two years older than me.

Lots has happened here since the hols. I'M IN A NEW DORM! As they didn't manage to finish renovating the bedrooms over Old Schoolroom I'm now in a brand-new dorm called Dorm C. It's at the end of lower school corridor and next door to Mr and Mrs Rose's flat. It's great, it's like an old barn, with all the old beams and I'm in with McKenzie, Hainsworth, Shreve, Tyler, Wade, Schmidt, Clarke and Nicholson. As I arrived last Jimmy saved the end bed for me, next to him. So I'm furthest from the door. But, how neat is this, on the other side from me, next to Shreve, there's a quarter sized door next to his locker which is a fire exit into the top floor of music department. I bet someone will be playing the violin one day and we'll all burst in on them!

It's definitely the best dorm in the school, but we've all got to be quiet as mice at night according to Mabel (Mrs R) because if she and Fleabag (Mr R) EVER hear us after lights out, we'll be gated. Schmidt's bound to get kicked out, but everyone else in the other dorms that aren't finished have been squeezed into the main school corridors, we're really lucky.

Lots of love,
Olly

PS: BTW when matron unpacked my case I seem to have your washbag by mistake? Sorry.
PPS: He who laughs last didn't get the joke till the end!

Sunday, January 30, Bloody Sunday

The British Army allegedly kills 14 unarmed nationalist civil rights marchers in Derry, Northern Ireland.

Friday, February 17, Beetles

Volkswagen Beetle sales exceed those of the Ford Model T when the 15,007,034[th] Beetle is produced.

This would certainly have been news between my father and me. I loved the Beetle's wrong way roundness. The engine in the back, not requiring any water to cool it down. Handy in Nigeria.

At Malsis, Mrs Rose spoils her boys in Dorm 13. Once a month, for half an hour before lights out, we are invited into her sitting room listening to her favourite Classical music. We would have sooner it was the Radio 1 Charts, but it's a treat to sit on a grown-ups carpet eating Arctic roll.

Letter Writing. Lesson 3

Dear Dad,
Last night Mabel asked if we'd like to learn about Beethoven and Mozart so we all put on our dressing gown as went out of the side door of the dorm into her and Fleabag's flat. It's huge and on three floors, and smells of Imperial Leather, which is nice and homey. Reminded me of Grandma and Grandad's house.

To get to their living room you have to go down a fantastic spiral staircase. She gave us all Arctic roll which was terrific. I really liked the music, she did a clever thing. She has a cassette recorder that plays two tapes. "I'm going to play you two serenades by these two famous composers and you have to tell me which one is Beethoven and which one is Mozart."

They were both good. The first one was loud and shouty and the second one was obviously Mozart cos it was tricksy and clever. We really should get both: Beethoven, wind octet in E flat, op. 13 and Mozart, serenade no 12 in C minor, K388. I'm really not sure who I liked best.

No one else seemed bothered, they just wanted seconds of Arctic roll. I thought it was rude to ask.

Got to go.
Lots of Love,
Olly

PS: How does Dolby work?
PPS: People in glasshouses, shouldn't undress with the lights on.

Friday, March 3, Amanuensis[49]

Letter Writing. Lesson 3

Hi Dad,
Last night in her flat, Mabel and Fleabag gave us each a glass of milk and a new biscuit called a Hobnob, which is amazing. Like a chocolate digestive, only a trillion times more nutty and satisfying, without having any nuts.

I now know who my favourite classical composer he's called Delius. His Christian name was Fred, and he was from Bradford (shame yeah I know,

---

[49] February 21 – February 28 – US President Richard M. Nixon makes an unprecedented 8-day visit to the People's Republic of China and meets with Mao Zedong.
February 22 – Aldershot Bombing: An Official IRA bomb kills seven in Aldershot, England.
March 2 – The Pioneer 10 spacecraft is launched from Cape Kennedy to be the first man-made satellite to leave the solar system.

WEST Yorkshire!!) and he went blind so a man called Fenby had to write down all his music for him. Anyway, we listened to both sides of the record and the first side was all serene and soothing, (In a Summer Garden and Brigg Fair) but the next piece was amazing. It was called, On hearing the first cuckoo in Spring. And you could actually hear the cuckoo!!

I think it's so clever when composers do that. Mr Rose wasn't sure if the cuckoo was a bassoon or an oboe. The Halle orchestra were AMAZING. We were able to stay up till 9.15, which was great but disaster, Shreve and Nicholson were then caught talking after lights out at 9.22, and now we won't have music next Thursday. I think Mrs Rose is as disappointed as we were cos I think she likes being a pretend aunty to us. She never mentions whether she and Fleabag have their own kids. I expect not they are nearly 50. Their flat is very posh and proper too.

Lots of love,
Olly

PS: Whitaker managed to get a six and the ball went through Mr Watts's study!! As it's not been done for over 50 years the WHOLE SCHOOL is now having ice cream for dessert all week as a reward.
PPS: A bird in the hand, can poop on your sleeve.

Wednesday, March 22, A Most Cheerful Individual

Malsis School, Cross Hills, Keighley, England

Malsis School Report
Name: Oliver Milner
Age: 10.7
Easter Term 1972.
Form: 3 B. Number of boys in form: 14.
Average Age of Form: 10.2
Position at the end of term: 1st.
Subject reports

English: An excellent term, full of good ideas and enthusiasm. His weakness is impetuosity. He is in so much haste to get everything down on paper that accuracy and presentation sometimes suffer. Exam position: 2/14.

Mathematics: a very good term. Although Oliver's work is below the standard expected for a boy of his age, his efforts this term have done much towards closing this gap. I hope that he will continue to work in this way in the future. Exam position: 2/14.

French: Top of a mediocre form as far as French is concerned. Tries very hard and is eager to please. Exam position: 1/14.

Trumpet: He tries hard and works well. He is keen to make progress and shows some talent. Tone production and fingering are satisfactory. I am well pleased with the work he has done this term.

Housemaster's report: Oliver is to be commended on an excellent term in the classroom: but it must be remembered that he will be rather old by the time he reaches a Common Entrance form. His excellent tally of Star points has helped the house considerably in a closely fought competition. As well as winning a *Bene* for his work (i.e. 100 Stars), Oliver sang an accomplished solo in the school concert.

Headmaster's report: Clearly, this has been Oliver's best term to date and I'm delighted to see him at the top of the form. We find him a most cheerful individual, with a delightful sense of humour and he is very popular among the other boys.

Next term begins on Tuesday, April 25, 1972.

Self, maintaining a stiff upper lip; a most cheerful individual, baby brother, and a not so cheerful sister – she probably hated the dress – almost certainly about to set off for the British Club in Dad's white Opel Rekord, in northern Nigeria, probably Maiduguri.

Friday, April 28, Three of the Worst

Letter writing. Lesson 3

Dear Dad,

Mr Watts has told me to write to you and apologise and explain why he gave me three strokes of the cane yesterday.

Shreve lobbed jam at me during semolina for lunch so I flicked it back on the end of my knife like a catapult. It went miles, really fast but it missed Shreve and unfortunately splatted Mr Won the back of his jacket. The cleaning bill will be added to my fees. Sorry. Sorry.

I got 3 strokes and Shreve 4. He blubbered in Mr W's study. I cried a bit when we went to get our strokes checked in the san, but Sister Sutton says they are just a bit blue and purple but we are off swimming for a week if we want to.

I still think It's hilarious that Tyler dived in the pool last term after he got caned and it hurt so much we weed and pooed all at the same time! Lucky I was ahead of him during lengths!! McKenzie says he got a mouthful of wee, but hasn't been sick yet.

Anyway, it's only the 2nd time in three years I've got the cane so I hope that's ok? It still hurts a lot. Were you ever caned?

The new music teacher is called Mr Hope. He is a really famous organist according to Tyler's mother. He takes us for choir but I won't get him for trumpet as he only takes strings, woodwind, piano and percussion.

Someone opened all the gerbils' cages last week and two have escaped. Hedges says Burton's python has eaten them. Whoever did it is in real trouble if they're caught.

You know how foxes or owls just leave feathers when they catch a pigeon? Yesterday on the 2nd XI pitch the grounds man was cutting the outfield with the gang mower and there was a ziiiip noise and just light brown fur and red. Which must have been blood. I think it was a gerbil. There was a bit of tail and toe left.

Have nearly finished the moon landing transfer scene. It's really cool! Except I think I've got the Apollo module upside down. Grrr. Will send it you next week. Hope the weather is nice in Nigeria. It is here.

All my love,
Olly

PS: Anderson had a late class with Mr Hopwood yesterday and missed tea. He cried all last night in the dorm. He wouldn't say why but I think Mr H must be really strict cos Anderson looked really scared after double piano.
PPS: Apologies for getting caned.

Saturday, May 6, Legends

WINNERS! FA Cup Final 1972. Allan Clarke scores the only goal, Leeds United 1 Arsenal 0. However, it's the banner in the Leeds end at Wembley, which steals the headlines: *Norman bites yer legs.*

Thursday, May 18, Special

Four troopers of the British Special Air Service and Special Boat Service are parachuted onto the ocean liner *Queen Elizabeth 2* 1,600 kilometres (1,000 mi) across the Atlantic after a bomb threat and ransom demand, which turn out to be bogus.

Friday, May 26, Salt

Richard Nixon and Leonid Brezhnev sign the Strategic Arms Limitation Talks, SALT I treaty, in Moscow, as well as the Anti-Ballistic Missile Treaty and other agreements.

Thursday, June 8, Vietnam

Associated Press photographer Nick Ut takes his Pulitzer Prize winning photograph of a naked nine-year-old Phan Thi Kim Phuc running down a road after being burned by napalm.

About this time, I am rehearsing for yet another school play. I love it. I am precocious onstage, possibly because I know my mother will never see me act, and the school's attention gives me confidence.

It's not always to my advantage to be the centre of attention.

Classroom Scene 1.34 pm, After Lunch

Master on Duty: Milner, 'here please.

OM: Sir?

Master on Duty: Is this yours?

[He holds a yellow packet of Wrigley's Juicy Fruit up to the class]

OM: Yes sir.

Master on Duty: We have a rule, don't we?

OM: Err, yes sir. No sweets in Detention.

Master on Duty: And what do we have to do if we bring sweets into a classroom?

OM: We have to share them sir.

Master on Duty: Very good Milner, yes. Proceed.

OM: But sir, there are only six pieces, and 24 in the room.

Master on Duty: In which case you'll need some scissors then to divide up your loot, won't you?

111

Scissors? Has anyone got any scissors, to lend to this Villainous Creature? Thank you, Montague.

OM: Thank you sir.

Master on Duty: Milner, what are you?

OM: A Villainous Creature, sir.

Master on Duty: Milner, my God boy. What are you doing? If there are 24 people in the class and six pieces of chewing gum how many portions do you need to cut each piece into? Why have you cut each piece into three?

[Sighs]

Incredibly your mathematics is *even* worse than your dire French! No wonder you're in Detention.

Get out. And take this… muck with you.

[Door slams. Fade lights]

Friday, June 23, Watergate

US President Richard M. Nixon and White House chief of staff H. R. Haldeman are taped talking about using the CIA to obstruct the FBI's investigation into the Watergate break-ins.

For my own part, I was doing much to scandalise my teachers with my own errant behaviour.

Yours truly, front right, talking to myself as per usual above Haworth, in West Yorkshire, just a lunchtime away from locomotive catastrophe.

The West Yorkshire town of Haworth is famous of course as the birthplace and home of the Brontës. For little boys, however, on an afternoon field trip by far the best attraction is the steam railway. About a dozen old locomotives are parked outside, and along the platform, it was possible to inspect the carriage and the engine locomotive itself.

Not unreasonably, Mrs Rose assumed that the empty driver's carriage was a museum piece, which remained stationary. However, what none of the adults realised was that all the locomotives worked and all had full water tenders, ready for when the driver needed to build up steam.

It was great fun pulling the levels and making imaginary toot noises on the whistle. I pulled one lever and suddenly there were shrieks along the platform as children and adults too were washed off the platform as I accidentally released tons of water instantly from the water tender.

I didn't receive the cane for that. In hindsight, the locomotives should probably have been better supervised with clear signs forbidding naughty ten-year-olds from crawling all over them.

113

Malsis School, Cross Hills, Keighley, England

Malsis School Report

Name: Oliver Milner

Age: 10.10

Summer Term 1972.

Form: 3 B. Number of boys in form: 14.

Average Age of Form: 10.2

Position at the end of term: 2nd.

Subject reports

French: Oliver has done well again this term. There is no need to worry about his moving down from 1st to 2nd will stop he should still do well. Exam position: 2/14.

Mathematics: Oliver has had a satisfactory term and has worked well, although I had expected a better mark in his examination. With a little more effort he could be top of his group in this subject. Exam position: 2/14.

History: A Disappointing examination mark spoiled what had been a good terms work. He has worked keenly and well in class this term. Exam position: 9/14.

Geography: A very good term. Oliver has produced some interesting work. Exam position: 2/14.

Scripture: He has listened attentively and made useful contributions to the dramatic work that we have attempted. His examination result was very good. Exam position: 2/14.

Science: Oliver is a keen and lively member of this form and has made good progress. Exam position: 2/14.

English: Another very good term, with more care taken over accuracy, and well-meaning – if sporadic – attempts to write neatly. Exam position: 1/14.

Trumpet: His sight-reading and trumpet technique are well up to standard. He works hard at all times, especially at the practical side. Theory, however, needs a little more attention.

Housemaster's report: Oliver has done well to maintain his position near the top of this form: I hope that he will try very hard to be first again next term, where he will be working with the same group of boys in IVB. It must be noted that Oliver is well above the Standard Age for this Form. This means that if he stays at Malsis until December 1974, which I understand is the present plan, it will still only be possible for him to spend one term in the Common Entrance form.

He has received one or two Conduct Marks this term for silly behaviour. For the most part, I have found him sensible and responsible, and I hope that he will avoid these lapses next term.

Headmaster's report: There is little I can add to these reports and for the most part we are well pleased with the progress which Oliver has continued to make. The point which Mr Moore has made in the Housemaster's report is certainly very valid and I would like to have a chat with you both about his term of entry to his Independent School when you are next on leave.

Best wishes to you all for the Holidays. *GE Watts*

Next term begins on Tuesday, September 12, 1972.

Saturday, July 15, Maiduguri

We fly out to Nigeria. The holidays can't start soon enough for me. It's been a pretty poor, unhappy and nondescript term for me at Malsis. I'm neither a Junior or anyone of significance in Middle School. Does everyone suffer this fate in their school years? I reckon we all must, at some stage.

The new house Dad takes us to is his latest residence in Maiduguri, where he is opening up the latest branch for Standard Chartered Bank.

It's an impressive building with a veranda, which overlooks the nearby British Club.

Maiduguri is the capital of Borno State in the northeast of Nigeria. It sits along the seasonal Ngadda River, which disappears into the Firki swamps in the areas around Lake Chad. Nowadays Boko Haram is headquartered in Maiduguri, but fifty years ago, it was a town on the edge of Empire and the Sahara.

One of the regular features of living in Maiduguri was that it being so far north the car was forever sinking into soft sand on one of the many weekend picnics we went on. I have a picture of my baby sister sitting on the parched riverbed. In the rainy season, the Ngadda would be a raging torrent, twenty feet deep. Now it's a dust bowl. The hippopotamuses and crocodiles are all down river, taking their summer in Lake Chad.

On such an afternoon, Mum and Dad were joined by their new found friends Bill and Fred. Bill and Fred were hydrologists. They'd spend three weeks in the bush drilling wells, looking for fresh water, and one week off, enjoying R&R.

Mum had been cutting Dad's hair on the veranda, and seeing this one Saturday afternoon, they sauntered over to the house to ask if she'd cut their hair.

Barbers in Nigeria just shaved their customers' heads. Anyone with rudimentary skills with a comb and a pair of scissors was a rare find. That afternoon turned into dinner at ours and later, more drinks, far into the night.

"You must let me get you something, to thank you for your hospitality," said Fred.

"Hang on, I've got something in the car you might like."

He came back with a record.

"You won't have heard of him yet, but my stepson Reg is quite excited about it. It's called *Honky Chateau*, it's just come out in America. My favourite track is Rocket Man."

So that holiday, on the edge of the southern Sahara, we played Elton John's LP on repeat all through the summer.

It was probably the only copy of the LP in Africa.

A gift from Fred Fairbrother, Reginald Dwight's stepdad.

Fred Fairbrother, aka 'Derf' to Elton John, Mum and my baby sister, in a dried out waddi, Maiduguri, northern Nigeria.

Friday, July 21, Bloody Friday

Twenty-two bombs planted by the Provisional IRA explode in Belfast, Northern Ireland; nine people are killed and 130 seriously injured.

Monday, July 31, Bloody Monday

The troubles intensify in Northern Ireland.

Claudy bombing 10:00 am: three car bombs in Claudy, County Londonderry, kill nine. It becomes public knowledge only in 2010 that a local Catholic priest was an IRA officer believed to be involved in the bombings, but his role was covered up by the authorities.

Operation Motorman 4:00 pm: the British Army begins to regain control of the *no-go areas* established by Irish republican paramilitaries in Belfast, Derry and Newry.

Friday, September 1, Chess, Cod, Terror

Bobby Fischer defeats Boris Spassky in a chess match in Reykjavík, Iceland, becoming the first American world chess champion.

The Second Cold War begins between the United Kingdom and Iceland.

Eleven Israeli athletes at the 1972 Summer Olympics in Munich are murdered after eight members of the Arab terrorist group Black September invade the Olympic Village; five guerrillas and one policeman are also killed in a failed hostage rescue.

Sunday, September 10, John Player Special

The Brazilian driver Emerson Fittipaldi wins the Italian Grand Prix at Monza and becomes the youngest Formula One World Champion.

He is also my favourite driver, for having by far the best-looking car, the black and gold JPS livery has never been bettered. Best of all, he also possesses the maddest, hugest sideburns in the world.

How do they even fit inside his helmet?

Monday, October 16, Life in the Dales[50]

Emmerdale, the British soap opera, debuts.

Wednesday, November 1, Reading Matters

Ezra Pound, American poet (b. 1885) dies. Nothing is said of this at Malsis that I can remember. Odd given our inspirational English teacher was so keen to keep us up to date with contemporary poetry events. Ted Hughes' *Crow* being a current classroom read. Also Leon Garfield.

My favourite book is currently *If only they could talk* by James Herriot, the first in a series of eight books set in the 1930s–1950s Yorkshire Dales about animals and their owners. A number of my classmates are from housing stock and refuse to read the romanticised view of farm life through the eyes of the, even by then, world famous vet.

The books are so good; I don't want to be a vet. I want to be a writer, like him.

Tuesday, November 28, Guillotined

The last criminal execution takes place in Paris. Roger Bontems and Claude Buffet – the Clairvaux Mutineers – are guillotined at La Santé Prison by chief executioner André Obrecht. Bontems had been found innocent of murder by the court, but as Buffet's accomplice, he is condemned to death as well. President Georges Pompidou, in private an abolitionist, upholds both death sentences in deference to French public opinion.[51]

---

[50] October 1 – DNA and the joy of sex – the first publication reporting the production of a recombinant DNA molecule marks the birth of modern molecular biology methodology. Alex Comfort's bestselling manual *The Joy of Sex* also pops out today.

[51] November 29 – Atari kicks off the first generation of video games with the release of their seminal arcade version of Pong, the first game to achieve commercial success.

November 30 – Vietnam War: White House Press Secretary Ron Ziegler tells the press that there will be no more public announcements concerning United States' troop withdrawals from Vietnam, due to the fact that troop levels are now down to 27,000.

Monday, December 11, Moon Dust

Apollo 17 lands on the Moon. The mission includes three astronauts and five mice.

Three days later, Eugene Cernan is the last person to walk on the Moon, after he and Harrison Schmitt complete the third and final extra-vehicular activity (EVA) of Apollo 17.

This still stands as the last time man has stood on the lunar surface. It is beyond sad.

Friday, December 15, Conduct Marks

Malsis School, Cross Hills, Keighley, England

Malsis School Report
Name: Oliver Milner
Age: 11.3
Winter Term 1972.
Form: 4 B. Number of boys in form: 16.
Average Age of Form: 10.7
Position at the end of term: 1st.
Subject reports
French: A Good result. Oliver is the best of a very limited form. He works to the best of his ability. Exam position: 2/14.
Mathematics: He has worked well but his level of attainment is very low for his age. Exam position: 5/14.
Scripture: His work throughout the term has been of a high standard and he is making good progress. Exam position: Exam position: 1/14.
Science: Oliver is a keen and lively member of this form and has made good progress. Exam position: 2/14.
English: An Excellent term, he has made great efforts, shown every sign of enjoying his long and lively compositions and has improved the appearance of his work. His list of books read is long and varied. Well done! Exam position: 2/14.
Housemaster's report: This is an excellent set of reports, and Oliver's fine score of Star Points week by week has been of great assistance to Lund in the House competition.

Again, Oliver has too many entries under his name in the Conduct Book. I have explained to him that, if he is habitually silly and tries to draw attention to himself, he must not be surprised if on occasions he becomes a butt for others. Obviously, every effort is made to prevent unpleasantness of this kind, and I have asked Oliver to mention it to me, if ever it recurs. I thought he made a splendid Muse in the school play.

Headmaster's report: It is very good to see Oliver at the top of the form, once again, although there are one or two weaknesses especially in his Mathematics. The second paragraph of Mr Moore's report is highly relevant, of course, the points have been made to Oliver and I hope that we will see an improvement next term.

Do please let me know your impressions of Bootham when you have visited.
G E Watts

Next term begins on Wednesday, January 17, 1973.

Conduct marks were entered into the Conduct Book by the MoD (Master on Duty) and were given to any boy who had misbehaved. Typically, they could be given for fighting, shouting, acts of vandalism, repeated untidiness, i.e. any act of behaviour that didn't warrant being caned by Gerald Watts.

Not only was it a black spot against your character, it was also damaging to your House score, because a point would be taken off your House's points tally. You were then also in trouble with your housemates, as well as in the staff room.

Ten conduct marks in a term would result in the miscreant being given a Conduct card, which in most boys' view were worse than being caned or suspended from school. If you were on a Conduct card, which lasted seven days, all school privileges, such as tuck shop, ice cream for dessert, TV, extended lights out were all withdrawn *for the whole school.* Boy, were you unpopular.

In the five years whilst I was at Malsis, there were about twenty Conduct cards handed out. Last term, I got two.

If you were on a Conduct card, you had to report to the MoD or PoD on the hour outside of lessons, and at the start and end of every break time from 06:30 when you got up to 20:30 lights out. In between times, you were on clearing away and sweeping rota every night from 18:30 to 19:30, after prep.

120

And if you missed *any* of the 12 signatures for the day, the Conduct card was extended by another day. So it was essential to always carry it with you.

To have to complete a week of such menial duties as an 11-year-old, smirked at by seven and eight-year-olds, who all knew you'd been a naughty boy, was shaming beyond measure. But it did the trick. It made me turn a corner and within 18 months, I was Deputy Head Boy.

Why I was such a naughty little boy in 1972 is anyone's guess. Perhaps it was borne out of frustration that I was constantly on the move? Harrogate – Malsis – Nigeria? Perhaps it was because I didn't spend long enough with the people I loved. But that changed over time. The next three years became some of the happiest in my life.

Better to be a bigger fish in a small pond.

Gerald and the rest of the staffroom knew what they were doing.[52]

Sunday, December 31, Wait Two Secs

For the first and last time, a second leap second is added (23:59:60) to a year, making 1972 366 days and 2 seconds long, the longest year ever within the context of Coordinated Universal Time.

---

[52] "Use what talent you possess. The woods would be very silent indeed if no birds sang there except those that sang best." – Henry Van Dyke.

Our very own Herbie. Just the sound of a rear-engined, air cooled VW sends me back to this picture. There were very few tarmacked roads in Nigeria in the 1970s, and the VW's robust build was perfect for driving along the pot-holed laterite roads. Yes, those are leather shorts I'm wearing. No, there's no rational explanation.

1973, Cross Hills, West Yorkshire, England. Jos, Nigeria

Wednesday, January 17, Five of the Worst

Easter term at Malsis begins.[53]

After another hot Christmas, this time in Jos where Dad was opening a new branch for the bank, the term started very much as the last one had ended, with my doing much better in class, but in trouble with authority.

This time however I was totally without blame.

On Saturday night, having had a troubled 24 hours with an asthma attack I was in the San. At around 8.30 pm, Sister Spickett came into the sick wing and said I had to go down to the headmaster's study where the whole of my dorm was waiting for me.

But as I put on my dressing gown, Sister made me put on my shorts and underpants under my pyjama trousers. Clearly, I was for the cane again, but why?

Dormitory 13 was at the end of the Middle School corridor, on the floor above the classrooms, and because of its distance from the housemaster's flat rarely received a patrol until it was time for lights out.

On this particular Saturday night, Fred Jones had dared Bertram Schmidt that he wouldn't be able to climb out of the window at one end of the dorm, onto the window sill outside and shuffle along the length of the dorm and into the window at the opposite end.

---

[53] January 1 – The United Kingdom, the Republic of Ireland and Denmark enter the European Economic Community, which later becomes the European Union.
January 14 – Elvis Presley's concert in Hawaii is the first worldwide telecast by an entertainer that is watched by more people than the Apollo Moon landings.
January 15 – Vietnam War: Citing progress in peace negotiations, US President Richard Nixon announces the suspension of offensive action in North Vietnam.

All was going according to plan until with two yards to go the Master on Duty came in to turn out the lights and caught Bertram in the act, on the wrong side of the window. Possibly, because of the fright this little escapade gave the MoD, he immediately called for the headmaster to administer the appropriate sanction.

Hearing what had happened Gerald demanded all eight of us in the dorm should assemble outside his study, because the six who had done nothing to stop such a dangerous game were equally guilty.

I can only assume that Sister Spickett had said something to Gerald because I received barely three taps across my dressing gown clad bottom.

The relief made me giggle, and inevitably, I then received two quite genuine thwacks, for insolence. Schmidt received six strokes, the next highest sanction being expulsion; the other boys were given four strokes each.

Monday, January 22, Knockouts

George Foreman defeats Joe Frazier to win the heavyweight world boxing championship.

A Royal Jordanian Boeing 707 flight from Jeddah crashes in Kano, Nigeria; 176 people are killed.

The next day, US President Richard Nixon announces that a peace accord has been reached in Vietnam. US involvement in the Vietnam War ends with the signing of the Paris Peace Accords.

America is still in no mood to support Britain, or France, their co-members of the UN Security Council, both countries steadfastly stood to one side over Vietnam. At the end of the month, Pan American and Trans World Airlines cancelled their options to buy 13 Concorde airliners, thereby making further production uneconomic. What a coincidence.

Saturday, March 24, It's a Gas

Pink Floyd's *The Dark Side of the Moon*, one of rock's landmark albums, is released in the UK. Without my own record player until 1978, I have to wait a few more years to discover Pink Floyd.

LETTER

From the Headmaster, Malsis School

Dear Mr and Mrs Milner,

It was such a shame you were unable to see Oliver's performance in the school production of Nicholas Nickleby, last week, but I appreciate Nigeria is a 9,000 miles round trip. He worked hard at his part in the play, and made of Newman Noggs the kind of caricature that I am sure would have pleased Charles Dickens.

It's fair to say even though he didn't have the lead role he stole the show. You would have been immensely proud, and he is the talk of the school.

How simple life would be if every boy was as willing a worker as he. Despite his age in relation to the Standard Age, he should be able to achieve a satisfactory standard at Common Entrance level for Bootham in six terms time. We are just preparing the end of school reports, which you will receive in due course, but I am very pleased to say that he was able to win a place in the House soccer side, as he has always been keen to participate in out-of-school activities and is of course one of our major Leeds United fans!

Oliver has for the most part continued to make progress this term along the right lines. I have been in touch with Bootham regarding his entry and have suggested to the headmaster that the right time for him to join would be in September 1975, even though he would be virtually 14 by then.

I was impressed with his performance in the school play and very much look forward to seeing him the lead in our next production. Possibly he may even consider a career on the stage? I think we could have an actor on our hands.

Yours sincerely,
Gerald Watts

It's a bit early to be thinking careers quite yet. Currently thinking: novelist, something in natural history; NASA; acting; music; teaching – English or history, or the army.[54]

---

[54] March 21 – The Lofthouse Colliery disaster occurs in Great Britain. Seven miners are trapped underground; none survive.

Saturday, May 5, Crestfallen

FA Cup Final 1973 Leeds 0 Sunderland 1. We watched on the TV from the settee of the headmaster's personal flat, itself a rare, once in a lifetime experience.

Anne Watts kept us supplied with crisps and cake as we waved our scarves and sang, "Marching on together/We're going to see you win/La La La La La/We are so proud/We shout it out loud/We are Leeds, Leeds, Leeds!"

Only Shreve, a Sunderland fan, left happy.

The rest of us are absolutely crestfallen.[55]

Monday, July 16, Watergate Scandal

Former White House aide Alexander Butterfield informs the United States Senate Watergate Committee that President Richard Nixon had secretly recorded potentially incriminating conversations.

Friday, July 20, Kung Fu

Bruce Lee, American actor, philosopher, founder of Jeet Kune Do, dies in Hong Kong of cerebral oedema (six days later his final film *Enter the Dragon* is

---

March 23 – Watergate scandal (United States): In a letter to Judge John Sirica, Watergate burglar James W. McCord, Jr. admits that he and other defendants have been pressured to remain silent about the case. He names former Attorney General John Mitchell as overall boss of the operation.

March 27 – At the 45th Academy Awards, The Godfather wins best picture.[3]

March 29 – The last United States soldier leaves Vietnam.

April 4 – The World Trade Centre complex in New York City is officially dedicated with a ribbon-cutting ceremony.

April 30 – Watergate scandal: President Richard Nixon announces that White House Counsel John Dean has been fired and that Attorney General Richard Kleindienst has resigned along with staffers H. R. Haldeman and John Ehrlichman.

May 1 – An estimated 1,600,000 workers in the United Kingdom stop work in support of a Trades Union Congress day of national protest and stoppage against the government's anti-inflation policy.

May 3 – The Sears Tower in Chicago is topped-out, becoming the world's tallest building at 1,451 feet (442 m).

[55] "Whoever said 'it's not whether you win or lose that counts,' probably lost." – Martina Navratilova

released). I remember being quite moved by this. Although – from memory – most of his Kung Fu films would have had an AA or an X rating so I'd not be too familiar with his oeuvre, aged 14?

Sunday, July 29, Death

Formula One racing driver Roger Watts dies in an accident, witnessed live on television, during the 1973 Dutch Grand Prix.

My first direct exposure to death. Excluding three goldfish and one tortoise. At least motor racing is safer now, but what a cost to get there, just for sport. The need for speed killed too many.

Tuesday, July 31, That Scary Man Again

Militant protesters led by Ian Paisley disrupt the first sitting of the Northern Ireland Assembly. The reverend was a daily constant on TV news. We *despised* him, in all candour forty years on I have no idea why. He was just so easy to confuse with the forces who wanted to kill the British Army – a prospect he would have baulked and screamed down.

If you've not seen the Reverend Ian Paisley in full spittle, I urge you to search his name on YouTube. It's unique, and frightening stuff.

As history goes, I'd say the scabs are still too raw to pick at; the mid-1970s were a really bleak time in 1970s Britain. Let others explain the troubles in PhDs a hundred years from now.

Monday, August 13, Pyramids

Peanuts not a nut of course at all but a legume that grows in bunches under the ground are a big export here in Nigeria. Hundreds of thousands of 50 kg sacks are stacked symmetrically in square based pyramids, equally as high as Egypt's minor pyramids, lined up for miles along the roadside.

Nigeria is a very fertile country. Pretty much every garden we ever had contained mature mango trees, which were not only delicious but great fun to climb.

Once I had to make a hasty retreat having climbed to get a massive fruit. Some mangoes left on the tree would just keep on growing and could easily grow as big as a rugby ball. As I stretched for the mango, the unseen snake I'd disturbed on the branch slithered towards me.

I fell out of the tree, which probably saved my life because the snake just kept slithering for me. As I ran across the compound, Musa saw me from the kitchen being chased. Carrying a massive machete, he just cut the snake in two and then horror of horrors picked it up and took it to his house at the end of the compound.

"Mamba be good supper," Musa said, to explain.

All snakes in Nigeria were mambas to Musa, but in fact, Nigeria had several venomous snakes of its own whilst mambas' territory is eastern Africa.

The country's different terrains from savannah, rainforest, woodlands and swamp meant that bush meat was plentiful, although Mum was never tempted when the hawkers knocked on the door offering raw lumps of meat, which could be anything from a monkey's leg to lizards on a stick.

We were all fascinated by the grey geckos' ability to catch flies whilst suspended upside down on the ceiling. Lizards would occasionally stray into the house and all hell would break lose as my mother jumped onto a chair whilst Musa and the houseboy chivvied it away.

Most of the lizards were common agamas, which could vary in size from two to three-inch long babies, which fled whenever you stepped too close to big mature lizards, which could grow 18" long. Just occasionally, when you approached, they might stand their ground, which could be a bit unnerving.

The males were especially striking, with bright orange heads and bright blue bodies. Most of the time they just spent their days basking in the sun, bobbing their heads up and down, as if they were doing press ups. Toning up for their ladies.

It was an especially good day if one would jettison its tail. I'd save around two or three tails in a matchbox during most holidays, to trade for picture cards back at school.

It wasn't only the wildlife you had to watch out for.

I'd be about seven when I made myself a magnificent den, hiding under what looked like enormous rhubarb leaves. That night my skin was on fire. Something on the stems of the plants was highly irritant. I can still smell the pink calamine lotion Mum and Dad smothered me in to bring down the itching.

Sunday, September 9, Champion

Nice sort of a birthday present (for me): Scottish racing driver Jackie Stewart becomes Formula 1 World Drivers' Champion when his Tyrrell 003-Cosworth places fourth in the 1973 Italian Grand Prix at Monza.

Back to the wildlife: the spitting cobras and carpet vipers kept themselves to themselves but were clearly a very real danger to the barefooted workers in the fields or roadsides. There was one moment of drama at home, when a snake had gone to sleep on the curtain pelmet and fell to the ground as Musa was drawing the curtains.

It was around the time when his blindness was becoming worse and his protestations that it had left via a window were none too convincing. We spent a very nervous 48 hours before believing the coast was clear.

Thursday, September 20, Champion and Heroine

The *Battle of the Sexes*: Billie Jean King defeats Bobby Riggs in a televised tennis match, 6–4, 6–4, 6–3, at the Astrodome in Houston, Texas. With an attendance of 30,492, this remains the largest live audience ever to see a tennis match in US history. The global audience that views on television in 36 countries is estimated at 90 million.

I've admired her ever since.

Friday, October 5, Thank You Reg

Elton John releases his most successful album, *Goodbye Yellow Brick Road*.

Wednesday, November 14, Thank You Ma'am

This was deemed so important at the time the whole school watched the televised service in the assembly hall. It was a welcome relief from lessons, but I wonder what the staffroom were thinking?

HRH Princess Anne married Captain Mark Phillips in Westminster Abbey (they divorced in 1992).

"Celebrity marriages, they never last…"

Friday, November 17, Oh, Yes, You Are

The Watergate scandal: in Orlando, Florida, US President Richard Nixon tells 400 Associated Press managing editors, "I am not a crook."[56]

---

[56] December 16 – O. J. Simpson of the Buffalo Bills became the first running back to rush for 2,000 yards in a pro football season. He later had a more colourful history, as an actor and murderer.

December 25 – The movie premiere of *The Sting* starring Robert Redford and Paul Newman is held.

December 26 – The movie premiere of *The Exorcist* starring Ellen Burstyn and Linda Blair is held.

1974, Cross Hills, England.
Zaria, Nigeria

Wednesday, January 16, Acting Up

Easter term starts at Malsis. Position at the end of term in form V: 1/14.[57]

"He worked tirelessly, in a most demanding part in *The Royal Pardon* without ever complaining about long hours of rehearsal, and made a delightfully unhinged Constable. I cannot now imagine anyone else taking the part!" *GE Watts.*

Friday, March 15, Catching Up

Form position at end of spring term: 4/14

"Despite his absences, this term through ill health Oliver has managed to do a good amount of work this term and has made fair progress towards improving his chances at Common Entrance.

---

[57] January 11 – David, Elizabeth, Emma, Grant, Jason and Nicolette Rosenkowitz are born in Cape Town, the first recorded sextuplets in the world where all six babies survive.

January 15 – *Happy Days*, a sitcom about life in the 1950s, debuts on US TV.

January 17 – Two commercial divers, Pier Skipness and Robert John Smyth, die from rapid decompression and drowning in the Norwegian sector of the North Sea after their diving bell abruptly surfaces from a depth of 320 feet (98 m).

February 12 – The first episode of children's television series *Bagpuss* airs in Britain.

March 4 – Following a hung parliament in the UK's general election, Conservative Prime Minister Edward Heath resigns and is succeeded by Labour's Harold Wilson who previously led the country from 1964 to 1970.

"After his absence at Airedale he was quick to make up what work he had missed, in his trial examinations the English Composition paper went well but in the Comprehension he unaccountably took a wrong turn and was unable to make up for the marks lost by his mistake.

"As you know he had an exceptional exam in History gaining a splendid result. 94% was the highest school has ever seen, similarly his Geography was exceptional.

"Oliver always plays a leading part in House affairs and he performed his duties as a Prefect with tact and efficiency displaying a commendable sense of responsibility.

"I look forward to hearing him play the trumpet in the concert on Saturday and wish him an enjoyable cruise in the holidays on SS Uganda. I'm sure that he will make up the lost ground in the early part of next term and achieve a thoroughly satisfactory result in June's Common Entrance examinations." *G E Watts*

Friday, March 29, Overseas History

The Terracotta Army of Qin Shi Huang is discovered at Xi'an, China.

Launch of the Volkswagen Golf in West Germany, a modern front-wheel drive hatchback, which is expected to replace the iconic Volkswagen Beetle, holder of the world record for the car with the most units produced.

It's quick, but it never quite catches up with the Beetle's numbers.

Sunday, March 31, Ba

Our much-loved BOAC is no more. Today it has become British Airways, and with it, much of the romance of international travel vanishes with it. In time too, the elegant VC10 is replaced with wider bodied jets.

The BOAC Junior Jet Club logbook is no longer relevant. All those miles, carefully recorded, and countersigned by the captain. No wonder BOAC went broke.

I mentioned this wistfully to my mother recently. "Are you kidding? By the end BOAC flights were so delayed we used to say it stood for Better On A Camel."

Saturday, April 6, My Waterloo

This month the world's population reaches four billion people, estimated by the United States Census Bureau.

Auntie Harriet's family and ours sit on her sofa, in Glossop, a village in Derbyshire, to watch Swedish pop group ABBA sing *Waterloo* to win the 1974 Eurovision Song Contest held in Brighton.

At supper, Harriet screams at me for taking an extra tomato. My cousin Peter and I have a fight on the stairs – possibly over the tomato crime – and have remained as incommunicado as North and South Korea ever since.

The UK entry to Eurovision was sung by (Australian?) Olivia Newton-John. The song, called *Long Live Love*, finished fourth with a score of 14 points. ABBA smashed it that night.

Saturday, April 27, Winners!

Leeds United win the 1973/74 First Division title, having started the season with a 29-match unbeaten run.

Legends: David Harvey; David Stewart; Norman Hunter; Gordon McQueen; Frank Gray; Trevor Cherry; Terry Cooper; Paul Reaney; Paul Madeley; Roy Ellam; Peter Hampton; Nigel Davey; Mick Bates; Terry Yorath; Billy Bremner; Johnny Giles; Eddie Gray; Peter Lorimer; Allan Clarke; Mick Jones and Joe Jordan.

You never forget the names of your championship winning team.

Wednesday, May 1, PFA Player of the Year

Norman Hunter wins the inaugural Professional Players' Association Player of the Year award. Recognition, if any, was still needed that my football hero is a football legend.

In 42 games of the 1973/74 season, Leeds United conceded only 31 goals thanks to the best defender – and player – in the country.[58]

---

[58] May 18 – Nuclear weapons testing: Under project Smiling Buddha, India successfully detonates its first nuclear weapon, becoming the sixth nation to do so.

May 24 – Duke Ellington, American jazz composer, bandleader and pianist, dies at the age of 75 in New York City of complications from lung cancer and pneumonia.

Thursday, August 8, Tricky Dickie's Exit Stage Left, Followed by a Bore

The Watergate Scandal: US President Richard Nixon announces his resignation on August 8, handing over the presidency to Vice President Gerald Ford.

We're watching this presidential announcement on the TV in the living room in 9 Oval View. Unusually, Cousin Julia and I are fooling about together when she pushes me and I fall on my shoulder.

We both of us heard the crack, but try as I might, I cannot convince my mother or Auntie Harriet that my arm isn't hanging naturally. In fact, I get sent to bed for being naughty.

June 17 – A bomb explodes in Westminster Hall, the oldest part of the British Houses of Parliament. The hall's annex, housing offices and a canteen are destroyed by the bombing, attributed by police to the Provisional wing of the Irish Republican Army.

August 9 – Vice President Gerald Ford is sworn in as the 38th president of the USA upon Nixon's resignation.

August 14 – Turkey invades Cyprus for the second time, occupying 37% of the island's territory.

October 30 – The Rumble in the Jungle takes place in Kinshasa, Zaire, where Muhammad Ali knocks out George Foreman in eight rounds to regain the heavyweight title, which had been stripped from him seven years earlier.

November 3 – Billy Joel released his song *The Entertainer (song)*, which was part of his album *Streetlife Serenade*.

November 16 – Thinking ahead: the radio telescope at the Arecibo Observatory on Puerto Rico sends an interstellar radio message towards Messier 13, the Great Globular Cluster in Hercules. The message will reach its destination around the year 27,000.

November 21 – Birmingham pub bombings: In Birmingham, England, two pubs are bombed, killing 21 people in an attack widely believed at the time to be linked to the Provisional Irish Republican Army. The Birmingham Six are later sentenced to life in prison for this, but their convictions are quashed after a lengthy campaign.

November 22 – The United Nations General Assembly grants the Palestine Liberation Organization observer status.

November 24 – A skeleton from the hominid species Australopithecus afarensis is discovered and named Lucy.

At some time in 1974, Rubik's Cube puzzle is invented by Hungarian architecture professor Ernő Rubik.

Sunday, December 10, Recurring Numbers

Let me share a confidence; I'm being stalked by a number.

It's not Pi, although that's pretty cool.

Nor is it Fermat's last theorem, which is even cooler. (See below.[59])

Before we move on, now seems as good as any to explain about 134…

Firstly, 134 was the school number assigned to me when I went to Malsis.

Initially, this was needed to help label things like my coat pegs, my hairbrush, and my changing room locker. But then, we noticed that the number started *following me around*; in my second year I found myself in Dorm 13, bed 4.

In my third year, the Milners scored 134 out of 200, in the School Christmas Quiz.

It wasn't just at Malsis the coincidences continued. When I was at Bootham, Auntie Joan and Uncle Des' new car registration contained the numerals 134.

In Sixth form, we were in study 134.

When I went to university, the address of my second-year accommodation was No. 134.

To get to my first full time job in London from Muswell Hill, you caught the 134 bus to Euston, of course.

Ask me what the time is and on a disproportionate number of occasions, it's invariably 13:40 hrs.

Or the bill for some drinks will come to £13.40, or for the weekly shopping, £134.00.

Recently I took part in a fundraising sleep out for Centrepoint, the charity which aims to end youth homelessness. I *could* have engineered the amount I raised but didn't. It was £1,340.

The streetlight in front of the house I'm living in at present has an identification number; it's no. 134.

Look at the page number on the left. Spooky? Coincidental? Of course it is.

---

[59] In number theory, Fermat's Last Theorem states that no three positive integers a, b, and c satisfy the equation $a^n + b^n = c^n$ for any integer value of n greater than 2. The cases $n = 1$ and $n = 2$ have been known since antiquity to have an infinite number of solutions. After 358 years of effort by mathematicians, the first successful proof was released in 1994 by Andrew Wiles, and formally published in 1995; it was described as a stunning advance in the citation for Wiles's Abel Prize award (the Nobel Prize for Mathematics) in 2016 for the world's most difficult mathematical problem.

In the morning, when my collarbone is pushing through my pyjamas, even Auntie Harriet screeches.

I enjoyed walking around with the hospital's sling for the next three weeks. Not least because I was pampered on hand and foot. But most of all, because my mother *the qualified nurse* knew, I'd told her so.

Richard Nixon wasn't the only person you couldn't rely in 1974.

1975, Cross Hills, England.
Zaria, Nigeria

Wednesday, January 15, Rugging

Back to Malsis for spring term.[60]

One of the essential items in every boy's school list was a bed rug. Essential for those bedrooms which didn't yet have central heating and reusable in later life as outstanding picnic blankets, sans tassels.

There was a reason no Malsis boy's bed blanket had its tassels. Before lights out, a call would go around the bed block for *silence and get into beds*. Then the

---

[60] January 1 – Stevie Nicks and Lindsey Buckingham join Fleetwood Mac.

February 4 – Natalie Imbruglia, the Australian actress and singer is born today.

February 11 – Margaret Thatcher defeats Edward Heath for the leadership of the opposition UK Conservative Party. Thatcher, 49, is Britain's first female leader of any political party.

February 14 – P. G. Wodehouse, English writer (b. 1881) dies.

February 21 – Watergate scandal: former United States Attorney General John N. Mitchell, and White House aides H. R. Haldeman and John Ehrlichman are sentenced to between 30 months and 8 years in prison.

February 28 – A major tube train crash at Moorgate station, London, kills 43 people

March 4 – Charlie Chaplin is knighted by Elizabeth II.

March 7 – The body of teenage heiress Lesley Whittle, kidnapped 7 weeks earlier by the Black Panther, is discovered in Staffordshire, England.

March 8 – The United Nations proclaims International Women's Day. First appearance of Davros in Doctor Who. Monty Python and the Holy Grail is released in the UK.

April 4 – Bill Gates and Paul Allen found Microsoft in Albuquerque, New Mexico.

April 17 – The Khmer Republic surrenders, when the Communist Khmer Rouge guerrilla forces capture Phnom Penh ending the Cambodian Civil War, with mass evacuation of American troops and Cambodian civilians. The next day, the Khmer Rouge begins a forcible mass evacuation of the city and starts the genocide.

MoD would check everyone was where they should be and turn off each dorm light on their final rounds.

Whilst we were waiting, one of the best games ever invented involved pulling off a tassel, chewing it for a few minutes and when it was really well worked, rolling it up into a tight ball and then flicking it using your comb at a spot on the ceiling just above a boy's head on the other side of the dorm.

Depending on whether the MoD was popular or not, the tassels might also be flicked so they stuck on the ceiling above the door.

If you'd applied the right amount of spit, the tassel would dry out and drop from the ceiling just as lights were going out.

Monday, April 28, Worst Lunches

Summer term. Back to Malsis for my last term there. Five years along, and still Monday lunch times are scarred. We always have mince, mashed potatoes and peas and semolina and jam for dessert. Two utterly disgusting courses that I will certainly not miss when I leave.

Tuesday, April 29, Roof Escape

Vietnam War: Operation Frequent Wind – Americans and their allies are evacuated from South Vietnam by helicopter. Within 24 hours, the Vietnam War ends with the Fall of Saigon: The Vietnam War concludes as communist forces from North Vietnam take Saigon, resulting in mass evacuation of the remaining American troops and South Vietnam civilians. As the capital is taken, South Vietnam surrenders unconditionally and is replaced with the temporary Provisional Government.[61]

---

[61] May 2 – Golden balls himself, David Beckham, English football legend, and tattoo exhibit, is born.

Friday, May 16, Top Brass

Letter Writing Practice. Lesson 3

Dear Dad,

    Why do people stamp on their hats? In my Lion this week, the Carson's Cubs story ended with the baddies jumping on their hats in the last picture. It wasn't a really good story I like it when you see more of the match. But if you'd already had a bad day why would you want to make it worse by spoiling a perfectly good hat?

    Can I learn the trombone for this half of term? We've got a new head of music who will take the choir and teaches brass coming.

    Apparently Tyler says his parents paid to hear him play the trombone at the Proms last year. So he must be ace.

    Please? Can you telex to Miss Birch, Mr Watts's Secretary and give your permission.

    PLEASE? PLEASE?

Lots of love,
Olly

PS: To do is to be – Socrates. Do be do be do – Sinatra
PPS: When God was dishing out brains Shreve thought he said trains, so he gave him small, quiet, slow one.

Wednesday, May 28, Bites Yer Ankles

European Cup Final, 1975: Bayern Munich 2 Leeds United 0. In the Stade de Paris, at the Leeds end is a huge *Norman bites yer ankles* banner, translated from the English into German and French: *Norman beisst euch in die beine, Norman vous moro les jambes!*

Football legend Norman Hunter died from Covid-19, aged 76, on Friday April 17, 2020.

Thursday, June 5, Oui

The Suez Canal opens for the first time since the Six-Day War.

The UK votes yes in a referendum to stay in the European Community.

In Uganda, British author and adventurer Denis Hills is sentenced to death by firing squad for referring to Idi Amin as a *village tyrant*.

Auntie Joan, 13-year-old me and Uncle Des squinting into the sun on the day I don't seem very pleased to be flanked by either of them, but then I wasn't. Mum and Dad were in Nigeria. I do like this picture though – see the number plate to our left. The photo negative was printed in reverse.

July 6, The End[62]

Malsis School, Cross Hills, Keighley, England

Malsis School Report
Name: Oliver Milner
Age: 13.11
Summer Term 1972.
Form: Common Entrance 5. Number of boys in form: 13.
Average Age of Form: 13.2
Position at the end of term: 1st.
Subject reports
Mathematics: study, application and determination to succeed have brought their own reward. Well done! Exam position: 3/13.
Science: Oliver has worked well and sensibly this term's and was rewarded with a good mark in the Common Entrance exam. My good wishes go with him. Exam position: 1/13.
English: as expected, Oliver maintained his efforts and achieved some good results in Common Entrance as well as a thoroughly sound term's work. I believe he has a promising career ahead of him in English and associated activities, such as acting. I look forward to hearing of his undoubted successes and wish him good fortune. Exam position: 2/13.
History: this has been a most successful final term as he has fully lived up to the promise shown over the last two years, and these results are very commendable. Exam position 1/13.
Geography: some further work of a high standard culminated in a splendid result in the Common Entrance exam for Bootham and he has done very well. Exam position: 3/13.
Scripture: Oliver has worked well in class and produced an excellent result in his Common Entrance Exam. Exam position: 4/13.

---

[62] June 19 – Richard Bingham, 7th Earl of Lucan is found guilty in absentia of the murder of Nanny Sandra Rivett.

June 20 – Jaws is released in cinemas and becomes a popular summer hit, setting the standard for Hollywood blockbusters for years to come.

July 5 – Cape Verde gains independence after 500 years of Portuguese rule.

Latin: After a very disappointing Common Entrance trial at the beginning of the term, he did much hard revision and seemed to recover some of his confidence. However his Common Entrance mark was rather disappointing. Nevertheless, very good try. Exam position: 6/13.

French: he has always worked hard, but this term his achievements have not been as great as we might have hoped. I wish him greater success in the future. Exam position: 11/13.

Trumpet: Oliver has made excellent progress this term although very busy with schoolwork. He worked hard for the music exam. I expect him to become a valued member of a brass group at his new school.

Housemaster's report: Oliver has enjoyed a splendid final term at Malsis. He performed very well over the Sprint distances in the Athletics League. He was awarded his tenth bene for his project on the cruise, for winning the Drama, History, Reading, Gardening and Music prizes. He was also successful in his trumpet exam. It was good to see his efforts being so well rewarded on Speech Day. As our visiting speaker on the day said Oliver's 10 Benes were achieved without the advantage of any rugby or cricket honours – I doubt we will ever see that achieved again. We shall all miss his lively sense of humour and enthusiastic participation both in and out of the classroom. His contribution to Lund's successes over the past few terms have been considerable.

Headmaster's report: I can but reiterate all that Mr Moore has written. Oliver has had an excellent final term, and although his marks in languages were just a little disappointing in the Common Entrance exams, those in the other subjects were very good indeed. He has enjoyed a most successful career here, participating and contributing much in a wide range of activities. I am sure that he will make the most of every opportunity at Bootham. My best wishes for every success there. *G E Watts*

Next term begins on: N/A.

Saturday, July 5 – Tuesday, July 15, Vom Milner

It was a school tradition after the end of the summer term that the leavers and their parents would join the more outdoorsy teachers for a ten-day camping holiday along the banks of some privately-owned land next to Lake Ullswater, in the Cumbrian Lake District.

Who knows what the grown-ups might have been doing after lights out, but we boys were taught to canoe, sail, fish, rock climb and cook outdoors. It was an amazing holiday.

On the middle weekend, we were even allowed to go into Kendal, unaccompanied, to spend our pocket money. Patrick, who I was sharing a tent with, somehow managed to buy a bottle of Campari, and not to be outdone, I bought a catering sized tub of brandy butter.

That night we had our midnight feast.

In the morning, I imagine it was Patrick's first hangover. It was certainly mine.

The combination of neat Campari – we didn't know it needed a mixer – and brandy butter was probably a world first. It was definitely the last time I've ever been able to face both. The mere sight of either on a supermarket shelf is enough to make me want to heave.

Thursday, July 17, Big Fish, Little Fish

Apollo-Soyuz Test Project: A manned American Apollo spacecraft and the manned Soviet Soyuz spacecraft for the *Soyuz 19* mission, docks in orbit, marking the first such link-up between spacecraft from the two nations.

On my way to Nigeria for the holidays, I'm very sad to be leaving Malsis.

I was in for a shock when I got to Bootham. Better to be a big fish in a little pond, I think.[63]

Friday, August 15, Hallelujah

Some members of Jehovah's Witnesses believe that Armageddon will occur this year based on the group's chronology and some sell their houses and

---

[63] Established on 14 May 1924, Malsis School's school motto was *Sto Pro Veritate* (I stand for the truth). Its motto caught up with it when with dwindling pupil numbers it was forced to close for good on 10 December 2014. The truth is preparatory boarding schools for boys have had their day. Malsis Hall is now a treatment centre for patients with psychiatric conditions. They could not wish for a more idyllic setting.

August 11 – British Leyland Motor Corporation comes under British government control.

September 4 – Mark Ronson, English DJ, record producer, and singer is born. He is immensely talented. It's just a little early to confirm this.

September 19 – The British comedy sitcom *Fawlty Towers* airs on BBC 2.

businesses to prepare for the new world paradise, which they believe will be created when Jesus establishes God's Kingdom on Earth.

Harrogate, 1975: Taken just before I go to secondary school – look I'm wearing my new school suit and the brown tie. Not even our mother displayed this photo. My brother's now bald, my sister has eschewed the Purdy basin and I am still waiting for the call from L'Oréal, because I'm worth it.

The Birmingham Six are wrongfully sentenced to life imprisonment in Great Britain. (They are released 1991.)

Tuesday, September 9, York

I turn 14 today and Joan and Des drop me, my trunk and tuck box off at Penn House, Bootham School, in York, England.

Tough to start a new school on one's birthday.

Tougher still to be a boarder when many of my Year 7 compatriots go to the school as day boys. And tougher yet the next day to find the clasp on my tuck box has been forced open, and someone has put a half-smoked cigarette in my Kellogg's All Bran.

[A friend of mine in the first week at his boarding school wrote and told me that they had a teacher with spectacular halitosis who would come up behind them during class and put his hand into their pocket and have a feel of their private parts. It was only the seats at the back of the classes where there was space for him to walk behind unobserved, so as you can imagine, everyone soon learned to move their desks further back, so their chairs were always against the back wall.]

Wednesday, October 1 – The Thrilla in Manila

Muhammad Ali defeats Joe Frazier in a boxing match in Manila, Philippines.

Wednesday afternoons after lunch are free from lessons, allowing for inter-school football or hockey matches. As I'm not yet in any school teams, Wednesdays are pretty boring. Which was why with nothing particular to do, I was hanging around in the library wondering what book to read.

As I was thumbing through something on terrapins, an old man walked in through the doors. "Ah, young man, what's your name? Good to find you in the library, do you know where the History section is?"

I didn't, but it was easy enough to find as all the categories were in alphabetical order. The old man continued to ask me questions about the school and explained that he had also once been a new boy at Bootham in 1914. As neither of us had anything better to do, would I mind if I showed him around?

Other than wondering whose grandfather the old man might be, I was quite okay doing what he asked. It was expected that we would always welcome Old Scholars, so I was only doing what was expected. We got lost once or twice, as I was still quite new, but we found our way back to the library, where the old man went back to the History section. There, he looked for a book and taking it down – horror of horrors – started writing in it.

"Sir, sir, I don't think you're allowed to do that. We'd better go to the staff room." Lucky for me, ushering the old man to the staff room to explain to the Master on Duty what had just happened was relatively easy as the rooms were quite close to each other.

When we got there, the old man just walked straight in. "Ah, hello, Alan," went the headmaster. "Did you enjoy your tour of the school? I saw young Milner showed you around."

"Oh, yes, it was great fun, and I think you may have a young historian in your midst. Oh, Oliver, you might like to have this," and he handed me *The Second World War, An Illustrated History* by A J P Taylor.

"Thank you for the tour."

I went back to the library to put the book back on the shelf in its rightful place. Before I put it back, I wondered what he'd written in it:

> "*To Oliver Milner,*
> *I enjoyed sharing our Bootham history together.*
> *Best wishes,*
> *A J P Taylor 1ˢᵗ October 1975.*"

Saturday, October 31, Tuck[64]

The Queen single *Bohemian Rhapsody* is released. It later becomes one of their most popular songs.

Hot on the heels of gorging on brandy butter, one idle Saturday afternoon – weekends at Bootham are already very boring – I make a rudimentary mistake whilst out shopping for snacks for my tuck box.

A tuck box is a padlocked chest about 2' x 2' x 18" for personal treats like Ritz crackers, Kellogg's variety packs and sweets. Dad made mine and I was initially very proud of it, until I saw the other boys' some of whom had boxes from Louis Vuitton. The fact ours was homemade just made us look cheap and poor. A major crime.

What Dad's tuck box lacked in finesse, it definitely made up for in strength. Nearly 50 years on, the box is currently being used as a side table in the room in which I'm typing this. It would almost certainly withstand a bomb blast. He made it to last.

---

[64] October 2 – An RAF Avro Vulcan bomber explodes and crashes over Żabbar, Malta after an aborted landing, killing five crew members and one person on the ground.
October 30 – Peter Sutcliffe (the Yorkshire Ripper) commits his first murder, that of Wilma McCann.

The tuck box room for the Year 4s was in the basement of Penn House, on the other side of the road from the school, and where our dorms were.

On this particular Saturday afternoon where someone was playing *Bohemian Rhapsody* on repeat, I bought myself a family sized jar of frankfurters. It was an odd choice, as I'd never had a frankfurter in brine before. As I opened the jar and took one, I ate it cold, of course, as I didn't have the means to heat them up.

I realised that without a fridge the 11 remaining sausages would probably go off pretty quickly. So that night, I ate them all.

Big mistake.

What with that and the incessant playing of *Bohemian Rhapsody*, Sunday was not a good day.

Somewhat tearfully, I rang home from the red call box opposite school. Most of us rang home on a Sunday, staying on the phone for as long as our 10 pence pieces allowed, until we ran out.

Whilst I was on the phone, talking to Mum, I noticed Richard Bridge out of the corner of my eye. He was a Third Year but much larger than me and already once or twice in corridors he'd deliberately barged into me, for no other reason than he was a bully.

He clearly wanted to use the phone box too but seeing I had at least seven more 10ps stacked up, he went away. Only to come back five minutes later.

This time he disappeared behind the phone box, and then started sprinting around and around it, as if unwinding something. It was cling film. He cling filmed me into the phone box. With a whole roll of cling film wrapped in layers around the phone box, there was no way I could open the door.

And there he left me. I would have stayed there for much of the afternoon had not Matron come back from her shopping.

"Who did this to you?" she asked.

Trying not to cry, but more than a little ashamed that I'd been intimidated by a boy 18 months younger than me, I said I didn't recognise him (I was still a new boy). Just that he was larger than me.

"I bet it was Bridge," she said. "He's a nasty piece of work. Leave it with me."

Indeed, Bridge was a nasty piece of work, every week he'd be reported for punching someone, or stealing something. It wasn't long before his next suspension became an expulsion. Then he simply didn't come back after half-term. The whole school breathed a sigh of relief, but I was especially relieved.

Saturday, November 29, Beginnings and Endings

The name *Micro-soft* (for microcomputer software) is used by Bill Gates in a letter to Paul Allen for the first time (Microsoft becomes a registered trademark on November 26, 1976).

Formula One world champion Graham Hill is killed when the Piper Aztec aeroplane he was piloting crashed in foggy conditions near Arkley golf course in North London.

Tuesday, December 23, Betty Gets the Chop

Comic and tragic scenes in the compound today. For the past three months, Musa has been fattening up an enormous turkey for the Christmas Day table. Standing over a yard tall, its huge red wattle flaps in the air and its beak, six inches long, is razor sharp.

For some reason my Dad's christened the turkey Betty.

Musa opens the stable door and knife in hand plans on mounting the turkey from behind and swiftly dispatching it with a slit of its throat.

That's the plan.

Just as Musa puts one leg over the turkey's back it catches sight of the knife and with a huge squawk hurtles through the open door of the stable. But Musa has one hand on its neck and they circle each other at high speed for several seconds. The turkey trying to slash Musa with its beak, and Musa trying to slash the turkey's neck.

Suddenly, there's an almighty yelp. Musa has slashed the turkey's neck and his other hand at the same time. The turkey seemingly oblivious pounds off like an ostrich across the compound. Each time it takes a step, its neck lolls backwards a little more each time, the wound spraying blood.

After five minutes running around the compound evading capture, it slows down, totally disorientated, its head now hanging by some skin the bird collapsed onto the floor.

It takes three men to carry the carcass indoors.

Weighing in at 40 pounds, it is far too big to go in the oven so there is no bird to carve on the day. But everyone, in our and Musa's family, ate turkey for most meals for the rest of the year.

Tuesday, December 30, Fashion Disaster

In my hand, I have a photograph of me taken some time in the summer, outside my parents' house in Harrogate. Oh, the joy of being a teenager in mid 1970s Yorkshire. Let's reflect on how things look: I have shoulder length hair; an Adam's apple the size of a cricket ball; high waisted, beige flares that occupy the whole pavement – I look dreadful, and rather uncomfortable.

Where is *Home*? I wonder.

Stood outside the house in Harrogate, I feel and look like a guest. Indeed all my life, even as an adult, I've always rung the front doorbell of my parents' house, and still don't have a front door key.

Home is certainly not school – although I spend more days in the year boarding there. And whilst Nigeria is always an adventure, seeing Dad is always a holiday.

I'm from everywhere and nowhere. Much as every other school boarder feels, I imagine.

However, I do have some new school friends I can count on the fingers of one hand in Alex Cairns, Bruce Simpson and Tim Jerome. And I have enemies I can count in their tens.

Nineteen seventy-six will surely be better. Won't it? Hmm…[65]

---

[65] Tiger Woods, later to become quite a well-known American golfer, is born.

1976, York, East Yorkshire, Northern England

Monday, January 12, Whodunit

Crime author Agatha Christie dies aged 85 in Oxfordshire, UK. Christie's link with Harrogate is of course famous. In 1926, fleeing from her husband who was having an affair she hid herself away in the Old Swan Hotel.

Rumours abounded as to what had happened to the famous thriller writer. Typical she should be found in Harrogate where hardly anything happens. Needless to say, Miss Marple and Poirot are reputed to have been conceived whilst Agatha Christie was talking the waters in my home town.

According to the website Deadgood in a plot twist worthy of her own novels, Christie disappeared for 11 days in 1926. It was a turbulent time for the young writer, her mother had just died and her husband was having an affair. So she simply got into her car and disappeared. The car was found abandoned and police feared the worst – dredging local lakes and tapping the phone of her husband. Christie surfaced 11 days later at The Old Swan Hotel in Harrogate never saying where she'd been. She had however checked into the hotel using her husband's mistress's last name.

My mother mentions that when my dad was working in Lloyds Bank's Pall Mall branch a decade earlier than today, Mrs Mallowan was one of his richer, charming customers.

Mrs Mallowan aka Agatha Christie.

Since we're talking pseudonyms, Christie wrote several romantic fiction novels under the pen name Mary Westmacott. (*That's enough Agatha Christie –* Ed.)

Incidentally, the Pump Rooms, which is now a museum to Harrogate's history as a spa town, still smells faintly of rotten eggs – hydrogen sulphide from the springs – to me.

Friday, February 13, Mayhem

General Murtala Mohammed of Nigeria is assassinated in a military coup.

Today I played a handball game for the first time, called Rugby Fives, it's like squash only you play with padded gloves and a ball the size of a golf ball that looks like a cricket ball.[66]

Bootham has one of the few courts in the country. I loved it.

Easter Term Report

Oliver is more relaxed and confident than last term, I feel. He still strives to do the right thing all the time without being pompous or self-righteous and is fussing much less now.

He continues to aim for and achieve high standards and always gives his best. His whole attitude to life is most commendable.

His Subject Masters' reports speak for themselves with one voice as it were. Keep it up.

David Robinson, Class Master

Monday, March 22, *Pseudemys Scripta Elegans*

Star Wars begins filming in Tunisia.[67]

We weren't to know the impact C3PO, R2D2 and friends would have on our lives, till later. Juxtaposed between my catching up on films like *Saturday Night*

---

[66] https://rugbyfives.com/what-is-fives/

March 1 – UK Home Secretary Merlyn Rees ends Special Category Status for those sentenced for scheduled terrorist crimes relating to the civil violence in Northern Ireland.

March 4 – The Maguire Seven are found guilty of possessing explosives and subsequently jailed for 14 years.

The Northern Ireland Constitutional Convention is formally dissolved in Northern Ireland, resulting in direct rule of Northern Ireland from London via the British Parliament.

March 16 – Harold Wilson resigns as prime minister of the United Kingdom.

[67] April 1 – Apple Computer Company is formed by Steve Jobs and Steve Wozniak.

April 3 – The Eurovision Song Contest 1976 is won by Brotherhood of Man, representing the United Kingdom, with their song *Save Your Kisses for Me*.

Fever, Jaws, The Sting and *The Exorcist*, I go off at a slight tangent from my peers, and out of nowhere become a precocious expert on the keeping of *pseudemys scripta elegans.*

The red-eared slider, also known as the red-eared terrapin, is a semiaquatic fresh water turtle belonging to the family Emydidae. It is a subspecies of the pond slider.

What it is not is an ideal pet.

Whilst they look great, doing breaststroke in fresh water or on a bank, soaking in the sun in a school, they need a herpetological lamp, a neon UV light to keep them warm and to stop dying of vitamin D deficiency, and they eat live bait.

So far so available – all the pet shops sold water larvae and tubifex (little red worms) for the aquatic fish trade. What they don't tell you is that whilst an obsessively well maintained filter in a decent size aquarium will keep the water clear, if you're lucky, what it won't do is stop the bacteria at the bottom of the tank building up from the dead meat the terrapins leave for later and giving your average teenage boy salmonella.

It took nearly 18 months for Matron to track my semi-permanent dysentery back to the pet shed. Meanwhile, I engaged in a long correspondence course with other members of the British Chelonia Group, mostly who were middle aged bachelors.

Terrapin keeping is a solitary business and not much of a spectator sport. But I thought they were great and a decade later when Hero Mutant Ninja Turtles on the TV started, a craze for buying baby red-eared terrapins my 19-year-old opinions were much in demand by Sunday supplement feature writers.

Mick, Keith, Bill, Charlie and Ronnie the terrapins, travelled backwards and forwards to Harrogate. One weekend we even went to Leeds University for a lecture, and when I was ill – with (undiagnosed) salmonella – for a month, the Natural History students looked after them for me.

Although I was still in Middle School, I entered and won the School Natural History competition. Essentially, I copied the only book about turtles in York City Library and pasted in photographs of my own 5-piece band in a massive booklet.

I then won it the next year, and would have swept a hat trick of wins had not my good friend and study mate been keeping a spawning trout, in a bath, on the top of the science lab. No one could compete with that.

But I got him back in our last year.

I think we'd eaten the trout by then.

Sadly, my potential career on the international conference circuit being Mr Turtle was abruptly ended by of all people the very Biology teacher who had encouraged my interest in the first place.

For the long summer holidays before my final year, Dr Pickering agreed to look after them whilst I was away in Bahrain with Mum and Dad. At some stage in the holidays, Dr Pickering became ill. (Now I think about it, I wonder if it was with salmonella). The filter on the tank eventually clogged up and stopped. The water all evaporated from the aquarium. All that was left on my return to school were the desiccated remains of my rolling stones.

Dr Pickering was as upset as I was. Rather than start again I gifted the tank to the school, and I think he entertained the junior school with something less exotic the next year, like an axolotl.

Monday, April 5, Stars and Stitches

James Callaghan becomes Prime Minister of the United Kingdom.

It's a particularly dull, bland and grey period of British history and within the school the monastic repetition the week's timetable can be pretty oppressive to young teenagers too.

Which is why at 2 am, Tim, Bruce and I find ourselves in the astronomy tower. Not especially interested in planetary bodies but the permitted excuse to go star-gazing late at night.

It is boring though. Only Bruce is sincerely interested so to occupy our time, Tim and I jump across the gap between the astronomy tower, which is above the fives court, and the science block. It's a gap of about six feet, so reasonably safe, even two storeys up.

The jump from the astronomy tower, which is higher than the science block roof, is reasonably easy. Jumping back is a little more dangerous because the smooth curved dome of the astronomy tower doesn't really provide many handholds to grab onto once you've jumped.

We're on our third attempt – it's quite a rush – when for some reason Tim decides to jump across without a run up. He doesn't quite clear the roof of the science block and slides down the wall catching his groin on an open window and with a grunt falls to the ground.

We thought he was dead.

153

Incredibly, he'd landed on a sloping flowerbed, which had cushioned the impact and we found him giggling, uncontrollably, presumably a shock response that he hadn't been killed. He was however bleeding quite obviously from the stain on his trousers.

There was nothing for it but to wake Matron who took Tim to hospital to get stitched up.

We stayed awake all night wondering if Tim would live and whether we would be expelled in the morning.

Being a Quaker school, corporal punishments and indeed any form of severe punishments weren't sanctions ever meted out for bad behaviour. Discipline at the school was really lax, the headmaster was a real wuss. Bruce and I were first admonished for behaving so recklessly, and then praised for acting swiftly to get help. Typical Quaker response.

Tim's ignominy was completed in A&E. The effects of a nurse moving his willy out of the way so he could be stitched up had the effect one might expect on a prepubescent teenager.

We did not go to the astronomy tower for several weeks after that.[68]

Monday, June 14

The trial begins at Oxford Crown Court of Donald Neilson. The killer known as the Black Panther, is defended in court by one of the UK's most brilliant barristers, Gilbert Gray QC. For a few terms, I sat next to Gilbert Gray's son in class at Bootham, for a short while, we were good friends before he went on to another school.

Everything about the Grays was remarkable not least the fact that they had a pet wallaby. One Sunday, I was invited to their house near Scarborough for Sunday lunch and there it was. Bobbing about and acting around the house like a small dog. Admittedly, they also had several acres of garden so the dear thing had lots of space, but from then, I was transfixed. Who doesn't want a pet wallaby?

---

[68] April 23 – The punk rock group the Ramones release their first album, *Ramones*. Jethro Tull release their album *Too Old to Rock 'n' Roll: Too Young to Die!*
June 1 – The UK and Iceland end the Cold War.

Given the Grays were much more sophisticated than us, what happened at lunch was therefore something of a surprise. In true Yorkshire style, they started very traditionally – but it was a tradition I knew nothing of, then.

Mrs Gray came in with a huge square Yorkshire pudding, one for each of us. I was slightly taken aback. Where was the Sunday roast I'd been expecting? But being a polite young man I said nothing and ate everything on my plate thinking that was lunch.

Then, in a gesture intended to praise Mrs Gray for her cooking, I said, "That was delicious, I wonder if there were seconds?"

Mrs Gray, somewhat taken aback, said, "Of course, Olly." And I waded through my second slab of Yorkshire pudding, this time which I filled to the brim with onion gravy.

Just as I was finishing, Mrs Gray then said, "Excellent. Who would like lamb or beef? Or perhaps both?" And then proceeded to lay out the biggest spread of Sunday roasts and vegetables I had ever seen.

I had no idea that the custom in their part of Yorkshire was to eat the ballast first and then tuck in to the nice bits.

I did my best. But I just felt sick.

Gilbert Gray QC had a remarkable career. The cases he defended being a roll call of some of the most the most famous in the 1970s and 1980s. Well worth looking up, although none of the obituaries mentioned the wallaby.[69]

---

[69] June 29 – Seychelles gains independence from the United Kingdom.

July 4 – Entebbe Raid: Israeli airborne commandos free 103 hostages being held by Palestinian hijackers of an Air France plane at Uganda's Entebbe Airport; Yonatan Netanyahu and several Ugandan soldiers are killed in the raid

July 21 – An IRA bomb kills Christopher Ewart-Biggs, British ambassador to the Irish Republic, and Judith Cooke, a Northern Ireland Office private secretary; two others are seriously wounded but survive.

July 27 – The United Kingdom breaks diplomatic relations with its former colony Uganda in response to the hijacking of Air France Flight 139.

September 6 – The Cold War: Soviet Air Force pilot, Lt Viktor Belenko lands a MiG-25 jet fighter at Hakodate, on the island of Hokkaidō in Japan, and requests political asylum in the United States.

September 13 – The Muppet Show is broadcast for the first time on ITV.

October 4 – The InterCity 125 high-speed train is introduced in the United Kingdom.

Wednesday, July 7, Captains of Minor Teams

David Steel becomes leader of the UK's Liberal Party in the aftermath of the scandal, which forced out Jeremy Thorpe.

I become Vice Captain of the school's Five's team. Not bad for a squirt in Middle School. Mr Gibson has been so impressed by my commitment to practise that I'm allowed off cricket in order to keep training.

The only problem is, I'm running out of opponents. My natural inclination to slaughter them on the court makes volunteers reluctant somehow.

Sunday, October 24, Friends

James Hunt wins a very political Formula One World Championship by just 1 point driving a McLaren M23-D as rival Niki Lauda retires from the Japanese Grand Prix due to heavy rain.

This year's motor racing championship has fascinated my best mate Alex Cairns and me. Found out in our first week that Emerson Fitipaldi was also his favourite motor racing driver that made us friends for the next five years.

Also in my dorm, which was in a converted office with no windows, was Tim Jerome. Tim and I were almost opposites in everything we did. He was good at sciences, I was better in arts subjects. He was short; I was relatively tall at that time, for our ages. I was good at swimming, he was better at tennis. But we were both reasonable hockey players, and when I became captain of the 2nd XI, he learned how to be one of the best goalies in York.

We were a good team.

Tuesday, November 2, Bunch of Fives

US presidential election, 1976: Jimmy Carter defeats incumbent Gerald Ford, becoming the first candidate from the Deep South to win since the Civil War.

In the Inter School Fives competition, I easily win the Middle School cup and lose in three sets in the seniors' competition. News that I might beat Gavin Lascelles soon gets around the school.

By the time we start the third set, there are nearly 100 people cheering me on in the gallery. But it's too much, I'm totally knackered after playing for nearly five hours, and lose 7–11, 11–9, 6–11.

Wednesday, December 1, Fuck

The Sex Pistols achieve public notoriety, as they unleash several four-letter words live on Bill Grundy's early evening TV show.

Christmas Term Report

Oliver has continued in his exemplary way this term and I am pleased that in Alex Cairns he has found a good friend and common interest.
Generally he has progressed very well this year and I feel that his professed happiness has become more genuine much more solidly based.
It is sad that his examination results did not always correlate well with their effort but this is something that Oliver will solve himself as he learns to work more effectively.
We are all pleased with his achievements in the Fives court. He is already one of the best players in the school and I'm told he narrowly missed out on winning the Seniors tournament only by having had to play and win the Middle School finals an hour previously.[70]
This has been a good year for Oliver and he has my best wishes for next year.

David Robinson, Class Master

Wednesday, December 8, You Can't Never Leave

Hotel California by the Eagles is released. If *Hotel California* forms the soundtrack of the holidays, my leisure time reading is provided by James Herriot.

The contrast of the Yorkshire vet struggling through North Yorkshire's snowdrifts and the baking heat outside could not be more stark.

You can take the boy out of Yorkshire, but you can't tale Yorkshire out of the boy. For a while, I seriously contemplated becoming a farmer – I wasn't good enough at the sciences to become a vet – but soon decisions that will affect our careers for life are being made.

Next year, we are starting our O'Level syllabuses and over the holidays have to make our subject selections.

---

[70] "The breakfast of champions is not cereal, it's the opposition." – Nick Seitz.

1977, York, England. Aprica, Northern Italy

Thursday, January 6, Baths

Record company EMI drops the controversial United Kingdom punk rock group the Sex Pistols.

There were three principal ways you could get dropped or expelled from Bootham: caught taking drugs; caught smoking or drinking; caught performing a homosexual act.

In my school career, I think the respective scores were 2, 4 and 0. The latter was the more remarkable given 350 adolescent boys would certainly have had a fair proportion of gay people in our midst. No one was openly gay although all through Middle School I was terrified that an accusing finger would be pointed at me. We all were.

The reason was that it was impossible not to be aware that some industrial strength wanking was going on whilst the baths were running in the washroom. In Middle School, bath night was once a week and dorms were on a rota as to who used the washroom on different nights. Each of the baths were separated by some extremely wobbly wooden partitions.

If you were in the end cubicle, the planking was so lose that *should* you wish to spy on your neighbour having a wank it was merely a question of choosing the spyhole of your choice.

The only way to demonstrate your heterosexual proclivity to your peers, and demonstrate that of course taking a sneaky peak through the planking was something you could never dream of, was to openly carry the latest dog-eared copy of *Private* magazine, usually featuring Mary Millington, into the bath with you.

Occasionally, a friend might ask you to lob the magazine over the partition. Just don't let it fall in the water, or you really would be unpopular.

There was of course the dilemma of knowing how to behave if you were being spied on. How could you report it? You couldn't prove it and who would admit to it?

Monday, January 17, Shot

Gary Gilmore is executed by firing squad in Utah (the first execution after the reintroduction of the death penalty in the US).

Three days later, Jimmy Carter is sworn in as the 39th President of the United States. He looked like a decent man. I felt he would have stopped the firing squad, if he'd been President.

One of his first actions is to pardon America's Vietnam War draft evaders. A decent gesture from a decent man, who seemed too spiritual to lead the world with the firm grip it needed in the 1970s.

First published in 1957, Stevie Smith's poem *Not Waving But Drowning* sums up Carter's presidency. Whenever his name is mentioned on TV or radio, something cataclysmic has just befallen the world.

Friday, April 1, April Fools[71]

The small market town of Hay-on-Wye declares independence from the UK, as a publicity stunt.

Hay on Wye it is that has the famous literary festival and fair to say I am enjoying myself hugely in English Literature lessons. Our teacher, Val Hall (whom we obviously all call Val Halla, not least because she is also built a bit like a Valkyrie) used to, in a former life, write for *Biker Monthly*. In particular, Val enjoys the poetry of Gerard Manley Hopkins and his poem *Nothing is so beautiful as Spring* – reduces her to tears when she reads it to us for the first time.

---

[71] February 4 – Fleetwood Mac's Grammy-winning album *Rumours* is released in the United States.

March 10 – The rings of Uranus are discovered. Fnaar, fnaar.

March 12 – The Centenary Test between Australia and England begins at the Melbourne Cricket Ground.

March 27 – Tenerife disaster: A collision between KLM and Pan Am Boeing 747s at Tenerife, Canary Islands, kills 583 people. This becomes the deadliest accident in aviation history.

Nothing is so beautiful as Spring –
When weeds, in wheels, shoot long and lovely and lush;
Thrush's eggs look little low heavens, and thrush
Through the echoing timber does so rinse and wring
The ear, it strikes like lightnings to hear him sing;
The glassy pear tree leaves and blooms, they brush
The descending blue; that blue is all in a rush
With richness; the racing lambs too have fair their fling.
What is all this juice and all this joy?
A strain of the earth's sweet being in the beginning
In Eden garden. – Have, get, before it cloy,
Before it cloud, Christ, lord, and sour with sinning,
Innocent mind and Mayday in girl and boy,
Most, O maid's child, thy choice and worthy the winning.[72]

Saturday, April 2, Snow

In a catastrophically misguided attempt to win me new friends, Mum and Dad booked me onto the Easter holidays school skiing trip to Aprica, in northern Italy.

No one in the family had ever been skiing before so excitement was quite high in the Milner household. As my parents were in Nigeria packing for the trip, I was left under supervision of Nana, and Uncle Des.

The only sport Nana ever watched on the TV was the Saturday afternoon wrestling on *World of Sport*. It would have been to the advantage of us all if she had watched just one episode of *Ski Sunday*, to gain an idea what the modern skier wore. Instead, she took her inspiration from Jeeves and Wooster and knitted me a beige ski suit.

It was a condition of the trip that Des and she having packed my suitcase, containing some treats, was not under any circumstances to be opened till we arrived in Italy.

Des had made his contribution by assuring me that the matter of the gloves, helmet and goggles in particular were all taken care of. Boots of course were supplied with the skis, so even I agreed wellington boots were probably a sensible addition.

---

[72] Source: Gerard Manley Hopkins: *Poems and Prose* (Penguin Classics, 1985)

The coach trip from York to Luton airport and the flight over were uneventful enough. Spirits were high.

In the morning, however, when I lined up on the piste with my other *chums* even the teachers, a kindly Quakerly bunch, howled with laughter at my appearance. Already sweating in the woollen one piece my gusset had begun to sag below my knees. However, it was the World War II motorcycle gauntlets and airman's flying cap and goggles that really set off the ensemble. Des and Nana had excelled themselves.

To avoid any further cruel taunts, Mr Peach came up to me during our lunch break and said if I wanted to go down the hill and explore the village in my civvies that would be perfectly fine. It was an enormous relief to see the school party snowploughing down the mountain away from me as I made my way up to the ski lift for the journey down.

The top of mountain was eerily quiet. It was so peaceful. I was absolutely on my own, there was no one else about. I caught the chair lift as it swept in a 180-degree curve at the top of the slopes and then started on its journey back down. Within seconds, I was twenty feet in the air with a magnificent view across much of Lombardy.

Just at that moment, at precisely 14:30 hrs, the chair lift stopped and restarted at 17:00 hrs to take the last of the skiers off the piste.

No one in the school party knew that on a Sunday afternoon there were usually no instructors on the snow so beginners only used the foot of the mountain. So the ski lift was switched off most Sunday afternoons.

I've hated snow, and skiing especially, ever since.

Tuesday, May 17, 25 Not Out

Elizabeth II begins her 1977 Silver Jubilee tour in Glasgow, Scotland.

Wednesday, May 25, Dominion

George Lucas's *Star Wars* opens in cinemas and becomes the highest grossing film of its time. It also makes sci-fi films very popular.

For a man who liked his astronomy, and tried to teach me physics, I find it odd that Mr Robinson never made mention of Star Wars. My main memory – in fact only memory – is the day he came into physics, and started the lesson declaiming Dylan Thomas' *And death shall have no dominion*, in the most hilariously strange way, the memory has lasted over fifty years.

It's highly possible that earlier that week his own father passed away and this was one of his ways of exculpating the pain and grief. I've laid out the first stanza very much as he declaimed it.

I'm afraid to admit his tears just embarrassed us.

And
        DEATH
Shall have
No
        DOMINION

Dead men naked they shall be one
With the man in the wind and the west moon;
When their bones are picked clean and the clean bones gone,
They shall have stars at elbow and foot;
Though they go mad they shall be sane,
Though they sink through the sea they shall rise again;
Though lovers be lost love shall not;
And death shall have no dominion.
And death shall have no dominion.
Under the windings of the sea
They lying long shall not die windily;
Twisting on racks when sinews give way,
Strapped to a wheel, yet they shall not break;
Faith in their hands shall snap in two,
And the unicorn evils run them through;
Split all ends up they shan't crack;
And death shall have no dominion.
And death shall have no dominion.
No more may gulls cry at their ears
Or waves break loud on the seashores;
Where blew a flower may a flower no more
Lift its head to the blows of the rain;
Though they be mad and dead as nails,
Heads of the characters hammer through daisies;

162

Break in the sun till the sun breaks down,

And death shall have no dominion.[73]

Monday, June 6 – Thursday, June 9, Jubilee

Jubilee celebrations are held in the United Kingdom to celebrate 25 years of Elizabeth II's reign.

Over in the British Club in Zaria, Nigeria, the Jubilee celebrations are marked by amongst other things, a barbeque and an inter United Kingdom children's swimming competition. The pool of course being the centre of the activities in the club.

Northern Ireland and Wales are seeded third and fourth given their smaller populations so to balance up the disparities in the teams' sizes are given the inner two lanes. Scotland and England the outside lanes.

There are three age categories: Under 5s, Under 10s and Under 18s. Dad, by now the de facto captain of the Welsh team, keen to demonstrate his son's prowess as a decent backstroker and breaststroker, enters me in the 25-yard races and the 4 x 4 medley, which to his immense pride; I win!

Then come the *long* 50-yard races. My three sprint victories behind me I'm content that's my evening done.

Rather than forfeit all points for the 50 yards butterfly for which we have no entry, Dad asks if I can swim that too and earn Wales the consolation point, just for finishing.

It's a race too far. My three consecutive victories have taken their terrible toll.

I started well enough but then by the turn I'm third and then, as my arms begin to feel like lead, and my legs barely lift me from the water I'm way back in fourth. And then disaster strikes. Utterly exhausted, almost blind with fatigue and nausea, barbequed butterfly prawns, steak and salad spew in a plume in front of me. A kaleidoscope of meat and lettuce shimmers and bobs across the surface of the pool.

Somehow, with prawn in my nostrils and steak in my hair, I touch the end of the pool at last. Big hands reach down and pull me from the water. The club

---

[73] Dylan Thomas, *Collected Poems*: 1934–1952 (Aldine Paperback) ISBN: 9780460020879

nurse wraps me in a towel and clucking after my father tells him what a fool he is.

The President of the British Club announces that as the pool now needs 24 hours to be properly cleaned, the races are abandoned, due to vomit.

It doesn't take long for the DJ to restart the party and I am soon restored to reasonable health. A toast is given to the Queen, with beer and bottles of Fanta, and the swimming gala is soon forgotten.

However, the captain of the Welsh team is the happiest man in Africa. The winning country of the British Club in Zaria, 1977 Jubilee Swimming Gala is: Wales.

By one point.

Saturday, June 25

American Roy Sullivan is struck by lightning for the seventh time.[74]

Summer Term Report

Oliver is coming along very well. He is mature, responsible and eminently reliable. His academic work continues well and while I hope he can reach an A grade once more there is no doubt that he is working well and conscientiously.

His spare time is very well spent in chess, woodwork and tending terrapins but above all in playing the trumpet he is most able and gives confidence which will come in time will do well. There has been something missing this term since his terrapins were quarantined in Leeds! Cultivating algae in the tank has not seemed quite the same.

---

[74] June 10 – The first Apple II series computers go on sale.

June 26 – Elvis Presley holds his last concert at Market Square Arena in Indianapolis.

August 19 – Comedian Groucho Marx dies of pneumonia at Cedars-Sinai Medical Centre in Los Angeles, at the age of 86 (born 1890).

September 7 – Treaties between Panama and the United States on the status of the Panama Canal are signed. The US agrees to transfer control of the canal to Panama at the end of the twentieth century.

Olly always seems well occupied, happy and polite and I anticipate that he will do well in the future.

Robin L Peach, Class Master

Friday, July 1, The Championships

At Wimbledon, Virginia Wade wins the Women's Singles title in the centenary year of the tournament, Wade's first and only Wimbledon title and her third and final Grand Slam title overall; she remains the last British woman to win the singles title at Wimbledon.

Sunday, July 10, And Now the Weather

A temperature of 48.0 °C (118.4 °F), a record for continental Europe, is monitored in Greece.

This is a remarkable summer in the UK too. It has been baking hot and hardly rained all year. Hosepipe bans mean that everyone's lawn is completely brown and the roadside verges look like…Nigeria's.

Since we're talking records, for the record, England's hottest recorded temperature occurred in 2019 when it was 38.7 °C. Still 10 °C cooler than Greece in 1977. (Although a little way off the hottest temperature ever recorded on Earth which was 56.7 °C in Death Valley in 1913, or the coolest temperature which was –89.2 °C at the Vostok Station in Antarctica, in 1983.)

Tuesday, August 16, The King is Gone

Elvis Presley, still the undisputed King of Rock and Roll, died in his home in Graceland, aged just 42. 75,000 fans line the streets of Memphis for his funeral, which occurred two days later.

Thursday, October 27, Staying Alive

British punk band The Sex Pistols release *Never Mind the Bollocks, Here's the Sex Pistols* on the Virgin Records label. Despite refusal by major retailers in the UK to stock it, it debuts at number one on the UK Album Charts the week after its release.[75]

---

[75] September 10 – Hamida Djandoubi's is the last guillotine execution in France.

Listening to this on Radio Luxembourg, under the blankets after lights out, I wonder if the Queen has heard the lyrics, and what she might think? I imagine the soundtrack to *Saturday Night Fever*, which is released on November, is more to her tastes.

Featuring five new Bee Gees compositions, it will go on to become the then bestselling album of all time. Interesting that in the intervening decades both bands still receive much the same airtime as they did when they first became famous.

Saturday Night Fever comes out in December and we're all pretending we're the next John Travolta, teachers included. The film launches his career and catapults the Bee Gees – who performed several songs on the soundtrack – to newfound success.

I imagine, being a fully qualified civil aviation airline pilot in his spare time, this announcement excites Captain Travolta as much as it does me. Concorde becomes a (not so) commercial airliner, as British Airways inaugurates its regular London to New York City supersonic Concorde service.

Later, Concorde famously arrived at Manama airport too, but the air density was too low for it to take off with a full planeload of passengers, so it had to leave some behind. Imagine that.

I so wanted to fly in it, but by the time I could afford even its shortest novelty flights around the Channel Islands, all the aircraft were grounded following the catastrophe in Paris.

Before the end of term, Egyptian President Anwar Sadat became the first Arab leader to make an official visit to Israel, where he meets with Israeli Prime Minister Menachem Begin, seeking a permanent peace settlement.

As a result of this, they later received the Nobel Peace Prize, something of course Bootham as a Quaker school followed closely. Indeed marching for peace was something Bootham was very keen on. Being pacifists, Quakers were very vocal campaigners against the expansion of the world's nuclear weapons. It was even said that Geoffrey Easton our woodwork teacher had been arrested whilst on a march for CND (the Campaign for Nuclear Disarmament).

A few of the teachers wore CND badges, but faithful to the Quaker way extreme positions were never thrust down our throats. For every guest liberal

---

October 26 – The last natural smallpox case is discovered in Merca district, Somalia. The WHO and the CDC consider this date the anniversary of the eradication of smallpox, a great success of vaccination, and by extension, of modern science.

166

democrat speaker we might host at a Sunday evening service, chances were the week later the contrary position would be argued by a parent who happened to be a ranking soldier in the army, navy or air force.

One of the legacies of my time at Bootham was my admiration of the Quakers' desire to see both sides. Which possibly explains why I joined the Territorial Army for nine years, leaving with the excuse *I'd become a pacifist*. I realised my commanding officer would have no come back on that argument, and he conceded that matters of conscience should be respected.

For that point too, I have huge admiration.

Christmas Term Report

Oliver's terrapins have returned – and his interest in them has borne fruit in the form of the school Natural History prize, for which we must congratulate him very much.

This is not to suggest that Olly has not occupied his time well with other matters. He has surprised us all – and I suspect himself – with his aptitude and love of Fives. His commitment to interest all of us to have a go is exemplary. You really should watch him play. (They never did).

His academic work remains very good. The drop to the B grade across the examinations being due in part to a more demanding standard of examination as we near the O-Levels.

I have confidence that Olly will show his accustomed good sense and hard work next year and do well as a result. This has been a very good year and I have every confidence that it will be followed by another one.

Robin L Peach, Class Master[76]

---

[76] December 25 – English comedian and silent film actor, Charlie Chaplin dies at his home in Corsier-sur-Vevey, Switzerland from a stroke at the age of 88.

1978, York, England. Ibadan, Southern Nigeria. Manama, Bahrain

Wednesday, January 18, Suntans

The European Court of Human Rights finds the British government guilty of mistreating prisoners in Northern Ireland but not guilty of torture.

During the holidays, the adults' conversation is all about Nigerianisation. It has become political policy to kick out white colonials occupying leadership roles, which the government would like to see Nigerians doing.

The process is quite systematic and ruthless, although violence against white families that flared up in southern central Africa does not take hold in Nigeria.

Family after family say their tearful farewells to each other in the British Club. This holiday we're in Ibadan, near Lagos where Dad is currently supervising his own removal from post.

It's a sad holiday. It's the last time I'll go back to school with a Christmas suntan from Nigeria.

Sometime after I fly back to school, Mum, this time accompanied by my brother and sister, repeats her journey of ten years before from Liverpool by ship. This time on the SS Accra, bringing all our Nigerian luggage.

When it's Dad's time to fly back, he arrives home in a suit and tie, with just a toothbrush for luggage. He always travels like this, much to my mother's chagrin whose entourage of children ensures she is always surrounded by teddies, feeding bottles, pushchair and losable hand luggage.

Wednesday, March 1, Ignominious

Charlie Chaplin's remains are stolen from Corsier-sur-Vevey, Switzerland. What a week this was:

March 5 – *Wuthering Heights*, the debut single by Kate Bush, charts at #1 in the United Kingdom, making her the first woman to have a self-penned number one single.

It's the first record I queue to buy having heard Wuthering Heights on the radio. When pictures of Kate are published too, just 19 years old, like every teenager in 1978 I am smitten. *The Kick in Side* is still my favourite LP, although *Dark Side of the Moon* and *Hell's Bells* run it a close second and third.

March 8 – The first radio episode of *The Hitchhiker's Guide to the Galaxy*, by Douglas Adams, is transmitted on BBC Radio 4. John Searle Barnes our young house master and my struggling politics tutor invites us to listen to it in his school flat. After the first episode, he's realised too that geeks of a certain age – like us – will accord it cult status immediately. For the rest of the term, everyone's conversation is peppered with references to Zaphod Beeblebrox and Arthur Dent.

March 17 – An oil tanker, *Amoco Cadiz*, runs aground on the coast of Brittany. Even the site of oil-smothered birds is *still* not enough to prick the consciences of the world's politicians that Earth is heading for an environmental disaster of humans' making.

Adjusting to life in the UK is very hard for both my mother, but especially so for Dad. Britain is going through an extended period of recession and finding a job with equal status to that he'd enjoyed in Nigeria is practically impossible.

But he's a resourceful man, and sometime during the Easter half term break he announces he's going for an interview in Lagos, for a French bank.

Ever the optimist my mother says, "But you don't even speak French." There's no doubt about it, she seems annoyed he's going to live abroad again, but equally they know they're better together apart.

Personally, 1978 is shaping up to be my best ever year, possibly, if only because I really love my first year sixth form A-level classes. As sixth formers we each get a study (a 10' x 10' cell) of our own, albeit to share with a friend, in my case Bruce.

Outside of lessons, we play our LPs pretty much all the time seven days a week.

Imagine how unhappy life could be if you didn't get on with your study mate, or at least his choice of music.

It seems terribly highbrow but in between Supertramp's, *Breakfast in America*, and Pink Floyd's *Dark Side of the Moon*, Bruce and I listened to the box set of all Beethoven's Symphonies played by the Berlin Philharmonic Orchestra and their maestro conductor Herbert Von Karajan.

It was study rule that a classical album *had* to be followed by a rock album.

Nearly fifty years later, we can still spot a Karajan recording at 100 paces.

Loudspeakers were the thing in 1978 at Bootham. Unless you had a speaker stack at least three feet high on each corner of your study, you just weren't normal. Even the lads who had no intention of going on to university had massive speaker stacks. Normally, all that interested them was food.

For some reason, it didn't occur to the teaching staff either that the combination of teenage boys highly fuelled with testosterone and Jaffa cakes, listening to a continuous diet of heavy rock confined two to a cell might be a recipe for trouble. Each of the studies was separated by nothing more than plasterboard.

On three occasions, at least, whole bodies came hurtling through the walls of the study corridor, usually following some dispute about the next choice of LP.

The plasterboard wall was thin, cheap and easily repaired. But you could hardly sulk quietly in the corner of your study if your study mate had pushed you through next door's wall.

But I was having a great time. And then I got a girlfriend.

Friday, April 7, Sand and More Sand

US President Jimmy Carter decides to postpone production of the neutron bomb, a weapon that kills people with radiation but leaves buildings relatively intact.

This is a relief to us all, but like most momentous world shaping decisions, is hidden from public gaze. This is still an era when governments are deemed to know what's best for the citizenry.

So at the time, we'd be none the wiser. Still I'm very grateful Mr President.

Whilst leaving Standard Chartered Bank of West Africa, must have been a wrench, Dad's experience was soon to earn him a new role for Banque de Paris et des Pay Bay, in Bahrain. Similar role, different continent.

This end of term, flying to Bahrain for the holidays rather than Nigeria is a much more exotic affair. For a start the Arab nation, about the same size of the Isle of Man, situated half way down the Arabian Gulf was emerging as a global financial powerhouse, an oil rich state where the ruling family presided over a country with one of the highest per capita incomes in the world.

And for fans of the Muppets, flying to Manama airport never ceased to amuse. Gulf Air flew some of the most luxurious jets in the air and with petrol 20p a litre, Dad's massive Pontiac Firebird had an air conditioning system bigger than the ones we had in our houses in Nigeria.

Air conditioning in the Middle East is essential for survival. Whilst life in Nigeria was colonial, in Bahrain the subordinate position of women and migrant workers was oppressive. Life in Bahrain was never as relaxed as it was in Nigeria, and Dad worked a six-day week, so we hardly ever saw him.

Whilst the Manamanams all took Friday and Saturday off as their weekends, the French bank expected its expatriate managers to work on Fridays. The local managers were all expected to work on a Sunday – a working day in the Middle East – so Dad only had 24 hours off, on a Saturday.

Wednesday, May 17, Less Ignominious

Charlie Chaplin's coffin is found some 15 kilometres (9.3 mi) from the cemetery from which it was stolen, near Lake Geneva.[77]

---

[77] June 1 – The 1978 FIFA World Cup starts in Argentina.

June 9 – The Church of Jesus Christ of Latter-day Saints extends the priesthood and temple blessings to all worthy males, ending a general policy of excluding Canaanites from priesthood ordination and temple ordinances.

June 16 – *Grease* starring John Travolta and Olivia Newton-John is released.

June 19 – Cricketer Ian Bootham becomes the first man in the history of the game to score a century and take eight wickets in one innings of a Test match.

Garfield, which eventually becomes the world's most widely syndicated comic strip, makes its debut nationwide.

June 21 – A shootout between IRA members and the British Army leaves one civilian and three IRA men dead.

June 22 – Charon, a satellite of Pluto, is discovered.

June 25 – Argentina defeats the Netherlands 3–1 after extra time to win the 1978 FIFA World Cup.

June 28 – The rainbow flag of the LGBT movement flies for the first time (in its original form) at the San Francisco Gay Freedom Day Parade.

Monday, July 17, Malaria

One advantage Bahrain has over Nigeria is the lack of malaria. Mosquitos were a scourge in Nigeria and even though we took a daily white tablet called Paludrine, mosquito nets were essential over each of the beds.

Before the mosquito nets went down each night, the houseboy would spray all the corners of each bedroom, and the nets themselves with Sheltox. Nigerian strength Sheltox spray came in a canister that was pumped out using a hand pump that the canister screwed onto. Catch too much of the cloud of spray and you'd struggle to breath. Small animals like geckos quickly succumbed too if they received a full-on squirt. I loved the smell.

In Bahrain, the biggest threat to our health at night was hypothermia. For some reason the air-conditioning seemed permanently set on *Winter*.

Another striking contrast between the two countries is the lack of rain in Bahrain. By comparison, it rained in Nigeria almost year around and with some of the most spectacular storms.

One of the most exciting afternoons of my childhood was taken standing by the front door of the house, where the rain was pelting down like a car wash, but outside the back door, all was dry and the sun was shining, the landscape completely different. Being on the edge of the storm front was one of the most surreal experiences I've ever had.

Summer Term Report[78]

Once more and we were delighted that he achieved the 11 O'Level results he so clearly deserved. This term he has been a little less worried than previously, although he certainly did not need to be anxious.

Once again Olly is to be congratulated on winning the Natural History competition for the second year running. I have no doubt he will be striving hard to make it a hat trick of wins next summer. I note from his music teacher that he produces a good bold tone on the trumpet but does not yet always use this to provide the strong lead in ensemble work that his ability enable him to do.

Enjoy your summer holiday and we look forward to inviting Olly back into the sixth form.

Robin Peach, Class Master

Sunday, December 10, Retakes

Back to Bahrain, carrying my school report in my suitcase. Slightly nervous as I failed my French and Latin O'Level in the summer and had to retake them.

---

[78] July 25 – Louise Brown the world's first test tube baby is born in Oldham, Greater Manchester.

August 26 – Pope John Paul I succeeds Pope Paul VI as the 263rd Pope

September 5 – Camp David Accords: Menachem Begin and Anwar Sadat begin the peace process at Camp David, Maryland.

September 7

In London, England, a poison-filled pellet, supposedly injected using an umbrella, fatally poisons Bulgarian defector Georgi Markov; he dies four days later.

Keith Moon, wild man drummer of the British rock band The Who, dies from an accidental overdose at age 32 in London, England.

September 28 – Pope John Paul I dies after only 33 days of papacy.

October 16 – Pope John Paul II succeeds Pope John Paul I as the 264th pope, resulting in the first Year of Three Popes since 1605. He is the first Polish pope in history and the first non-Italian pope since Pope Adrian VI (1522–1523).

October 27 – Egyptian President Anwar Sadat and Israeli Prime Minister Menachem Begin win the Nobel Peace Prize for their progress toward achieving a Middle East accord.

I scrapped through with grade C passes in both. Now giving myself a ridiculous number of O-Levels: 13.

Christmas Term Report

Oliver has been fully involved during the term. He has carried his for A-Level subjects extremely well and in addition he has had to work at the two language 'repeats'. His classroom work reveals much promise and Oliver is always prepared to follow up each class with reading and questions. It is just in this way that his confidence is likely to grow.

I have been especially pleased with the time and consideration that Oliver has managed to give to activities involving the junior boys.

He is looked up to in the Junior House and his work with the Fives Club has been heroic. These are rare qualities today and Oliver deserves all credit. Indeed, he should look back at his first term in sixth form with considerable satisfaction.

Michael E Allen, Class Tutor

The heroic act referred to was borne out of what I perceived to be a huge injustice. The school to my horror announced that the science block was going to be extended, a new astronomy tower constructed and two squash courts built on the site of the fives court, which would be demolished.

How could this be? Our fives court was one of less than twenty courts in the country. There must be twenty squash courts in York. I wrote to the Mayor, York's MP, the Chief Executive of the council and then with the help of a friendly solicitor applied to English Heritage to get the court Grade II listed.

But my 17-year-old's efforts were too late. By the time we came back after Christmas, building work had already quickly started on the new science block and squash courts. More experienced heads than mine knew that once demolished no retrospective cases could be heard.

Wednesday, December 27, Nana's Funeral

She died on the 18th, at home in her own bed, temporarily downstairs in the dining room as she hadn't been able to manage the stairs. How convenient too that she should have been born in 1900, calculating how old she was being one of the easier pieces of anniversary arithmetic.

I cannot bring myself to go to the funeral. I lie to my mother that it's one of the last things Nana said to me, that she would rather I didn't. Instead, I fiddled with the napkins on the dining room table and pretended to be busy until the mourners descended on the house to eat our sausage rolls.

I hope she had a good life. It was certainly very tough and very full. Two world wars, pony and carts, Saturn V, the NHS, me.

Her cancer in her final weeks certainly put paid to her having a good death, and I rarely ventured into the dining room where we'd moved her bed, to see her for fear she would die in front of me if I went in to swap over a teacup. Or take in another slice of unwanted toast.

Instead, I wish I'd taken solace that the poets have all thought deeply about death and love and loss before us. It's best left to them, like W B Yeats, in *When you are old.*[79]

---

[79] Source: *The Collected Poems of W. B. Yeats* (1989)
December 31 – The Soviet Union nuclear weapons stockpile exceeds the United States nuclear weapons stockpile.
The Space Invaders arcade video game is released by Taito Corporation.

1979, York

Monday, January 29, Tell Me Why I Don't Like Mondays

Brenda Ann Spencer opens fire at a school in San Diego, California, killing two faculty members and wounding eight students and a police officer.

Her justification for the action, "I don't like Mondays," inspires the Boomtown Rats to make a song of the same name.

Given I am a teenager, constantly glued to my Walkman, this next news is alarming. In early February, former Sex Pistols bassist Sid Vicious is found dead, aged 21, of a heroin overdose in New York, the day after being released from a 55-day sentence at Rikers Island prison on bail.

In Iran, the Ayatollah Khomeini creates the Council of the Islamic Revolution, which no one pays attention about until all hell breaks loose globally. We little realise it at the time what the long-term impact will be. Suddenly we're aware there are both Shi'a and Sunni Muslims.

Supporters of Ayatollah Khomeini take over the Iranian law enforcement, courts and government administration; the final session of the Iranian National Consultative Assembly is held.

The Iranian army withdraws to its barracks leaving power in the hands of Ayatollah Khomeini, ending the Pahlavi dynasty. A little later in the year, ironically on April Fool's Day the government becomes an Islamic Republic by a 98% vote (really though?), overthrowing the Shah officially.

My father once met the Shah. I say met, I think Dad was on manoeuvres with the Royal Parachute Regiment, training some elements of Iran's Special Air Service. My father frequently recounted tales of what happened when vehicles pushed out of the air transporters experienced parachute failures. Sadly, he was invariably a little too graphic when describing similar events that had happened to comrades.

Even when he worked for a bank, much to my mother's relief, he still had stories of gruesome death. Lift failures were few in Nigeria, as there were so few lifts, but maintenance of those that were there was haphazard at best. The same was true of safes and vaults were bullion was stored.

Occasionally, my father would come home and over dinner explain how so and so's chest had been compressed by the automatic safe door, or so and so lost a finger today.

However, even he was shaken by the fate of the maintenance worker who working alone at the weekend was checking on the cylinder pressures of the xenon gas, which would extinguish a fire in a vault. Important given all the printed notes stacked inside.

He had not noticed the door close behind him. Using his lighter to find the way out the flame tripped the xenon gas extinguisher and he was suffocated.

Thursday, February 15, Dangerous Places

A suspected gas explosion in a Warsaw bank kills 49.

Wednesday, March 28, Politics

As an A-Level Politics student, there was much to get my teeth into this term. The A-Level the school taught was Economics and Politics, but as I was such a dunce at Maths I found the Economics deadly dull and practically impossible. There was an examination board that offered just Politics and rather nobly our young teacher John Searle Barnes offered to learn and teach me the syllabus.

His only challenge was that I was rather more interested in the subject than he was and often read ahead of him.

This term, in particular, UK political history was unfolding before our very eyes and ears. James Callaghan's minority Labour government lost a motion of confidence by one vote, forcing a general election, which was to be held on May 3.

In March, Airey Neave MP, a World War II veteran and Conservative Northern Ireland spokesman, was killed, presumably the work of the Irish National Liberation Army bomb in the House of Commons car park.

A month later, Pakistani Prime Minister Zulfiqar Ali Bhutto was executed by hanging for the murder of a political opponent. That doesn't happen very often.

Then on May 4, something unique occurred. Counting in the previous day's British general election showed that the Conservatives have won and Margaret Thatcher has become the country's first female Prime Minister, ending the rule of the Labour government.

Easter Term Report

Oliver deserves particular credit for the enthusiasm and leadership which he has given to the revived House system and as always he has kept himself remarkably busy, editing the school magazine, representing the school at hockey.

Olly has proved to be an enthusiastic member of the Second XI and captained the team exceptionally well. It is a pleasure to teach someone with such an obvious interest in English, History and Politics

He is beginning to tighten up his essay style and is obviously reading widely and sensibly. In Politics, I hear reports that Oliver has been almost excessive in his work output this term and the teachers have sometimes felt swamped by the volume of words he has written. Although his output has been prolific it was always been of a satisfactory quality and his style of writing is much improving.

I am sure the holidays will give Oliver an opportunity to read further round is academic subjects in which he is doing so well.

Michael Allen, Class Tutor

Friday, June 1, McDonald's Introduces the Happy Meal.[80]

Friday, June 22, London

The Muppet Movie is on general release today, and in the Sixth form, we are on a cultural field trip to Tate Britain Art Gallery, in Pimlico, London. As we

---

[80] June 2 – Pope John Paul II arrives in his native Poland on his first official, nine-day stay, becoming the first Pope to visit a communist country. This visit, known as nine days that changed the world, brings about the solidarity of the Polish people against communism, ultimately leading to the rise of the Solidarity movement.

approached in our coach, the exciting sites of the Houses of Parliament and the River Thames hove into view. Inside the gallery, Whistler's view of London, looking across the mist to Westminster Bridge resonates precisely with mine, and Wordsworth's.

As I look at the picture, and the poem alongside it in the notes about the artist I wonder if Whistler and Wordsworth ever met. On this bridge, perhaps?

Composed Upon Westminster Bridge, September 3, 1802

By William Wordsworth
Earth has not anything to show more fair:
Dull would he be of soul who could pass by
A sight so touching in its majesty:
This City now doth, like a garment, wear
The beauty of the morning; silent, bare,
Ships, towers, domes, theatres, and temples lie
Open unto the fields, and to the sky;
All bright and glittering in the smokeless air.
Never did sun more beautifully steep
In his first splendour, valley, rock, or hill;
Ne'er saw I, never felt, a calm so deep!
The river glideth at his own sweet will:
Dear God! the very houses seem asleep;
And all that mighty heart is lying still![81]

Val Halla tells us of a famous exchange between James McNeill Whistler and a sitter for one of his portraits, possibly in the gallery before us. "It's not a great work of art," says the model.

"Perhaps not, but then *you're* not a great work of nature," replies the artist.

Sunday, July 15, Lacking Confidence

President Jimmy Carter addresses the nation in a televised speech talking about the *crisis of confidence* in America today; it would go on to be known as his *national malaise* speech.

---

[81] *Collected Poems*, William Wordsworth, ISBN 13: 9781853264016

Surely, I think, if he's in charge of the country, shouldn't he be doing something about the conditions that brought about the national malaise he's so vexed about?

Anyway, in less than a month Michael Jackson releases his breakthrough album *Off the Wall*. The US has its mojo back. It sells seven million copies in the United States alone, making it a 7× platinum album.

Monday, August 27, IRA's Revenge

Striking at the heart of the Royal Family, the IRA kill Lord Mountbatten of Burma and two others with a bomb concealed in their rowing boat. Mountbatten was a British admiral, statesman and an uncle of The Duke of Edinburgh.

On the same day, the Warrenpoint ambush occurred, killing 18 British soldiers. Possibly because Margaret Thatcher's stance against the IRA and terrorist acts is so intractable the country braces itself for a long and worrying fight ahead. Neither side will back down.

Sunday, September 9, Foot Stomping

Mum and Dad are sitting either side of me in the Harrogate Theatre, on the occasion of my 18th birthday. George Melly and John Chiltern's Feetwarmers are the act.

Their live jazz is amazing, and George Melly, who I'd never heard of, tells the most outrageous blue stories imaginable. Perhaps because he's in prim and proper Harrogate, he really turns it on.

It's so outrageously naughty I'm embarrassed for my mother in particular. But it's a good way to enter adulthood. George may have even given me a shout out to wish me happy birthday. I think he did. I just personally wasn't too keen when he broke into song. It held up the dirty story telling.

Tuesday, October 30, Crocii

Tonight, Mischief Night at Bootham, we planted crocus bulbs rather than seeds (we were so posh and stuck up, thinking back) in the flower border in front of John Gray, the headmaster's office.

JG = twat

Years later, I went back to the school as a parent to talk about my eldest daughter's admission to Bootham, I sneaked a look at the flowerbed as the headmaster was pouring us tea in his study.

There was now a magnificent deep blue ceanothus bush where the flower border had once been. Much safer. Was that a dash of purple underneath? Perhaps.

My year group's efforts to cause mischief paled into insignificance compared to the brains who went before us. It had long been common practice on Mischief Night for groups of boys, ten or so, to lift any car that was parked in the forecourt and *park* it somewhere else, possibly facing the other way, or on one celebrated evening in between the doors of the assembly hall ensuring it could neither be moved backwards or forwards. Eventually, the fire brigade had to jack up Matron's car and slide it out, sideways.

However, the year group before mine were a much brainier lot. Many went on to Oxbridge and had careers in high office, even ascending to the House of Lords in one case at least.

On this Mischief Night, they parked the new, young science teacher's car on the flat roof of the science block. Poor Mr Jamieson must have missed the warning in the staff room to park his Mini Metro off site on 30 October. Being the Master on Duty that night, he was a complete innocent.

After dark, finding his car missing, and nowhere in the grounds he reported it to the police as stolen. But in the morning, his bright orange car was visible for miles around – and certainly to all of us trailing into assembly for morning meeting.

It remained a mystery how the car appeared four storeys up, totally undamaged, and still in perfect working order, when after three hours of crane work the fire brigade finally returned it to the ground.

Mr Wilkinson the physics teacher and Mr Cartwright the Sixth Form maths tutor were still to be seen after lunch in the dining room hard at it poring over diagrams showing pulleys and cantilevers and formulae. The issue seemed to be that there was no apparent room to employ any levers big enough, or fixing points strong enough for any pulleys. Nor did anyone hear or see anything in the dead of night, which took the fire brigade an 80-tonne crane and lots of grunting and shouting to remove in broad daylight.

How did the Mini Metro get onto the roof? Was it dismantled and reassembled – in the dark – or was it carried up the fire escape, which was surely too small? Was it hoisted up the wall in a sling, but where was there space on the roof for a team on the other side to pull it up?

How, and who, put the car on the roof?

Nobody knows. Or rather, I'm not telling.

Friday, November 9, Guilty

The Carl Bridgewater murder trial ends in England with all four men found guilty. James Robinson, 45, and 25-year-old Vincent Hickey are sentenced to life imprisonment with a recommended 25-year minimum for murder. 18-year-old Michael Hickey is also found guilty of murder and sentenced to indefinite detention. Patrick Molloy, 53, is found guilty on a lesser charge of manslaughter and sentenced to 12 years in prison.

Nuclear false alarm: the NORAD computers and the Alternate National Military Command Centre in Fort Ritchie, Maryland, detect an apparent massive Soviet nuclear strike. After reviewing the raw data from satellites and checking the early warning radars, the alert is cancelled.[82]

To Parents of Boys in Sixth Form

Dear parent,

In this important year in your boy's academic school life we think you will appreciate a brief report on his progress. All boys hoping to go on to university should have completed their UCCA forms by half term and the forms will have been sent off with the headmaster's testimonial by the end of the month, or very soon thereafter.

---

[82] November 12 – Iran hostage crisis: In response to the hostage situation in Tehran, US President Jimmy Carter orders a halt to all oil imports into the United States from Iran.

November 14 – Iran hostage crisis: US President Jimmy Carter issues Executive Order 12170, freezing all Iranian assets in the United States and US banks in response to the hostage crisis.

November 15 – British art historian and former Surveyor of the Queen's Pictures Anthony Blunt's role as the fourth man of the Cambridge Five double agents for the Soviet NKVD during World War II is revealed by Prime Minister Margaret Thatcher in the House of Commons of the United Kingdom;[15] she gives further details on November 21.

This report places emphasis on how well your son is working rather than on the standard he is reaching. Sometimes a pupil does not do himself justice in the summer A-Level examinations because he has not begun effective preparations early enough. Our comments will enable you to make an assessment of your son's progress. If you have comments or questions please address them to me his sixth form class tutor or the headmaster.

Oliver has been working diligently and effectively this term often producing written work that has not been specifically set. He appears interested in all his subjects and he makes it plain that he is anxious to improve and to do well in the summer. At the moment he appears to be heading for three very sound[83] passes with good grades. Whether he can attain A grades remains to be seen but it has been encouraging to observe his readiness to be a little more experimental and a little bolder with his essay style.

Yours sincerely, Michael E Allen, Class Tutor

---

[83] The school's lack of enthusiasm in my ability to achieve three A grades consigned me to not apply to Oxbridge. I might still have gone to London, but it would have been nice to have had the option. I've not forgiven them.

November 21 – After false radio reports from the Ayatollah Khomeini that the Americans had occupied the Grand Mosque in Mecca, the United States Embassy in Islamabad, Pakistan, is attacked by a mob and set fire to, killing four, and destabilising Pakistan-United States relations.

November 30 – *The Wall*, the rock opera and concept album by Pink Floyd, is first released.

December 9 – The eradication of the smallpox virus is certified, making smallpox the first of only two human diseases that have been driven to extinction (rinderpest in 2011 being the other).

1980, York. Camden, North London

Thursday, February 14, Valentine's Day[84]

An extraordinary thing happened this morning. I received a Valentine's Day card, pushed under the door of my study. Immediately, I opened the door to find John Searle Barnes.

Seeing my immediate disappointment, he explained, "I was at the Mount this morning taking Lower Sixth for history. Jenny Kirkham asked me to give you this. I think you have an admirer."

Smiling, he turned on his heels and disappeared.

Jenny Kirkham was in the school year below me, at the Mount. The Quaker girls' school on the other side of York. Having a pash for someone was okay, but it was unheard of for anyone to go out with someone in a different year group. And of course being asked out by a girl was even rarer.

JSB smiled for good reason. Jenny had a mane of natural ginger hair that fell to her waist and an hourglass figure. She wore little round wireframe glasses at the end of her nose and dressed with real style compared to most of the other girls in the sixth form who used the free dress code to either dress as Goths or nuns.

I was a lucky lad.

Over the next twelve months, Jenny taught me how to have a girlfriend.

---

[84] January 4 – President Jimmy Carter proclaims a grain embargo against the USSR with the support of the EU.

February 13 – The 1980 Winter Olympics open in Lake Placid, New York.

February 22 – The United States Olympic Hockey Team defeats the Soviet Union 4–3 in the semi-finals of the Winter Olympics, in the Miracle on Ice. An ideological and bigger propaganda victory over the Cold War foe could hardly be bigger.

March 4 – Robert Mugabe is elected prime minister of Zimbabwe.

Our first date the next Saturday afternoon was a bit of a rocky affair. Jenny came dressed to kill in a beautiful Chanel cardigan. We mooched around York, not holding hands. At the end of the afternoon outside the gates of the Mount she asked me, "What on earth has happened?"

"It's your cardigan. It's got buttons."

Far from chucking me on the spot for being a weirdo, she understood.

Whenever we went out again Jenny never wore jackets or cardigans but jackets or coats with zips, jumpers, T-shirts, or my favourite, tight long woollen dresses.

It was all I could do not to cuddle her all the time.

Thursday, March 20, Taking on Water

The Mi Amigo, the ship housing pirate radio station Radio Caroline, sinks off the English coast (the station returns aboard a new ship in 1983). Listening to them trying to broadcast whilst the ship was taking on water was one of the most dramatic and funny events of 1980. No one drowned.

In spite of the distraction of Jenny in a tight woollen dress all my mock A-Level results are A's or B's, and still with plenty of time still left to improve. English Literature-I is my favourite paper. I know Hamlet and Macbeth our two comparative Shakespeare plays almost by heart now. Fifty years on, I can still recite many of Macbeth's best lines.

How come when I try to learn a new poem today I struggle to remember even the second line!

> Tomorrow, and tomorrow, and tomorrow,
> Creeps in this petty pace from day to day,
> To the last syllable of recorded time;
> And all our yesterdays have lighted fools
> The way to dusty death. Out, out, brief candle!
> Life's but a walking shadow, a poor player,
> That struts and frets his hour upon the stage,
> And then is heard no more. It is a tale
> Told by an idiot, full of sound and fury,
> Signifying nothing.

The last sentence of that speech might even make the front-page blurb of a decent book.

185

Wednesday, April 30, Fact Better than Fiction[85]

Without doubt, one of the most dramatic televised events on British soil ever made. The Iranian Embassy siege in central London took place live, in front of TV news crews. Six Iranian-born terrorists took over the Iranian embassy.

A week later, the SAS retook the embassy, tear gassing the rooms and saving the lives of all the hostages. Only one terrorist survived.

Tuesday, June 10, There Is a Corner

The African National Congress in South Africa publishes a statement by their imprisoned leader Nelson Mandela. Mandela's imprisonment makes me think of lines from The Solider somehow.

It was good to be alive and see one of the miracles of history unfold when Mandela walked free in 1990. Rupert Brooke wrote *The Soldier* with death on his mind. Mandela escaped a similar fate, although we'd all expected he'd rot and die in Apartheid South Africa. But he didn't and he laid the foundations of a Rainbow Nation. Still, my thoughts turn to *The Soldier*:

> If I should die, think only this of me:
> That there's some corner of a foreign field
> That is for ever England. There shall be
> In that rich earth a richer dust concealed;
> A dust whom England bore, shaped, made aware,
> Gave, once, her flowers to love, her ways to roam;
> A body of England's, breathing English air,
> Washed by the rivers, blest by suns of home.
> And think, this heart, all evil shed away,
> A pulse in the eternal mind, no less
> Gives somewhere back the thoughts by England given;
> Her sights and sounds; dreams happy as her day;
>
> And laughter, learnt of friends; and gentleness

---

[85] March 21 – US President Jimmy Carter announces that the United States will boycott the 1980 Summer Olympics in Moscow because of the Soviet invasion of Afghanistan. March 26 – A mine lift cage at the Vaal Reefs gold mine in South Africa falls 1.9 kilometres (1.2 mi), killing 23.

In hearts at peace, under an English heaven.[86]

Monday, June 23, WWW

Tim Berners-Lee begins work on ENQUIRE, the system that will eventually lead to the creation of the World Wide Web in 1990.

Back at Bootham for the second half of term. Are there any more empty days, when A-Levels finished all you're waiting for is the end of school, and the rest of your life?

One of the changes we noticed is in the staff – certainly, the younger ones with whom we get on the most have started to treat us as adults, if not as equals.

Val Halla, my favourite teacher, is one such and I'm delighted when she invites me over to help out at a weekend barn dance and barbeque she is helping to organise in the village in which she lives. Long Marston is a gentle bike ride from the school and I have a pass to stay at her house overnight.

The house is an old farmhouse, full of character and probably several hundred years old. On the night, my first job is to supervise the parking of all the cars, in a spill over area through the gate and onto a field newly mown earlier for that purpose.

The Yorkshire weather is kind to us for a change and first the barbeque and then the barn dance are both a great success. Around midnight, I am performing my last duty, which is to clean up any discarded litter and make sure the gate is shut after the last car has left.

"Everything all right?" Val asks when I come in.

"Sure, all locked up. A funny thing happened though just as I was going down the drive. Out of the corner of my eye, I saw three riders go through the gate and then disappeared. It just seemed strange they didn't acknowledge me or wave goodbye? I thought it was a bit rude. Perhaps it's a bit late to be riding. Although it's not dark tonight."

After a nightcap we all went to bed.

In the morning, I helped Val with the last of the washing up.

---

[86] Selected from *Poem for the Day (Book One)* (ISBN 185619499X) in their footnotes on Brooke explains that he died in 1915 from blood poisoning on the Greek island Skros, where Winston Churchill telegrammed that he should be buried there, adding: "We shall not see his like again." Rupert Brooke was only 28 when he died, immortalised forever by his poetry but also joie de vivre inspiring Walter De la Mere to remark of him that "he flung himself into the world, as a wasp into a cake shop, Hotspur into the fighting".

"Those riders you saw last night," Val said, "they weren't in fancy dress were they?"

"Well, I didn't mention it last night, but yes. They had feathers in their hats and all looked like old soldiers."

"Ah, that explains it. It's never happened to me, in the thirteen years I've lived here. But you've seen the three Cavaliers. The farm is on the site of the Battle of Marston Moor, it took place in the meadow behind the farm on July 2, 1644.

"It's no wonder they didn't stop to chat, they were trying to escape. Oliver Cromwell won a famous victory here. The Royalists were heavily defeated; it was the turning point of the Civil War. The story goes that as the Royalists rallied together around the farm for one last effort, the farmer's young daughter ran to open the gate for them, but she was so small they didn't see her and she was knocked down and tragically killed.

"You do believe in ghosts, don't you?" asked Val with a smile.

"I'm not sure."

But I know what I saw.

Years later when it was time for me to buy a bigger house for the family, my wife and I were looking at a nice detached house in Grewelthorpe, a quaint village in North Yorkshire.

"You go on, have a look upstairs, the bedrooms are nice and roomy," said the estate agent. "Easily big enough for an en suite, if you want one. I'll just be here by the front door."

My wife and I went and explored upstairs. The bedrooms were indeed quite large and the master bedroom especially so. Then something quite peculiar happened. Both of us had an overwhelming sense that we were being ejected from the room and *persuaded* down the stairs.

We both rushed pass the estate agent and into the warm summer afternoon.

"Ah, both seem a bit shaken?" enquired the estate agent.

"We don't seem to be able to sell this one. I take it you sensed *the presence*?"

Indeed, we had.

At the *Financial Times*, one of my friends had cause to regret a house she and her husband bought. It wasn't on the particulars when they bought it. But try as they might whenever they wallpapered their bedroom dark patches would show through the paint or the double lined wallpaper.

Eventually, they decided to sell up. But not before the estate agent suggested that mentioning the previous owner had murdered his wife in that room, by slitting her throat, might not be such a good idea.

Saturday, July 19 – Sunday, August 3, Moscow

The 1980 Summer Olympics are held in Moscow. 82 countries boycott the games; athletes from 16 of them participate under a neutral flag.

End of School Report, 20 July, 1980

Oliver completed preparations for the examinations as thoroughly as had been anticipated. He should have faced them with confidence and I believe that he did. It is pleasant to record that in what was for Olly his most crucial term he has felt able to sustain his all-round activities. It was fitting that he won the Natural History prize, for the third time. He spoke extraordinarily well in the Speech Competition and his participation in school affairs and events have served as a model to other boys.

I'm sure that he will succeed in his chosen course at university and we hope to retain contact with him when he becomes an Old Scholar. He deserves to get the high grades he needs and I am hopeful that he will do so. I wish him well and trust that as in Law justice is not only done but seen to be done.

Though I know he gets exasperated by inefficiency and sloth he has contributed magnificently to the life of the school and he has my warmest thanks.

Warm good wishes,
John Gray, Headmaster

Monday, August 4

A-Level results day. I call the school for my grades: A; A; D. (D in History, but then I did panic and write about Robert the Bruce and King Alfred, instead of the Tudors and the Weimar Republic).

My place on the LLB (Bachelor of Laws) course at UCL is secure, although they'd have preferred ABB.

I really enjoyed the Moscow Olympics from the front room of 9 Oval View. These five would have won golds for Britain, even without the boycott.

Allan Wells – Athletics, Men's 100 metres, pale and Scottish

Steve Ovett – Athletics, Men's 800 metres, tough as nails

Sebastian Coe – Athletics, Men's 1500 metres, quicker than Ovett

Daley Thompson – Athletics, Men's Decathlon, best athlete alive

Duncan Goodhew – Swimming, Men's 100 metres Breaststroke, bald

Sunday, August 31, Solidarność

Lech Wałęsa leads the first of many strikes at the Gdańsk Shipyard in the Polish People's Republic. The Gdańsk Agreement is signed, opening a way to start the first free (i.e. not state-controlled) trade union in the communist bloc, Solidarity (*Solidarność*).

It was an amazing summer.

September 2 – Ford Europe launches the Escort MK3, a new front-wheel drive hatchback.

Tuesday, September 9, Still a Lanky Youth

My 19th birthday. This was my eldest cousin's best attempt at describing me to her friends who were spotting me off the train at King's Cross station. I've forgiven her for lanky, but not youth.

Friday, September 19, Crummy Camden

Moved in to my University College , London (UCL) Halls of Residence, Evans Hall today, on Camden High Street.

Built in the 1960s, the concrete pebbledash walls have zero personality, but the location is convenient for lectures in Euston and the tiny bedroom, eight in each wing, are functional.

To avoid the tiny cells completely replicating a prison experience there is a large shared kitchen and dining room at the end of the corridor, and off from these a communal shower room and toilets. None of the bedrooms is en suite.

I imagine this is exactly what an open prison might be like, except my cellmates are even more unusual than cons.

They're all mature students, from Nigeria.

Someone in the registry office must have thought I would welcome the opportunity to share my first years with them, given my background. It was a potentially kind gesture, but as I was at least five years' their junior, the accommodation block was somewhere I spent no more time in than actually necessary.

I was still a teenage boy, and three of the men were married and had children back at home. And their Ibo, Yoruba and Hausa occasionally proved explosive, often whilst we were cooking.

Occasionally, they did eat together on feast days but as one was a tribal prince and the others of lower birth life in block was fraught. The authorities ultimately moved them all out when it came to light they were slitting live chickens throats in the shower.

It wasn't a great start to being an independent adult.

Wednesday, October 1, Newspapers and Cars

In London, Associated Newspapers announces that *The Evening News* will close and merge with the *Evening Standard*. Strangely affected by this. The news is definitely in my blood, which is probably why I bought the first edition of *The European* and *The Independent* and *Today* and the last edition of *The News of the World*.

October 3 – English rock band The Police release their third studio album, *Zenyattà Mondatta*. Still my favourite album of Sting's.

October 5 – The now defunct British Leyland launches its new Metro, a three-door entry-level hatchback, which is designed as the eventual replacement for the Mini. It gives BL a long-awaited modern competitor for the likes of the Ford Fiesta and Vauxhall Chevette.

List of the cars I've owned or company cars

1. Ugly tank: Bronze Vauxhall Cavalier
2. Hairdresser's delight: White Rover 200 Cabriolet
3. Totally tango'd: Orange Mini Metro
4. Poor man's MG: Red Mazda MX5
5. My sweetheart: British Racing Green MG
6. Poor man's Land Rover short wheel base (but brilliant): Grey 3 door Suzuki Vitara
7. Hairdresser's Land Rover (not quite such fun): White 5 door Suzuki Vitara Automatic
8. The Lord of the Manor has arrived: Mustard Range Rover
9. Look, Mum, I'm in the army now: Grey Short wheel-based Land Rover
10. Sounds like a whale, less useful: Blue Suzuki Baleno
11. Car shaped: Red Suzuki SX4
12. Wishes it was a Vitara: Red 5 door Kia Sportage
13. Dad's hand me down to Daughter #1: Silver Renault Clio
14. Even more car shaped: Red Kia Venga Automatic
15. My sweetheart II: Midnight blue MG F
16. Daughter #2's run around: Blue VW Up!
17. Daughter #2's replacement Up: White VW Up! Automatic[87]

Monday, December 8, Shot

In bed, in Halls, I turned the radio on. "The English musician John Lennon has been shot dead outside his apartment in New York."

Suddenly, there's a commotion in the corridor as students knock on each other's doors. "Have you heard the news? Have you heard the news...?"

---

[87] October 15 – James Callaghan announces his resignation as leader of the British Labour Party.

October 27 – Six Provisional Irish Republican Army prisoners in Maze prison in Northern Ireland refuse food and demand status as political prisoners; the hunger strike lasts until December.

November 4 – 1980 United States presidential election: Republican challenger and former Governor Ronald Reagan of California defeats incumbent Democratic President Jimmy Carter to become the 40th president-elect of the United States, 1 year after the beginning of the Iran hostage crisis.

For my generation, it's a day of similar magnitude to that of my parents' generation, who all know where they were when JFK was assassinated.

If what we read is true, Lennon was difficult, violent and possibly abusive. Nor was he even my favourite Beatle so I'm surprised at the magnitude of my melancholy on hearing of Lennon's assassination. It is such a waste. The man was unnaturally gifted.

It's a rite of passage demonstrating how unfair and random and cruel life can be.

I don't want to face the world today, so stay in bed. All day. It's my first – and only ever – duvet day.

Let it be.

Thursday, December 16, Take Away

During a summit on the island of Bali, OPEC decides to raise the price of petroleum by 10%. The world is not really looking after itself.

Life is also especially hard in London. Even as a student on a full university grant some days I have to choose, will I eat a meal today, or not?

Whilst I'm really not enjoying the capital, there are treats though. Jacqueline Alderton a fellow first year lawyer, in Halls with me, have a Chinese takeaway blow out on the last Sunday of the month. There's a well situated takeaway less than five minutes from our gates.

I don't know whether Jacqueline ever became a barrister but driving up High Street Camden some forty years later I was delighted to see the Chinese takeaway is still going strong.

Later in the month, I go back home to spend Christmas in Harrogate.

I put on a brave face, but I'm not really enjoying life in London. Although Law is okay.

1981, Camden, North London

Friday, January 2, Silence in Court

One of the largest investigations by a British police force ends when serial killer Peter Sutcliffe, the "Yorkshire Ripper", is arrested in Sheffield, South Yorkshire.

It's hard to express how much fear the Ripper's murders instilled in women, especially across the north of England. One of the consequences of which was that for most of my time in the sixth form at Bootham, it was not just the gentlemanly thing to do, to accompany a girlfriend back to the Mount. It was mandatory. For the past three years, the Ripper's murders had made women wary of ever walking on their own. It's so sad that forty years later women rarely feel safe venturing out at night alone.

He was a curse.

The trial of course would be held at the Old Bailey and as criminal law students we thought it was our duty to queue to see it from the public gallery.

In the following months whilst the trial was on, I queued and queued and queued. And so did several thousands of others too.

I never got to see the trial of the century.

In hindsight, hearing how Sutcliffe killed some of his victims with hammer, I'm embarrassed I even thought it was a spectacle worth queuing for.

Friday, February 13, Lucky For Some[88]

Tomorrow being my first Valentine's Day with Jenny, I have fairly elaborate plans prepared. I aim to go to York, having saved the day return rail fare, wait till classes finish and – now I am *an adult* – take her out to Wong's, for the Chinese of her dreams, before she has to go back to the Mount, for Evensong.

That's what I had planned.

Saturday, February 14, Valentine's Day

I hope she got my card. It's huge, with a teddy bear on it, from *Guess who?* xxx

Clearly, her Valentine's card to me won't be able to fit in my pigeon hole when I check my post, so I'll probably have to check in with the porters.

I do check my pigeonhole though. And there's a letter, with my address written in Jenny's handwriting.

"Olly, we've had a lovely year. Now you're at university I'm sure you've met lots of lovely girls. I'm going to go out with Theo Morley (Head boy, Bootham School).

"All my love, Jenny xxx."

I'm guessing Theo wasn't aware he was going to go out with Jenny, until he received her Valentine's card, as I had done a year ago.

He's a lucky lad. And Jenny's got a point. It's time I grew up.

---

[88] January 15 – Pope John Paul II receives a delegation led by Polish Solidarity leader Lech Wałęsa at the Vatican.

January 16 – Loyalists shoot and seriously wound Irish nationalist activist Bernadette Devlin McAliskey and her husband.

January 20 – Iran releases the 52 Americans held for 444 days minutes after Ronald Reagan is sworn in as the 40th president of the United States, ending the Iran hostage crisis.

January 21 – The first DeLorean automobile, a stainless steel sports car with gull-wing doors, rolls off the production line in Dunmurry, Northern Ireland

March 1 – 1981 Irish hunger strike: Bobby Sands, a Provisional Irish Republican Army member, begins a hunger strike for political status at HM Prison Maze (Long Kesh) in Northern Ireland, dying on May 5, the first of 10 IRA hunger strikers to die.

Sunday, March 29, 26.2 Miles

The first London Marathon is held today, with 7,500 runners. The event receives a huge build up and the crowd is considered enormous. So too are scare stories. Will half the non-elite runners hit *the wall* at 19 miles and die of heatstroke or exhaustion?

I have a more than curious interest in the event as Lucy Lee, a girl I've sort of started going out with from the Athletics Club, is competing with her university kenjutsu team mates.

Lucy had taken a curious interest in my fives ability – UCL unusually had access to two courts – and I just thought kenjutsu was hitting people with sticks. So we started hanging out together.

After the event, the plan was to weave our way back to Halls where I would cook for her.

Lucy didn't die. She went for a bath and I cooked a marathon reviving dinner. Opened some wine, lit the candle and called her to come through. And called and called. But she was nowhere in the flat.

She had left a note though. "Sorry forgot to mention, the kenjutsu lads are taking me out tonight. Cooking smells nice."

Perhaps it was naïve of me to think I could compete with men in masks who thought waving bamboo about was fun. It put me off fives too.

Saturday, April 4, Making Your Mind Up[89]

Perhaps the clue was in the song that Bucks Fizz sang at the 1981 Eurovision Song Contest. Incredibly, *Making Your Mind Up* won and emboldened by the noble victory, I decided to ask someone else out. This time I tried closer to home.

As a first-year lawyer like myself, Jacqueline Alderton was significantly easier to track down, as all of us spent such a lot of time in the law library. "Do you fancy going out to a concert next Saturday?" I asked.

And she said, "Wow, that would be great. I don't mind who we see, you decide."

---

[89] March 30 – Attempted assassination of Ronald Reagan: US President Ronald Reagan is shot in the chest outside a Washington, D.C. hotel by John Hinckley, Jr.; two police officers and Press Secretary James Brady are also wounded.

I left it too late and by Friday, I panicked. The only tickets I could afford were to see Dennis Waterman (*I could be so good for you*), Sheena Easton (*9-5*) and Kajagoogoo (*Too shy*).

It was a catastrophe.

Jacqueline insisted I keep it a secret who we were seeing until we arrived at Wembley Arena. I was only moderately concerned at some of the outfits one or two of our fellow Tube travellers were wearing, but concern turned to dismay when we arrived at Wembley Park. Was it children's night? The average age of our concert party was about 12 years old.

Jacqueline had no intention of letting me take her home again, where she had a boyfriend waiting anyway (I never knew). She'd been expecting Wagner, or the Royal Philharmonic at least.

I couldn't even give the tickets away at the door. The touts seemed to have overbought Dennis Waterman too. There was no prospect of my watching the concert on my own. I'd be arrested for loitering near children. I'm still embarrassed.[90]

Wednesday, May 13, Divine Intervention

Not a great day for Pope John Paul II who was shot and nearly killed by Mehmet Ali Ağca, a Turkish gunman, as he entered St Peter's Square. However, JP II as pontiffs go was really cool and it was with genuine relief that the world learned he'd survived surgery and would later make a full recovery.

The law library is once again where I call on divine providence and write a note to Andrea Thompson, a first-year anthropology student, that if she is free on Saturday would she like to go for a pizza. She wrote back *Yes* underlined three times, which I thought encouraging.

Before we'd even ordered dough balls, I realised I didn't fancy her. I hadn't noticed that she was quite a lot larger than me, and in heels towered above me like a Valkyrie. I know it's not very modern of me but being on the same eye line is quite important.

---

[90] April 11 – 1981 Brixton riots: social unease erupts against the police stopping and searching people of colour; petrol bombs are thrown, the police attacked and shops were looted.

April 15 – The first Coca-Cola bottling plant in China is opened. Progress, of sorts.

May 11 – Jamaican singer Bob Marley dies aged 36 from cancer in Miami, Florida.

Sitting down, the effect was lessened, but then she sprang the next surprise. She didn't laugh, she brayed, oblivious to all the stares she attracted across the restaurant.

I didn't know what to do. All my chatting up technique relied on me being able to make the other party think I was *Monty Python, Not the Nine O'clock News* and *Fawlty Towers* encapsulated in one body.

Now, my only stratagem was to be as unfunny as possible, anything not to make Andrea laugh.

Over the Sloppy Giuseppe, I suddenly acquired a verbal tic, which try as I might just grew worse and worse. I started inserting the word actually into the end of every sentence, actually.

Even Andrea began to tire of this and by the time ice cream came, she was quite cross with me. She insisted we split the bill and she let me know that she was now off to see her boyfriend.

I was horrified. Looking back at no stage in the wooing process had I ever asked if she was going out with anyone else, so it was my fault actually.

Friday, May 22, Waiting's Over

Over at the Old Bailey, Peter Sutcliffe, the Yorkshire Ripper, was found guilty and sentenced to life imprisonment on 13 counts of murder and 7 of attempted murder in England.

With no more queuing to do, this left me just enough time either side of lectures to try and find another suitable girl to ask out. And I was in luck.

Julie Stewart was an English literature first year who I'd bumped into through mutual friends, and with whom the laughing strategy had seemed to work.

But I didn't rush and in fact it was Julie who asked me back to her bedsit after we'd been to the pictures. The night was going so well in fact that Julie got into bed and I nipped into her bathroom to brush my teeth. "There's a new spare toothbrush in the cupboard," she said, and something else I didn't quite catch.

I needed to use the loo too, so trying not to make any noises was grateful for the loo paper. When I flushed loo, the cistern didn't work, there was no water in it.

"You'll have to use the loo down the hallway. The plumbing's blocked, so they've turned off the water to our cisterns," Julie called out. But it was too late. I'd filled the toilet pan.

The evening ended pretty abruptly soon after.

Neither of us could hide our embarrassment at the intervention I felt obliged to make, and I carried my poo home in my rucksack.

It was a shame Julie and I could never meet again after that. She was obsessed with David Essex, but holding me close wasn't something either of us ever felt up to after that.

It was probably for the best. My end of year exams were about to start.

Friday, July 3, Tensions

The Toxteth riots started in Liverpool after a mob saved a youth from being arrested. Shortly afterward, the Chapeltown riots in Leeds began after increased racial incidents.

The tension around the country was certainly mounting. There was growing unease with the Thatcher government whose hard-line approach to law and order pleased their own core voter but not the rest of the electorate.

Some of our lecturers even went on to attack the brutality of the police in the press and on late night news shows. One even describing how one of his children described a mounted policeman as a *pig on a horse*.

My first three exam papers have all gone according to plan, but for the Roman law paper the wheels fell off, literally.

From our halls, walking into Euston to the law faculty was about a 45-minute walk, 30 minutes if the bus was a bit late, or 15 minutes on a bike. So most of us cycled.

The morning of my Roman law, I'd maintained exactly the same routine as for the other papers, leaving myself a good 45 minutes to cycle onto the campus. However, when I went to the bike shed to my horror someone had stolen my new back wheel.

The previous weekend I'd replaced the old tyre, which was buckled slightly and rather rusty. The new wheel had clearly caught someone's attention.

I'd sort that out later. In the meantime, I was less than 30 minutes away from the start of my exam.

All my peers were concerned that I might have missed the exam completely and failed the year when I didn't show up for the start. I waited for a bus, but none came and so eventually, I ran in arriving about 15 minutes late, hot and sweaty.

Thursday, July 16 – Tuesday, 21, The Headingly Miracle

Waiting for my First-Year results, I'm killing time just watching the cricket on the TV. The longer I watch the worse England does. Australia score 401, a huge score, in their first innings and declared. England does so badly scoring only 174 they are made to bat again *asked to follow on*. With nothing to lose, Bootham goes nuts and scores 149 not out, still giving England no chance but a little respectability.

Cross that I am glued to the TV when the weather is so glorious outside – especially for Yorkshire – Mum gives me £2 for the fare and a sandwich wrapped up in silver foil and tells me to take myself off to the cricket. It's only 25 minutes away and as it's the final day and really nothing to play for, entry is also free.

The odds of England winning are 500–1.

England become the first team in over 100 years to win a cricket Test match after the follow-on when they beat Australia by 18 runs at Headingly cricket ground, Leeds, England.

And I was lucky enough to see Bob Willis take 8 wickets for 43 runs.

The following week is one that millions remember too. Which we also watched on TV. A worldwide television audience of over 750 million people watch the wedding of Charles, Prince of Wales, and Lady Diana Spencer at St Paul's Cathedral in London.

Celebrity marriages…

Thursday, July 30, 1%

Unfortunately, my results for my First-Year exams at UCL follow a pattern established in my A-Levels. Great passes in Criminal law, Constitutional law and Property law – in fact I win the Year One prize for my 87% in constitutional. But in Roman law my 49% is one mark off a pass. If only I hadn't started 15 minutes late.

I have to re-sit – the same exam paper though – on August 30, before confirmation of my place can be given for starting Year 2.

It's the same paper, after all. And I'll have the full two hours next time.

I am disappointed, but I can revise model answers and have the next four weeks. What could possibly go wrong?[91]

---

[91] August 24 – Mark David Chapman is sentenced to 20 years to life in prison after pleading guilty to murdering John Lennon in Manhattan eight months earlier.

Monday, September 7, Pliny Pah

Sister's birthday. It's a Monday.

Today we hear about my marks for the Roman law re-sit I took last week, a week before UCL's next academic year begins.

I sit nervously at the bottom of the stairs next to the phone. Promptly at 10 am, it rings.

It's the kindly head of department who delivers the verdict. I impressed Professor Guest in the viva very much, but extraordinarily this time, having re-taken *the same* Roman law Year 1 exam paper I score 16%...?

How this happened will remain an unsettling mystery for the rest of my career.

This is an absolute disaster. My career as a barrister has been felled by Professor P J Thomas, Emperor Augustus and Pliny the Younger, and the Elder come to that.

I burst into tears. My mother bursts into tears. But by teatime we've both stopped crying. What am I going to do? Aged 20 on Wednesday, I'm already almost old enough to be a mature student, but I still haven't even passed my first year. And will the government ask for its money back as Mum got a 100% grant, given Dad isn't domiciled in the UK.

The registry at UCL explain my options:

1. The government will *not* ask for its maintenance grant or tuition fees back so long as I don't drop out or take a year out.
2. The rest of my UCL marks were sufficiently high for me to be offered a place as a first year again on the LLB course. But I will have to re-sit the whole of Year 1 again. That would mean still facing the dreaded paper 4: Roman law.
3. In spite of coming top or second in the contract, constitutional and property papers, I really don't have the heart to relive the same course again. And who knows, I might even score a minus mark in Roman at my current level of ineptitude.

August 27 – North Korea fires a surface-to-air missile at a US SR-71 Blackbird spy plane flying in South Korean and international airspace. The missile misses and the airplane is unharmed. Just including this to show they're still as bonkers now as they were then.

4. There are still some places left on Clearing at those universities who have vacancies on their less popular courses. I could apply for a new degree. But not at UCL. No department wants me.

My mother and I discuss option 2 and spend Monday on the phone desperately waiting to get through to UCCA. We agree that following a degree subject in which I have good A level grades would be sensible, as this is an emergency.

Every single English, History, Economics or Politics course is full.

We ring Clearing again and again, but the line is constantly engaged. It's nearly 5 pm and we're getting desperate.

At last: "Yes, hello. Yes, it's been a busy day."

There are three places left. To do linguistics (which is kind of Englishy, isn't it?); Hull (too close to home); Aberdeen (much too cold); the University of Wales Institute of Science and Technology (UWIST) – I'd get an ology – in Cardiff. And it's where my dad is from (just right).

We call Cardiff. They seem a bit apologetic. "Are you quite sure? Your ABD A-Levels are about 180 points more than we require for Modern English Studies.

"Formal registration has closed, but so long as you attend the first lecture we can catch up on the paperwork then.

"It's tomorrow, at noon. We start a week before the universities in England."

Harrogate to Central Cardiff railway station takes around 5 hours and 48 minutes today. Forty years ago, it took even longer.

But we pack a suitcase and I'm on the bus to the station. Next, I'm on the train to York, the single ticket to Cardiff costs a month's grant money. At York change at Birmingham New Street. At 2 am is there a more depressing place in Britain? It still looks like the basement of a multi-story carpark, even today. Next, change at Crewe and eventually rattle into Cardiff Central, stiff and bleary eyed, at 9:45 am.

Although the course I've chosen no longer exists – nor does UWIST – it was absorbed into the University of Cardiff during a bloodless academic coup in the late 80s, we study Chaucer and Early English, modern phonetics, dialect, Victorian literature, linguistic notation, twentieth-century poetry and journalism. I love it all. The Early English nearly catches me out in the first-year exams, but I'm not going to fail a second time.

202

As I leave the station suitcase in hand, Cardiff Arms Park looms huge in front of me and the strong smell of hops and barley from Brains brewery hangs heavy in the air.

I ask for directions to UWIST and set off.

In just 24 hours, we have turned my fortunes around. So fast in fact, I forgot to say goodbye properly or even thank my mother for getting me back to university.

Thanks, Mum.

Wednesday, September 16, Splott

My first landlady in Cardiff is a lovely eighty-year-old called Sadie Richards. Her neat terraced house is in Splott, the area in Cardiff my father, Shirley Bassey and Tom Jones were all born in, or so he tells us.

By contrast to the hours spent in lectures and in the Law Library, Modern English Studies has a total of nine hours of lectures or supervised seminars *a week.*

Better yet, there are 27 women on the course and only 3 men.

In my first few weeks in UWIST, I sign up for all the societies I can: gliding, natural history (naturally), the editorial team for *Impact* magazine, chess club and on a whim, the Officers' Training Corps (OTC)[92]. The OTC is sub-unit of the Territorial Army based at many universities across the UK and aimed at finding its next star recruits. Or failing that, officers.

I instantly fall in love with a woman from Scarborough called Beverley who writes articles for *Impact*. She is in her second year but on the same degree course as me, so we feel a natural bond. I fancy her something rotten, but she's all about the words. She wants to be a journalist and likes me only because I enjoy writing, as she does.

I instantly fall in love with a woman I meet on parade at the OTC called Sally. She is a first year engineer and thinks my attempts to look like a professional soldier in my oversized beret hilarious. Somewhat pathetically, I beg her to be my girlfriend. She thinks I'm amusing – or possibly funny/odd – and we do become friends, but she initially steadfastly refuses to go out with me, or anyone. She's at university to get a degree.

---

[92] "Eighty percent of success is showing up." – Woody Allen.

I instantly fall in love with a woman from Poland called Nadia who has her own glider. She asks if I would like to go up with her and I of course can't wait. We do go up in the glider and she loops the loop, showing off.

I beg her not to do it again, and subsequently spend the rest of the afternoon washing the vomit from the canopy of her grounded glider. Strangely, she does not seek my company again.

Wednesday, November 25, OTC

A group of mercenaries led by Mike Hoare take over Mahe airport in the Seychelles in a coup attempt. Most of them escape by a commandeered Air India passenger jet; six are later arrested.

After one of our early OTC training evenings, in the Mess bar, we discuss this daring coup attempt. What would it take to take over an island? How many people would you need? We are all looking forward to our long weekend training session. This term we've been going through our counter intelligence and security module.

A tattered note, ironically quoting one of Wales's favourite sons pinned to the noticeboard of the officer's mess always makes me smile. "Join the army and see the next world." – Dylan Thomas.

Recently I've been sending in articles to a new magazine called *Combat and Survival*. Amazingly, they accept the first of my submissions. It's a small *box-out*.

BOX-OUT

Tips for Searching Some Makes of Cars

1. VW beetle

The dashboard is accessible from under the front bonnet and provides a good hidden space.

2. Renault 4

The rear wheel arches extend high into the bodywork enabling small arms to be safely stashed.

3. Hillman Avenger

The rear panel above the bumper is double skinned. A hole can be cut from the boot to gain access.

4. Maxi

Large voids in the air hoses under the front wings deserve extra examination.

5. Mini

Some models have a boot floor instead of a mat to cover the spare wheel – where weapons can be stored.

Monday, December 11

Muhammad Ali loses to Trevor Berbick; this proves to be Ali's last-ever fight.

Life in Cardiff has settled down to a pattern. I'm a regular contributor to *Impact* magazine. This is encouraged by the Head of the Department who realises that our degree course will probably spawn some careers in journalism.

Impact is hardly journalism, but it's good fun. The editorial meetings are louche affairs with beers from 10 am and the hippies smoking joints blowing their smoke out of the windows.

Curiously, I'm never tempted to take a puff.

There's organised chaos and a flurry of activity in the two days before publication, but miraculously, the page layouts get done. Adverts – which keep the enterprise going – are placed where the purchasers have asked. Inside front left, facing matter, costing three times more than behind the staple, below the fold, at the back.

And I'm in print.

But not bold enough to admit that the *funny* stories sent anonymously to *Impact* by Weasel is actually me. Just occasionally, one or two of the anonymous pieces are a hit and make people in the office laugh out loud.

More often than not, the editors just crumple Weasel's words into the bin. "More shit from the weirdo."

My alter ego enjoys being a Junior Officer Cadet in the Officer Cadet Corps, which is practically next door to the Students' Union, and we couldn't be a bigger contrasting group.

Within minutes of learning how to bull my boots and shape my beret – so I no longer look like a Frenchman – I have fallen in love.

I am totally smitten by Sally and we become best friends. Which is not what I want at all. She's a mechanical engineer, on a course with over 100 men and three women. I'm on a course with 27 women and just three men. It is pointed out to us that these are pretty decent odds, and what are the chances you'd fancy someone in a uniform, in the OTC.

So I live in hope that one day, we might not just be friends. Still it's nice someone laughs at my jokes.

The other person who finds me mildly amusing is Ralph Atkinson, an altogether superior being, with a slight stammer. He is doing an MA in chemical engineering, so is a few years older than we are. However intellectual he may be, but he is incapable of marching or leading a group and he looks a crumpled mess.

Sally even volunteered to iron his lightweights (green trousers), so that we all pass on parade. But within minutes, they're crumpled. He is forever being shouted at, but he has a unique skill. He can strip down and reassemble the GPMG (General Purpose Machine Gun) even faster than the full-time staff. When it comes to guns, Ralph has a gift, and so somehow, he manages not to get sent off the squadron by a whisker.

Our training is surprisingly intense, which is fine when most of us have no exams. We travel the country in the back of 10 ton trucks on exercises just as Territorial Army forces are trained. Just occasionally, we take the ferry across to Rosslare and drive north often delivering equipment to Thiepval Barracks, in Lisburn, Northern Ireland.

As Ralph has a grandmother in Belfast, it's a good opportunity for him to meet her for free too.

I prefer the exercises that centre around us using the communications systems. The command position is a Land Rover and I can't see any advantage by being outside in the rain getting your carefully ironed uniform wet, so I concentrate on aspects of the roll that enable me to sit down. It gives me the excuse of sitting up front with Sally too.

As we're getting ready to go home for the Christmas holidays, she asks if I'd like to spend Christmas in Exeter. Yes, of course!

Maybe we'll become more than friends after all.

In Exeter, her three brothers, all Marines, treat me like some exotic creature fascinated that their sister has fallen for someone who wants to write for a living. And she has a twin sister, Rosemarie, a policewoman who may or may not be home for Christmas.

There's something familiar about the warmth emanating from the family and it's a few days before I realise where I've experienced it before. Then the realisation comes clear, of course. Living here is like living with Musa and his family again. Everyone looking out for each other, everyone making sure if someone's down, it's their role to help cheer them up.

In fairness, the family are amongst the most optimistic bunch you could ever care to meet – just like Musa's family. It's the little attention to detail moments that send my thought back to Musa. Learning that I'm left-handed, Sally's mother the next day lays my place at the table with the knife and fork the right way around for me. She didn't ask, she'd just noticed I'd swapped my fork into my right hand at dinner the night before.

She also told Sally to swap her cardigan for a jumper when she came down for breakfast the next day. In fairness to them both neither laughed at my aversion to buttons. Her brothers thought I was bonkers, but then I was from Yorkshire, so perhaps everyone from the north was odd?

Her parents treat me like a fourth son and within a few days, it's as if I've always lived there.

Then this happened.

Sunday, December 20, Disaster

The Penlee lifeboat disaster occurred off the coast of South-West Cornwall.

The tragedy makes the national news, but for once, the ebullient family are totally glum. They have friends on the Penlee lifeguard station.

After Christmas, we all go to the funeral service which follows. It's a moving, sad end to the year.

1982, Cardiff, South Wales

Sunday, January 10, Arms and Armour

The second brutal cold snap of the winter sends temperatures to all-time record lows in dozens of cities across the United Kingdom. It includes the national record from February 1895 being equalled; it would be equalled again in December 1995.

Typically, we're on some blizzard lashed moor trying not to get hypothermia in our bivouac. It's another OTC weekend. Ralph, Sally and I – all in the same squad for this weekend – are trying to cut some tinder for the fire with the useless equipment we're supplied with. "What we need are some proper logs," said Ralph, and from behind his back removes a gleaming Gurkha kukri.

"Where the hell did you get that?" We both gasped.

"My d-d-dad was given it in the war."

"But how come it looks brand new?" I asked.

"I'm a horologist. I've just given it a bit of a polish. You know what a horologist is? I c-c-collect and mend valuable watches and clocks. We're one of the UK's leading repairers. We're hoping we'll get our Royal Warrant this year. You should come over one weekend when we're not doing this."

And so the next weekend we did.

The shop front in Holland Park in west London was smart enough but concealed within were grandfather clocks and huge grandiose golden monuments that might have come from Versailles.

"That's exactly right," said Ralph. "I've b-b-been working on that for nearly a year. It's probably worth over £1 million now."

"Who buys all these?" I asked looking at rows upon rows of Breitling and Rolex watches in a case.

"Oh, there are lots: sheiks; Tory grandees; Russians; arms dealers, pop stars, footballers. They're all a p-p-p-pretty shady bunch actually."

Back in Cardiff, it's bone chillingly cold. But I'm determined to keep producing little pieces of writing for publication.

My next piece for *Combat & Survival* earned me £150. £1 per word based on the National Union of Journalists' freelancers pay rates. Very generous.[93]

BOX-OUT

Some Types of Explosive Device

1. Time-delay

This is attached to a simple timing mechanism such as an alarm clock; it could be concealed in the glove compartment.

2. Pressure switch

This activates an explosive device when touched; for example, when the accelerator pedal is pushed down.

3. Release switch

This pulls a tripwire when a door is opened, or a chair lifted; can be used and can be made using an ordinary close peg.

4. Tilt switch

This is set off by tilting movement and so is quite suitable for attaching around axles. It can be detonated by jacking the car up to look underneath.

---

[93] In the intervening years, the rate barely changed. Ultimately, the attractive career that journalism posed in the 1980s did not continue to be as attractive in the following decades. The internet all but killed off a handful of quality media outlets. Why buy a newspaper, when you can read the content for free? Why wait for broadcast news, if you can see it online as it happens by someone actually present?

5. Heat switch

This could be located in the engine compartment, or on the exhaust pipe, when the device explodes upon reaching a certain temperature.

6. Remote controlled device

This could be quite sophisticated. Radio control allows the operator to detonate the charge from a safe distance at the time when it will cause the most damage.

ENDS

(150 words)

Wednesday, January 27, Secrets[94]

Christmas with the Holders had only helped me to fall in love with the whole family. She looked just as good in her uniform as out of it to me. The family were all superheroes. She could run, climb and carry faster, higher and heavier than me. She wouldn't however let me call her a girlfriend.

She refused to go out with me. We were just friends.

We spent a lot of time together – often in the OTC at training weekends – I was particularly interested in the new communications equipment we were being asked to test. This term we were learning all about Signals Intelligence. The Clansman system was being superseded by something called Bowman. And we were guinea pig testers.

One day the CO saw us and after parade said: "Ah, the lovebirds Holder and Milner!"

Sally ground her teeth.

"Don't worry your secret's safe with me. Didn't I see you holding hands by the Student's Union last Thursday? We can't expect university First Years not to experience all the fruits of a university education, can we, and in any case you're doing very well with us in the OTC as well.

---

[94] January 11 – Mark Thatcher, son of British Prime Minister Margaret Thatcher, disappears in the Sahara during the Dakar Rally; he is rescued January 14.

"So much so, I wonder if you'd mind signing this? Next week we have some warrant officers coming over from the Royal Corps of Signals and the Intelligence Corps. They want to meet anyone I'd recommend considering the army as a career. Might you both be interested? I've asked that chap with the stammer that you hang out with, Atkinson, too."

Sally signed, and then I did and so did Ralph. It was the Official Secrets Act.[95]

To be honest, I would have signed anything that kept me close to Sally in those early months. I found her Devon burr absolutely hypnotic. But we were just friends.

Modern English Studies was also living up to its full potential. Even now from our year group of 30, it was beginning to emerge who was likely to be a teacher, who a speech therapist and who a journalist. (For the record, I thought I could be any one of the three.)

There weren't many candidates for full time poet but Year 1 Twentieth-Century Poetry Tutorials were events we would never skip. Here's an example why.

An Irish Airman Foresees His Death

by William Butler Yeats (1918)

I know that I shall meet my fate
Somewhere among the clouds above;
Those that I fight I do not hate,
Those that I guard I do not love;
My country is Kiltartan Cross,
My countrymen Kiltartan's poor,
No likely end could bring them loss
Or leave them happier than before.
Nor law, nor duty bade me fight,
Nor public men, nor cheering crowds,
A lonely impulse of delight

---

[95] The penalty for breaching the Official Secrets Act is a maximum jail term of 14 years if the crime relates to spying or sabotage under the 1911 or 1920 acts. The Acts were updated and consolidated in 1989.

Drove to this tumult in the clouds;
I balanced all, brought all to mind,
The years to come seemed waste of breath,
A waste of breath the years behind
In balance with this life, this death.[96]

Thursday, February 25, Three Cheers

The European Court of Human Rights rules that teachers who cane, belt or tawse children against the wishes of their parents are in breach of the Human Rights Convention.

Wednesday, March 10, Camp Sites[97]

We're all wondering where this year's OTC Annual Camp is going to be. Every year the army gets to control our lives for two to three weeks to see if they might want us. For the students its two weeks of *bull*, and to see if we might want

---

[96] This and many other poems in this book are also to be found alongside helpful side notes such as this in *Poem for the Day (One)*. The Irish airman Yeats wrote about was Robert Gregory, killed in action over Italy in 1918. Of his son, Major Gregory said that the months since he joined the Army had been the happiest of his life…leading his squadron…mind and hand were at one, will and desire.

January 24 – Super Bowl XVI sees the San Francisco 49ers and game MVP Joe Montana capture their first National Football League championship by beating the Cincinnati Bengals 26–21 at Detroit's Pontiac Silverdome. It's on my bucket list to see an American football game one day. Ideally in America, of course.

February 5 – London-based Laker Airways collapses, leaving 6,000 stranded passengers and debts of $270 million.

[97] March 3 – Elizabeth II opens the Barbican Centre in London. Is there an uglier building in the world?

a career in the army: BAOR/Bielefeld[98]; SHAPE[99], Templar Barracks[100]; Catterick; Brunei or Stanley/East Falklands.

In total, I attended seven annual camps and over one hundred weekend training exercises. I dreaded going on each one. But by the end regretted they had ended so soon. In hindsight, I might have enjoyed a commission as a regular army officer, instead of joining the TA. But as Lance Corporal I think I've seen more, done more and had more fun.

Apparently, there are three places for the top in the class going to Brunei; those wanting to join the Intelligence Corps are all going to Templar Barracks in Kent; there are six places to go on a Speed Driving and Close Attachment course in Stanley, wherever that is, and the rest are going to practise their marching and drilling in Catterick, North Yorkshire.

After tonight's class, we all fall in and WO2 Dobson – Dobbo – calls out our names and the annual camps we've been assigned to.

Whisper, Tallboy – and Sally – all get Belize.

Spontaneous applause breaks out and we are shushed back to at ease.

The spies are all off to Templar Barracks, which we knew anyway.

---

[98] British Army on the Rhine: A legacy of World War II and the Cold War facilities in Germany are no longer strategically useful, therefore, British Forces began withdrawing from Germany in 2010; in 2015 21,500 troops remained in the country.[29] The deployment will have been phased out by 2020, although concentrations of installations and troops in the Paderborn / Bielefeld / Gütersloh area and at Mansergh Barracks will remain until late in the decade.

[99] Supreme Headquarters Allied Powers Europe (SHAPE) is the headquarters of the North Atlantic Treaty Organization's Allied Command Operations (ACO). Since 1967, it has been located at Casteau, north of the Belgian city of Mons, but it had previously been located from 1953 at Rocquencourt, next to Versailles, France.

[100] British Army Military Intelligence Headquarters was based in Templar Barracks near Ashford, which was also the location of the Joint Services School of Intelligence and the Joint Service Interrogation Wing. The Intelligence Corps is responsible for gathering, analysing and disseminating military intelligence and also for counter-intelligence and security. British Military Intelligence is conducted via The Intelligence Corps, not MI5 or M16, but we still called them spies. Within the army, the Intelligence Corps is also known as the Green Slime, on account of their green berets.

If you want more intelligence, call them, on: 0345 600 8080.

RESULT – Ralph and I are both selected for the SPEED DRIVING COURSE. But where on earth is East Falkland? He doesn't know either, but we're heading off for two weeks of sea and sun, we assume, in June.

Not quite.

Friday, March 19, Queue?

Argentine scrap metal workers (infiltrated by Marines) raise the flag of Argentina on South Georgia in the Falkland Islands, a British overseas territory.

Thursday, April 1, Invasion

This is not an April Fool. Although in hindsight, foolish to jerk the British Lion's tail.

The 1982 Argentinian invasion of the Falkland Islands begins when Argentine military forces land near Stanley, beginning the Falklands War.

The next day, unable to match the firepower of the tanks on the lawn of the governor's lawn Rex Hunt, the British governor of the Falkland Islands surrenders the islands to Argentine forces leading to their occupation.

Saturday, April 3, Attention

Argentine forces begin the invasion of South Georgia.

The mood is very serious and thoughtful at the OTC tonight.

All our serving officers are deploying to the Falklands Task for within the next few days. We are immensely proud. There's also a lot of gallows humour. "If we do happen to tread on a mine, sir, what do we do?"

"Normal procedure, Lieutenant, is to jump 200 feet in the air and scatter oneself across a wide area."[101]

The parade ground is alive like I've never seen before as any spare kit – including our weapons, Land Rovers and Clansman comms equipment – is tightly packed into all our 10 ton lorries. I get the thrill of slowly driving Betsy, our section's long wheelbase Land Rover, gleaming now and bristling with antennas, onto the massive vehicle transporter.

---

[101] Lieutenant George and Captain Blackadder, *Black Adder Goes Forth*

It takes two days for us to make everything ready from our OTC for loading onto the SS Atlantic Conveyor. The Malvinas will soon be the Falkland Islands again. And I *will* get to my SPEED DRIVING COURSE…

Monday, April 26, Retaken

British troops retake South Georgia Island during Operation Paraquat.

Sunday, May 2, The Belgrano

The British nuclear submarine HMS *Conqueror* sinks the Argentine cruiser *General Belgrano*, killing 323 sailors. Operation Algeciras, an attempt to destroy a Royal Navy warship in Gibraltar, fails.

Tuesday, May 4, Exocet

HMS *Sheffield* is hit by an Argentine Exocet missile and burns out of control; 20 sailors are killed. The ship sinks on May 10.

Saturday, May 8, Fatal Crash

French-Canadian racing driver Gilles Villeneuve is killed during qualifying for the Belgian Grand Prix.

Tuesday, May 18, Special

The British Special Air Service launches Operation Mikado to destroy three Argentinean Exocet missiles and five Super Étendard fighter bombers in mainland Argentina. It fails when the Argentineans discover the plot.

Friday, May 21, War

HMS *Ardent* is sunk by Argentine aircraft, killing 22 sailors.

Sunday, May 23, War

HMS *Antelope* is lost.

Tuesday, May 25, War[102]

British ships HMS *Coventry* and SS *Atlantic Conveyor* are sunk during the Falklands War; *Coventry* by two A-4C Skyhawks and the latter sunk by an Exocet.

Betsy and all the OTC's equipment sank to the bottom of the Atlantic that day.

Of the 12 men killed in the sinking of Atlantic Conveyor six were from the Merchant Navy, three from the Royal Fleet Auxiliary and three sailors from the Royal Navy. I still think of them today whenever I'm on board a sailing vessel. Death at sea is not how I'd choose to die.

I hope their families have been able to find some peace after all these years. Their lives were not lost in vain.

Friday, May 28, Pope's Can Be Cool

Pope John Paul II's visit to the United Kingdom, the first by a reigning pope, begins.

This is another of those, *where were you when...?* moments. Genuinely, I have no recollection, other than I'd be in Cardiff as it was still term time.

A cool guy in a white frock shakes hands with lots of people. What's to report? (This is my history, after all.)

Friday, May 28 – Saturday 29, War[103]

The Battle of Goose Green: British forces defeat a larger Argentine force.

British supply ship RFA *Sir Galahad* is destroyed during the Bluff Cove air attacks. The daring of the Argentinian Air Force pilots can't be questioned.

---

[102] May 26 – Kielder Water, an artificial lake in Northumberland, is opened.

[103] June 8 – President Ronald Reagan becomes the first American chief executive to address a joint session of the Parliament of the United Kingdom.

June 11 – *E.T.: The Extra-Terrestrial* is released in the United States; this will become the biggest box-office hit of the rest of the decade.[11]

June 13 – The 1982 FIFA World Cup begins in Spain.

June 19 – The body of God's Banker, Roberto Calvi, chairman of Banco Ambrosiano, is found hanging beneath Blackfriars Bridge in London.

June 21 – Prince William is born at St Mary's Hospital in Paddington, West London.

July 11 – Italy beats West Germany 3–1 to win the 1982 FIFA World Cup in Spain.

Unlike their army counterparts, who are mostly reluctant conscripts. The planes come in low, weaving around the terrain so as to give as much cover against the British gun emplacements.

Monday, June 14, Victory

Argentine forces in the capital, Stanley, conditionally surrender to British forces. Four days later, Argentina's military dictator Leopoldo Galtieri resigned in the wake of his country's defeat in the Falklands War.

Friday, July 2, Nuts

Lawnchair Larry flight flies 16,000 feet (4,900 m) above Long Beach, California, in a lawn chair with weather balloons attached.

Sunday, July 11, Tidying Up

Another OTC weekend. There's a lot of sorting out of the equipment to do, some of it which has come back from the Falklands and a group of us volunteer to spend a week in Lisburn barracks, where it's been assembled to help sort some of it out.

Ralph visits his grandmother, and the disorganised oaf that he is, misses the ferry home!

Monday, July 19, Blackmail

William Whitelaw, British Home Secretary, announces that Michael Trestrail (the Queen's bodyguard) has resigned from the Metropolitan Police Service over a relationship with a male prostitute.

Tuesday, July 20, Sefton

Hyde Park and Regent's Park bombings: the Provisional IRA detonates two bombs in central London, killing eight soldiers, wounding 47 people, and leading to the deaths of seven horses.

My next offering for *Combat & Survival* arrives too late to help.

Eight Steps to Make Searching Simpler

1. Look for evidence of recent activity.
2. Ask yourself where you would hide something.
3. Look above and below as well as at eye level.
4. Keep thinking where the spaces are and how to reach them.
5. Have a change of kit handy; you might get dirty or messed up.
6. Strong smells of talc or perfume may be hiding the powerful smells of explosive.
7. Get the driver to open the bonnet and the boot. Don't do it yourself.
8. Look carefully at the driver; is he or she nervous?

Wednesday, July 21, Commander's Intent

HMS *Hermes*, the Royal Navy flagship during the Falklands War, returns home to Portsmouth to a hero's welcome.

Hard not to think of this without welling up, even now. Wow.

In their book *Made to Stick*, Chip and Dan Heath illustrate how a commander's intent should be boilable down into a single sentence. This was clearly in evidence across the Falklands campaign, every British soldier, sailor and aircrew knew exactly what the prime minister's aim was: take back the Falklands.

And they did.

Something else in *Made to Stick* has certainly stuck with me and it's how our brains look for patterns in words. It wasn't something we were taught in linguistics, but I wish it had been. Until it was pointed out to me, I had no idea what this jumble of letters signifies: J FKFB INAT OUP NA SAIS IS.

Now look at the footnote.[104]

---

[104] Try now: JFK. FBI. NATO. OUP. NASA. ISIS.

July 23 – The International Whaling Commission decides to end commercial whaling by 1986.

A coroner's jury returns a verdict of suicide on Roberto Calvi, who was found hanging under Blackfriars Bridge.

The apogee of sophistication at the time was to take tea at the Ritz.

Today being my 21st birthday would have been an ideal time to take a girlfriend, but Sally had made it quite plain we were just *friends*. Besides, she had no intention of missing lectures for a sandwich in London.

Perhaps taking pity on me, Jenny kindly agreed to be my consort for the day. I ask her to dress in her best frock, as I have big plans.

We'll have tea at the Ritz followed by a cocktail in the Savoy. Then I've booked a pre-theatre table at the Café Royale for supper, after which we have a box to see the West End's latest hit, *Steaming*, a play by Neil Dunn, which is apparently quite saucy.

It is my hope of course Jenny will melt into my arms with all this lavish expenditure, and who knows what might happen later.

Stood in the concourse of Green Park Tube station in my dinner jacket and black bow tie I am not as self-conscious as I might be, as lots of people are getting out of the Tube on their way to sophisticated afternoons down Piccadilly.

As Jenny appears up the escalator, my heart sinks. There's straw in her hair, mud on her nose and she's wearing a really tight T-shirt and jeans. She still looks fabulous but I'm crestfallen.

"What have you been doing?"

"I've been picking late summer strawberries in the fields for Dad. We've been up since dawn."

"They'll never let us into the Ritz with you looking like that."

"Sure, they will." She winked. She's a good deal more confident than I remember her, that's for sure.

The doormen at the Ritz take a look at Jenny and open the doors with a smirk. "She's with me, we have a table booked for tea at 3 o'clock," I explain, all grown up in my tux.

"Of course, this way, sir. *Madam*."

We're sat down and in the beautiful all white chintz of the Ritz, waiters buzz and fuss at the tables, backwards and forwards. We are however aware that Jenny's casual appearance is causing others to stare.

"Wait there, I'll freshen up," says Jenny, and heads for the ladies.

Dainty sandwiches and cakes are served whilst I wait for her, but my 21st is ruined.

This is not what I had planned at all.

I'm aware the guests are staring again over my shoulder. There behind me is Jenny. Her hair pinned up, wearing a gold sheath, defying gravity, held up with only a strap over one shoulder.

She is just mesmerizingly beautiful.

I'm only hoping when we get to the box in the theatre that there might be a little privacy...

Tea at the Ritz is a ritual almost Japanese in the way it's performed.

We skipped the Savoy but walked hand in hand in St James' Park until it was time for supper at the Café Royale. To my intense embarrassment, the whole menu was in French that I couldn't translate at all.

Jenny bailed me out by ordering for us both in impeccable French – she was after all going to study it at Newcastle University.

Steaming was every bit as steamy as I needed it to be for my nefarious intentions. Except that when I looked across to Jenny, I was clearly alone. Exhausted by the early start in the fields, the fresh air, the alcohol and now a comfy warm box, she'd drifted off fast sleep.

Eventually, *Steaming* ended and Jenny didn't even wake up through the applause.

I ordered a taxi to Liverpool Street Station and made sure she caught the King's Lynn train. Putting a cardigan around her shoulders, she waved as she went through the ticket barrier.

I realised my 21st birthday was over. She was someone else's girlfriend, after all.[105]

---

[105] September 19 – The first emoticons are posted by Scott Fahlman.

October 1 – Helmut Kohl replaces Helmut Schmidt as Chancellor of Germany through a constructive vote of no confidence. One Helmut after another. Only the Germans could have constructive vote of no confidence.

In Orlando, Florida, Walt Disney World opens its second theme park, EPCOT Centre, to the public for the first time.

October 11 – The Mary Rose, flagship of Henry VIII of England that sank in 1545, is raised from the Solent.

October 13 – The Ford Sierra is launched in Europe, replacing the Ford Cortina.

October 19 – John DeLorean is arrested for selling cocaine to undercover FBI agents (he is later found not guilty due to entrapment).

November 2 – Channel 4, a British public-service television broadcaster, is launched, with Richard Whiteley's *Countdown* being the first program to be broadcast.

November 7 – The Thames Barrier is first publicly demonstrated.

Sunday, December 12, Give Peace a Chance

A war won and the Prime Minister's approval rating sky high you have to admire the campaigners at the Greenham Common Women's Peace Camp who defied all authoritarianism. No doubt, some teachers from Bootham joined with the 30,000 women who held hands to form a human chain around the 14.5 km perimeter fence of RAF Greenham Common in England in a protest against nuclear weapons. I hope there were. It would make me proud to think so.

Monday, December 20, Oops

Christmas is around the corner and we're all spending it in Bahrain with Dad. It's a novelty as it's our first Middle Eastern Christmas.

The day ends badly when a gust of wind slams the upstairs door shut. Dad's house had a flat roof with built up sides where we sunbathed in total privacy, and where my younger brother played with his toys. His little fingers were on the door when it slammed and the end knuckles on his middle two fingers were totally crushed.

It was difficult to define what was worse. The bloody mess at the end of his hand, his screaming, or my mum, a qualified SRN nurse fainting.

It was sorted by Dad with a trip to the American hospital.

The next day, being on holiday too Dad took us to the poolside of the Hilton Hotel. It was a perfect day and we ate like kings, but that night I began to experience immense pain in my ear. It was as if a lizard was running around inside my head.

It was sorted by Dad with a trip to the American hospital. I'd perforated my eardrum, possibly whilst diving into the deep end of the pool. Lots of rest, quiet and dark were prescribed and in time it healed itself.

On Christmas Day itself, Mum had a treat for Dad. She'd brought over some blackcurrants from the bushes in our garden in Harrogate to make into a crumble for him, rather than a Christmas pudding, which nobody liked.

She'd also forgotten to defrost the turkey. Much to her dismay, we all had to eat corned beef hash for Christmas lunch instead. But there was the consolation of the blackcurrant crumble. Which flipped out of her oven gloves as she took it

---

November 30 – Michael Jackson releases his sixth studio album, *Thriller*, in the United States, which will go on to be the greatest selling album of all time at 110 million units sold worldwide.

221

from the oven and the Pyrex dish it was in smashed into splinters across the kitchen floor.

We'd wanted ice cream anyway.

Christmastime scene in the Middle East: Mum and me standing alongside a nodding donkey, pumping oil by the roadside, between Manama and the Sheik's Beach. Presumably, we're posing by this one because it's been painted.

Sunday, December 26, Beach Day

One of the attractions of living abroad in a hot climate at Christmas is that if you're lucky enough to live near a pool or the beach you feel like kings, whilst everyone is shivering or hiding from the rain at home.

Better yet to feel like a king on a king's beach.

To try to salvage what had not been the best of weeks, Dad drove us all as a Boxing Day treat, to our favourite place in Bahrain, the Emir of Bahrain's private beach. Certainly, no Bahrainis were ever allowed to go on it, but privileged Westerners, with permission, were.

Sheikh Isa bin Salman Al Khalifa was the first Emir of Bahrain from 1961 until his death in 1999 and he was a Europhile. For such a powerful man it was quite remarkable that we quite often saw him when we played on the beach and he would ask our names and say hello.

There was no one else on the beach when we arrived. Perhaps Boxing Day was treated more traditionally by the other Westerners in Bahrain.

But sometime in the middle of the afternoon, a solitary man could be seen walking towards us. It was the Emir.

"I say, would you like some tea? I normally take some at around this time."

"Well, that would be delightful," said my mum covering her bikini a little. With that, the Emir walked back to his palace and within 15 minutes, an entourage appeared bearing rugs, tables, tea and cakes.

And that's how we spent Boxing Day 1982, having tea on the Emir's beach.

I think he was just lonely and wanted some company.

1983, Cardiff, South Wales

Monday, January 31, Clunk, Click, Every Trip

Seatbelt use for drivers and front seat passengers becomes mandatory in the United Kingdom. It is the Easter term back at UWIST.

Fishing around for a suitable subject for my third year 20,000-word dissertation, someone says, "Olly, you like outer space. Have you heard of the Martian School?" Err, no.

Poet Craig Raine becomes my total obsession. He is already at the zenith of the poetry world having published *A Martian Sends a Postcard Home* in 1979. Which is handy for me as there are lots of reviews from worthy admirers. So my dissertation becomes an exercise in editing them together.

My shallow essay probably received just one review. I doubt the examiner read it all.

This, however, will live forever. As will most of Raine's stunning work. Would that I could come up with just *one* couplet. You'll have to read *A Martian Sends a Postcard Home* in your own steam as it's still copyrighted. But well worth buying the stamp. I'd explain what one of those was, if you already knew that a postcard was. But then it would probably take me the rest of this 'caxton' to do it. Just… buy it.[106]

1983 diary entry: 'From now on, I will read a poem every day.'
(Lasts about a fortnight.)

---

[106] *A Martian Sends a Postcard Home*, Oxford University Press, 1979. ISBN 0-19-211896-X.

I start well enough but soon realise how my girlfriend in the engineering department might think I am turning into a fey dilettante. The 1980s South Wales expects its bards to drink hard, chase women, and play rugby.[107]

Wednesday, March 16, Odd

The 1983 West Bank fainting epidemic erupts. Researchers point to mass hysteria as the most likely explanation.

Saturday, March 19, Freezing

This weekend, the OTC is yomping about in the Brecon Beacons, a mountain range in southern Wales, billeted in Sennybridge Camp on a training exercise. Mass hysteria or not I'd much rather be in Israel, it is freezing cold and worse, we are camping out Saturday night/Sunday morning. Worse, we are all issued with SLRs an enormous, heavy rifle, which is made even longer by the addition of a bright yellow BFA, blank firing attachment. The BFA is added to the end of the rifle to avoid any potential blank rounds accidentally discharging into someone. It doesn't do to enquire how they found out why the BFA had to be invented.

This training weekend, I'm thoroughly miserable. If I wanted to be in the Infantry, I'd have applied, but the OTC existed to train all potential Officer Cadets in all branches of the army. It's the grunts' turn this weekend. Suckers.

Late in the evening, we are given our orders for the next 12 hours. Strike camp, make ourselves a warming stew and set up two hourly guards, patrols or *pickets*, as an ambush is expected – hostile forces know we are in the area. Oh, bollocks.

There are twelve of us in our detachment, so we break into four groups. "Your dinner's in the Land Rover. Reveille's an hour before sunrise, i.e. 5:14 hrs tomorrow. Be alert. Stay alert. Stay alive." Bollocks.

---

[107] February 2 – Giovanni Vigliotto goes on trial on charges of polygamy involving 105 women.

February 24 – Bermondsey by-election (UK): Simon Hughes's defeat of Peter Tatchell is criticised for alleged homophobia.

February 28 – The final episode of *M*A*S*H* airs, setting the record for most watched television episode and reaching a total audience estimated at 125 million, which remains unsurpassed.

In the back of the Land Rover is dinner. Four live chickens.

Well, it's hopeless. Within a minute, we've all given them names. Diedre, Enid, Agnes and Daphne – DEAD – each suffer different fates. The countryside sports types – including Ralph – have no qualms about despatching their Diedre, with a quick snap of her neck. They ask the vegetarians if they can take Enid off their hands, which they do.

Agnes's group are mustering up the courage to slit her throat when she escapes and makes a bold dash for freedom.

And we are left with Daphne. She's beautiful, clucking about and lifting her neck up for a stroke. We vote on it. For the sake of filling our stomachs during a training exercise, we all agree Daphne doesn't need to die.

We freed her into the night, and I hope she was able to scratch a life in the sub-zero tundra of the Brecons in the midst of winter. Inadvertently, she probably suffered a worse fate than Diedre.

We shared a Mars bar for supper instead.

Later that night, exhausted and not alert, the enemy overran us in seconds. And we spent the rest of the exercise arguing whose fault that was, as prisoners, in the back of a 10 ton truck.

Anything was better than yomping, advancing on a pretend enemy with a thirty-pound rucksack on your back and a rifle that just went bang.[108]

I was happy.

After End-Ex, as we're unloading the 10 tonners in Handel Street, Ralph asks if I'd like to join him for a Guinness in the O'Neill's pub. He's meeting some friends. I didn't realise Ralph had any friends, he is just a geeky horologist with

---

[108] For about six months after the Falklands War, the OTC didn't have live weapons; they were all at the bottom of the Atlantic. So for a number of weekends when we didn't have rifles as a substitute, we were given heavy sticks and had to go bang on contact with the enemy.

March 25 – Motown celebrates its 25th anniversary with the television special Motown 25: Yesterday, Today, Forever, during which Michael Jackson performs Billie Jean and introduces the moonwalk.

April 4 – Talking of the moon, The Space Shuttle Challenger is launched on its maiden voyage: STS-6. However, I think at heart I only had eyes for the Apollo missions.

April 11 – Spain's Seve Ballesteros won the 47th PGA Masters Tournament.

May 11 – Aberdeen F.C. beat Real Madrid 2–1 (after extra time) to win the European Cup Winners' Cup in 1983 and become only the third Scottish side to win a European trophy.

a stammer when he's not with us…Barely able to lift my kitbag, I say no. All I want is a chicken biryani, a bath and bed.

Wednesday, May 25, The Force

Return of the Jedi opens in cinemas.

Sally and I go to see this together. She doesn't object when I put my arm around her in the cinema. Perhaps the Force is with me.

It is. She gives me a kiss, and we start going out as boyfriend and girlfriend. It surprises no one when I make a big announcement as they thought we were anyway.

Thursday, June 9, Writing

Britain's Conservative government, led by Margaret Thatcher, is re-elected by a landslide majority.

As all the Third Years are now deep into their finals, or have even left, it is up to Mike and me as the sole survivors of the editorial team to produce the next issue of *Impact*. The next edition is rude, lewd, very funny and nearly gets us kicked out of Cardiff. The 3,000 copies go so fast we have to print another 3,000. They all fly out of the stands too.

More remarkable is the fact that UWIST only has 5,000 students, which means the Cardiff University students must be picking it up rather than reading *Gair Rhydd*. We are delighted.

Doubly delighted, as under the list of numerous contributors we describe ourselves as Editors: Hugh Dunnett and Oliver Milner.

From memory, we always struggled to get any contributors too. It was Mike's ideas to make up names, so it looked like a colossal production. In fact, we wrote it all.

Filler Copy for Impact, pp. 4–6, By *Weasel*
The Life of Sherlock Holmes

It was a grey Autumn day in London fog hung in thick layers like a funeral shroud over Baker Street, my residence.

I was playing my violin. Unfortunately, it was better at chess than I was. *"It's your move," I said as I surveyed the chess pieces, thoughtfully. The violin said nothing. Dr Watson, my constant companion in adventure, looked up and said, "I say, Holmes, you're cheating."*

I leapt across the room and quickly got him into half nelson. "I know," I said. "I just can't stand losing to inanimate objects."

Tightening my grip, I spoke again. "I received a very strange letter this morning, Watson, what do you say to that?"

"Let go?" he screamed, painfully. "You're breaking my arm!"

"Don't worry, Watson," I said. "I know what I'm doing."

There was a loud crack. And a yelp.

As Dr Watson sat resetting his broken arm, I described the contents of the letter to him. It was a cry for help from an old friend. Watson asked me how I knew?

"Elementary, my dear Watson," I said. "I'll read it to you. It says: 'I am an old friend...Help.'"

[This goes on for several pages – Ed.]

[Abridged...]

"Well, Holmes," said Watson from his wheelchair, "another case successfully dealt with."

"Yes," I replied. I noticed that Watson was slowly recovering from the wounds he had carelessly picked up. "And even better than that we've got an RKO contract to make another picture. It's going to be called The Wound of the Baskervilles." [Surely Hound? – Ed.]

"Top ho. Splendid," Watson ejaculated.

It was just another case, and it was just another incident, in The Life of Sherlock Holmes.

ENDS

[1,362 words. Chop it down to 1,200. From the front. It gets better as it goes along. The fight's quite funny. – Ed.]

Sunday, October 2, 4x4

Neil Kinnock is elected leader of the British Labour Party.[109]

Back for the Christmas term in UWIST, and in the offices of *Impact*, we are hard at work, but not on the next issue.

Co-writer Beverley and I have ambitions to enter BBC Wales's competition looking for new writers under 25. It's a play for TV in which each of the characters' scenes plays out after a poem they've internally recited is heard.

So for instance, one of the characters – the girlfriend – is deaf, but all her friends have learned to sign so she's a central narrator to the story. Another character, a teacher over whom dark suspicions loom (unjustly), rows out to sea, on his own, accompanied by Kate Bush's *The Man with the Child in His Eyes:*

[We see him paddling a small rowing boat out to the middle of the sea at dusk, and them clumsily rolling out of the boat and into the water. As day breaks, the rowing boat lies empty, bobbing on the ocean.]

And then as the end credits play, Kate Bush's beautiful voice and lyrics lap the waves.[110]

We have a final scene all worked out too. The girlfriend internalises Craig Rayne's evocative poem *The Onion, Memory,* which is another poem for your bookshelf.[111]

It's what happens in the middle of our episode that we're still struggling with.

---

[109] Thursday, July 21 – This factoid escaped us on the day, perhaps we had already gone to press, but we would definitely have included it in *Impact*.

Sunday, September 25 – Maze Prison escape: 38 Provisional Irish Republican Army prisoners, armed with six handguns, hijack a prison lorry and smash their way out of HM Prison Maze in Northern Ireland, in the largest prison escape since World War II and in British history.

Monday, September 26 – 1983 Soviet nuclear false alarm incident: Soviet Military Officer Stanislav Petrov averts a worldwide nuclear war by correctly identifying a warning of attack by US missiles as a false alarm as the Emergency Broadcast System goes off for multiple television and radio stations in the United States.

[110] *The Man with the Child in His Eyes,* by Kate Bush © Sony/ATV Music Publishing LLC.

[111] *The Onion, Memory,* Oxford University Press, 1978. ISBN 0-19-211877-3.

Saturday, October 8, Hooters

As you might imagine, the OTC is much cheered by the announcement that *Hooters* has opened in America. The girls as much as the boys, surprisingly. When will there be one in Belfast my squad in the back of the ten-tonner muse.

Another weekend exercise in name camp, Belfast. I am particularly looking forward to this one as we are learning to drive HGVs, with a view to passing our HGV licence at the end of term. It's compensation for not having got to the Falklands, I suppose. On Saturday night, we have R&R, so Ralph takes the opportunity to visit his grandmother and stays the night. There's no roll call this weekend so he re-joins us for breakfast on Sunday.

Saturday, November 5, Bonfire Night

We've been looking forward to bonfire night for ages. The Students Union has really gone to town with our subscription money and the whole of Cardiff have come to watch the fireworks and the bonfire being lit.

"I have something to tell you, Olly," says Sally in between the ooos and aahs. "I'm pregnant."

"What? How? Well, I know how. What are you going to do? What are we going to do? What would you like me to do?"

"Well I can't tell my mother. And I can't have it. Can you help?"

"Well, yes of course, anything you want. Let me find out what to do."

The arrangements for having an abortion were unknown to us both. I knew if I rang my father in Bahrain, he'd know what needed to be done, but telephoning the Middle East wasn't as easy then as it is now.

That Monday night, Sally and I were both in the phone box together, having reversed the charges to Manama. Dad explained that clinics existed to take care of pregnant mothers and depending on how advanced the pregnancy was could terminate it or arrange for the child to be adopted.

Dad wired £500 to my bank account, more than enough money for us to go to a clinic he'd booked in Leamington Spa, which was at a discrete distance from Cardiff, but not so far to require spending two nights away from university during term time.

The clinic had the atmosphere of a country hotel. Everyone was very kind and Sally was ushered into an upstairs room for an initial examination. I read back copies of *Country Life* in the reception.

Twenty minutes later, she re-emerged. "False alarm. There's no foetus. Sorry."

It was I who was sorry. What a thing to put her through. Made easier by the unconditional support a father gives his children, there when I needed, just at the right time to help us.

Thanks, Dad.

Sunday, November 13, What Price Peace[112]

The first United States cruise missiles arrive at RAF Greenham Common in England amid protests from peace campaigners.

---

[112] November 26 – Brink's-Mat robbery: In London, 6,800 gold bars worth nearly UK £26 million are taken from the Brink's-Mat vault at Heathrow Airport. Only a fraction of the gold is ever recovered, and only two men are convicted of the crime.

December 19 – The Jules Rimet Trophy is stolen from the Brazilian Soccer Confederation building in Rio de Janeiro. As of 2018, the trophy has not been recovered.

December 31 – The Second Nigerian Republic is overthrown.

1984, Cathay's Terrace, Cardiff

Sunday, January 1, Is Big Brother Watching?

So, we all made it, 1984. Will Orwell's dystopian come to pass this year? No.[113]

Saturday, March 3, Lucky Jim

Ralph and I go on a training exercise with the OTC to Belfast. Ralph goes off to visit his grandmother while we all go to the pub and then catches up with us before we fly back to Handel Street.

Whilst we are having beers in the mess, we are joined by another OTC from Newcastle University. Second Lieutenant Jim Roberts and I strike a chord. He is without doubt the best mimics of county accents I have ever heard.

My telling him I am graduating with a degree in Linguistics sets him off on contest, can I spot the accent. He takes the rip out of the Edinburgh burr; Irish lilt, to be sure, obviously; Yerkshire, north and south; North East, diven't worry; Devon, Sally tries not to take offence, and Norfolk.

"I bet you won't guess that one."

"Well, actually, I went to school with a girl who sounded like that. Her dad was a mustard farmer just outside King's Lynn. We went out with each other in the Sixth Form. Her name was…"

"Jenny Kirkham!" Jim and I said, simultaneously.

"We've just started going out, in Newcastle."

"It wasn't on Valentine's Day by any chance?"

---

[113] February 3 – STS-41-B: Space Shuttle Challenger is launched on the 10th Space Shuttle mission. On February 7 – Astronauts Bruce McCandless II and Robert L. Stewart make the first untethered spacewalk.

February 23 – TED (conference) founded. Passed me by at the time.

"Yes. How did you know?"

"It's not important."

After that, Jim and I became inseparable friends. Every week, we'd send each other a postcard and always sign off with an ambitious bucket list challenge compiling lists of things we'd like to do before we *kick the bucket*. Most of mine seem to be travel or natural history related.

POSTCARD

Date stamp: 08.03.84
Dear Jim,
Great to meet you last weekend.
Send my love to Jenny.
Bucket List item: #33 Arrive by seaplane.
Kind regards,

Olly

Wednesday, March 14, Coconut

Sinn Féin's Gerry Adams and three others are seriously injured in a gun attack by the Ulster Volunteer Force.

POSTCARD

Date stamp: 15.03.84
Dear Olly,
Was pleased to read the IRA got a slap in the mush.
Great to meet you too.
Jenny doesn't remember you (jokes).
Bucket list item: #32 Drink a cocktail from a fresh coconut. (Ideally a deux.)

Au bientots,
Jim

Saturday, March 17, Just Like That

Welsh magician and comedian Tommy Cooper suffers a massive heart attack and dies while performing live on TV.

POSTCARD

Date stamp: 19.03.84
Dear Jim,
Could hardly believe my eyes, did you see Tommy Cooper die on TV?
The audience thought it was a joke and just kept laughing.
You can tell Jenny I've gone right off mustard.
Bucket list item: #31 Learn how to fillet fish properly.
Kind regards,
Olly

POSTCARD

Date stamp: 23.03.84
Dear Olly,
Jenny is enjoying these postcard exchanges, a little too much, in my opinion.
What an old trout. I shall endeavour to entreat her favours further.
I can show you how to fillet and pin bone a trout/aka Jenny.
Bucket list item: #30 Travel on as many different modes of transport in a day as possible.
Au revoir,
Jim

POSTCARD

Date stamp: 29.03.84

Dear Jim,
I really like your last Bucket List item.
Travelling onto and off a plane might actually take the longest time in transition?

Have you ever been on a hovercraft, tuk-tuk or hang-glider?

Would a penny-farthing and a tandem count as two bikes?

Bucket list item: #29 Break a Guinness World Record

Kind regards,

Olly

POSTCARD

Date stamp: 04.04.84

Dear Olly,

Yes I've been on all three. Good call on the bikes, definitely count separately.

Had a very good OTC weekend, looking at the Middle Eastern issues.

About bleedin' time g'vnor.

Bucket list item: #28 Watch England play at every Test cricket ground.

Au revoir,

Jim

Tuesday, April 17, See Also, The Police Memorial Trust

Woman Police Constable Yvonne Fletcher is shot and killed by a secluded gunman, leading to a police siege of the Libyan Embassy in London.

POSTCARD

Date stamp: 18.04.84

Dear Olly,

What a cowardly act, shooting an unarmed WPC.

I reckon the SAS will storm the embassy 'ere long.

Yes, I remember my Finals being a pain in the a. as well. Don't worry about writing back.

Bucket list item: #27 Release baby turtles into the sea.

Best of luck,

Jim

Monday, June 4, Finals

Bruce Springsteen releases his seventh album *Born in the USA*.

POSTCARD

Date stamp: 10.06.84

Dear Olly,
Not much is going on up here at present.
My dissertation is nearly finished. Thanks for asking, not.
It's great that it's shirtsleeves weather on Parade so early.
You should buy the Springsteen album, it's very good.
If you're bored with revision try this for starters:
Bucket list item: #26 Learn how to say supercalifragilisticexpialidocious backwards.

Best of luck, again,
Jim

I remember the weather during Finals being fantastically hot. I was relieved just to have got to the end of my degree. Although I revised, I didn't enjoy any of the six papers and really didn't do myself justice.

Nevertheless, I was still gutted to get a 2:2. Immediately known as a *Desmond* of course, after South Africa's inspirational Archbishop Desmond Tutu.

In my year group, no one got a First and only one person was awarded an Upper Second. It might have been on odd course for the University of Wales Institute of Science and Technology to have run, but that was no reason for marking our Finals overly harshly to compensate, in my opinion.

Sunday, July 1, Emancipation

Liechtenstein becomes the last country in Europe to grant women the right to vote.

POSTCARD

Date stamp: 05.07.84

Dear Olly,

The good burghers of Liechtenstein have seen fit to give Sheila's the vote. What's that you say, yes, I agree, let's not go visit.

When are you coming to see us? You're a FREE MAN.

I'm thinking of joining the Artillery for a full 22-year stretch. What say you?

Bucket list item: #25 Step foot on Antarctica.

E.G.Y.P.T.,
Jim

POSTCARD

Date stamp: 10.07.84

Dear Sirs,

URGENT TELEX My best friend has taken leave of his senses STOP Stop his application STOP He is not sufficiently ugly or thick to join up STOP Besides, he's going to be an Explorer STOP How otherwise will he step foot on Antarctica, or: Bucket list item: #24 Bathe an elephant

ENDS

Kind regards,
Olly
PS: E.G.Y.P.T.?

POSTCARD

Date stamp: 18.07.84

My dear old stick,

You appear to know me better than I know myself.
Ma agrees with you: I should join this trekking company, give it a go
and if it's a dud, apply for a commission in the new year.
Meantime I'm going to write a *Hiker's guide to Dorset.* Do you fancy
joining me?
Bucket list item: #23 Eat an ostrich egg
Ever Gripping Your Pink Tits, (E.G.Y.P.T.)

Jim

PS: Heard this from Bob Monkhouse recently on the TV, made me
laugh: "I can still enjoy sex at 75. I live at 76, so it's no distance."

Friday, July 20, Graduating By Degrees

I don't remember anything about my graduation ceremony, other than I
invited Sadie Richards to be one of my guests, as a thank you for looking after
me in my first year.

And here she is. My lovely landlady, Sadie Richards xxx

In the meantime, between the end of finals and graduation we all had a whirlwind of job interviews or applications for graduate management trainee scheme to apply for, all around the country.

POSTCARD

Date stamp: 28.07.84

My dear Jim,

Life is pretty shite at present. Most of my interviews are in London. No bites yet.
I'm living behind the settee of a school friend's house in London.
You're doing the right thing going to Nepal for six months.
Have you written the book yet? sorry I didn't come.
Bucket list item: #22 Have a picnic in an igloo.

NORWICH,
Olly

Most of the interviews were in London. Luckily, Tim Jerome and his girlfriend Anne were there already, Tim doing his PhD at King's College. They were renting a tiny flat near Penge station, in south London. So I slept behind his settee at night, after they'd gone to bed. And crept out of the house before they got up. For about a fortnight, Anne didn't know I was there.

The prize job for graduates in 1984 was deemed to be Marks & Spencer's Graduate Management trainee scheme. I applied like thousands of others for one of their 120 places but most of us were rejected.

Somewhere down the rankings of great graduate management trainee courses was the one British Home Stores had just initiated. On the basis that if you can't beat them copy them, BHS decided to copy M&S and was looking for 18 candidates.

Lucky for me, the interviews were held in the Cardiff store. The group exercises were all familiar enough and we were a motley collection. Evidently, applications had been in their tens rather than thousands so the rumour was anyone not sent home by lunchtime had a fair chance of getting on their course.

The glorious sunny weather continued through that July and I remember the interview rooms were baking hot and smelt of chips wafted in from the staff canteen.

At the end of a fairly depressing day, they let us know that we'd hear on August 1st if our applications were successful.

The race to work anywhere but BHS continued apace.

Unilever even put those of us who made the final selection round for their graduate management scheme up at the Waldorf hotel in London. For three days, we were interviewed, completed group tasks, gave presentations and ate like kings and queens at night.

For some of the tasks, my familiarity with military presentations and teamwork exercises helped. For others, I was like a fish out of water and my course buddy, Stephen Aldborough an astrophysicist from Oxford, was also rejected.

I'm quite grateful a rocket scientist wasn't finally selected to help design new combinations of washing up liquid or fly spray. But something must have clicked at the Waldorf, Stephen was later one of the ushers at my wedding.

I went up to London to be interviewed by Price Jamieson who had numerous editorial roles on their books, none of which they considered appropriate for me.

In Surrey, I was interviewed for *Scrip*, a twice weekly business publication. But my lack of knowledge of the pharmaceutical sector was *a concern*.

Hard News, Channel 4's new weekly series investigating the practices of the press, decided not to investigate my application beyond a rejection letter.

Back to London, this time in Hammersmith, I did my best to convince the editor, Shirley Shelton, that I was just the type of features editor that *Home & Freezer Digest* needed. She gave me the cold shoulder.

As the editor of my university's AWARD-WINNING magazine – Hugh and I gave ourselves an award for our final issue, which we splashed on the cover I was really hopeful for a career in journalism. In between interviews, I wrote speculative letters to publishing houses hoping my offer to be a freelancer might result in a full-time role.

LETTER

10 July 1984

Dear Ms Faulkner,

I am writing to enquire whether you would be interested in commissioning any editorial pieces?

Although I edited *Impact,* the University of Wales student magazine, I do not currently write for a living. I have had holiday positions as a cub reporter for the *Yorkshire Post* and the *Bridlington Free Herald* and currently have an offer of place on the postgraduate course at the Cardiff School of Journalism.

Recently I completed a series of articles for a Marshall Cavendish magazine *Combat and Survival*, that is now run its course consequently I am looking for some alternative topics to write about and wonder if the enclosed piece might be of any interest to you?

I would be interested in writing on his wide and varied a strategic matter as is necessary, although I do have an inexhaustible supply of source material regarding overseas residential property.

Yours sincerely
Oliver Milner
Enc…

LETTER

Nicholas Publications Ltd
14 July 1984

Dear Mr Milner,

Thank you for your letter of 10 July 1984.

It is not this company's policy to commission any new writers at present. However the situation may change in the near future.

With this in mind, I have returned your feature enclosed and placed you on our files for future freelance work.

Thank you for your interest.

Yours sincerely,
M Faulkner
Editorial Director
Enc. Returned herewith/...

So, You Thought You'd Go Abroad...? (Abridged)

Ever thought of being ill or suffering an accident whilst abroad? If you travel to Egypt, a Which? survey revealed that an enormous 58% suffer from at least some form of illness, the most common of which is a stomach upset.

So how can you insure against or avoid such illness spoiling a visit abroad? Organising inoculations and reducing the risks of becoming ill should be the highest of all priorities. Exotic locations often require vaccinations as a legal entry requirement against cholera, typhoid, polio, tetanus, yellow fever and malaria.

Lists are available in most doctors' surgeries as to what is required for each country. Tour operators also normally point out certain recommendations, but these are not always entirely accurate. There are no mandatory requirements for the Seychelles, but my ever-cautious GP suggested it would be prudent if he jabbed the family with yellow fever, cholera and tetanus. It was. Two weeks into our arrival and an outbreak of cholera was reported on neighbouring islands. The Bureau of Hygiene and Tropical Diseases at Kepple St, London WC1E 7HT tell (01) 631 4408 can be sought for a most authoritative opinion on what is required.

The summer of 1983 in Greece proved to be a fatal example of the effects of heat exhaustion. Holidaymakers actually died because their symptoms of giddiness, tiredness and headaches, which are the first symptoms of heat stroke, were not spotted in time. The prevention is so simple it made the fatalities so much more tragic. So long as you take more non-alcoholic drinks than usual, wear loose light fitting clothes and take it easy, you are likely to avoid the ruinous effects of heat exhaustion...

Nothing spoils a holiday more quickly than sunburn. Fortunately, public awareness and experience abroad make this less of a problem. However, those with very pale skin and especially children need to use a sun cream with a high protection factor. The highest is 50, which is a total sun block. Two points are often forgotten most suntan oils wash off in the sea or pool so always needs to be replaced on emerging. Secondly, that it is possible to burn even when the sun is behind cloud because the harmful ultraviolet rays still penetrate the haze.

If all this sounds as if the whole exercise of going abroad is normally one horror after another, the easiest way to relieve your troubled mind would be to visit your GP as a preparation before packing your suitcases. Sound out their opinion and take their advice. Some countries could view the medication you take as drugs of addiction. How for example would you explain your syringes if a diabetic?

A note from the doctor could make all the difference at customs, between getting a suntan or getting sent home!

ENDS

(465 words)

Absolutely desperate I'd write anything, for anybody. In the sheaf of articles in front of me now apparently I wrote about: fountain pens; the Seychelles; kiwi fruit (aka *Zesprii*); sauterne; underlay; philately; how to build a villa in Turkey; Chelonia (turtles and terrapins); sales techniques; surveillance; motorway pile ups; Bridlington beach; fish and chips; power station cooling towers...

I was prepared to work and write for anyone.

LETTER

Highlife magazine, Headway Publications Ltd
15 July 1984

Dear Mr Milner,

Thank you for your letter of 11 July 1984 and the enclosed 465-word article.

Unfortunately we do employ regular contributors and cannot therefore accept your contribution.

We return your article here with.

Yours faithfully,
K M J
Secretary to the editor

LETTER

Insight Publications Ltd
16 July 1984

Dear Oliver,

Thank you for your letter of 12 July 1984, and the article which I read with interest.

Unfortunately we no longer publish travel magazines and have no need of writers at this time.

I wish you luck with your writing and hope you find success in placing work.

Yours sincerely,
D Trebilcock
Managing Editor

LETTER

Reader's Digest Ltd
17 July 1984

Dear Mr Milner,

Thank you for your letter of 13 July 1984 and for your article "So you thought you'd go abroad?"

We have read it with interest but have regretfully decided it does not quite meet our requirements.

In returning it to you, however, we would like you to know how much we appreciate the opportunity to consider your material.

Yours sincerely,
Patricia Myers
Research Editor Encl.

LETTER

Home & Family, The Mothers' Union
18 July 1984

Dear Mr Milner,

Thank you for your letter of 14 July 1984. As we are a Christian magazine run by a charitable organization, I do not think we should be able to offer you the kind of work you have in mind.

Perhaps you did not consider the precise target audience when you sent us your article which surprisingly contains a profanity which might upset some of our readers.

We do appreciate your offer, however, and will certainly keep your name on our files.

In the meantime I return your article here with, with our thanks.

Yours sincerely,
John Martin
Editor, *Home & Family*

LETTER

Country Living
19 July 1984

Dear Mr Milner,

Thank you for your letter of 15 July Suggesting articles for *Country Living*. The piece you enclosed is an odd choice for us given we only run features with some country connection.

If you would like to send over more relevant features to us on a speculative basis, we would be very happy to read them.

Thank you for thinking of us.

With best wishes,
Katie Brown
Features Editor

LETTER

Radio Times
20 July 1984

Dear Mr Milner,

Thank you for your letter of 16 July 1984. Thank you for your letter and the sample piece of writing which I am afraid is not the sort of piece we publish.

However, I shall pass your details on to our features Department and should any opportunities for freelance work arise I am sure they will be in touch with you.

Yours sincerely,
Nicholas Brett
Editor

LETTER

Midweek
21 July 1984

Dear Mr Milner,

Thank you for your letter of 17 July 1984. I'm sorry, but the enclosed piece you sent me isn't actually for us.

I'm always interested though in London angled lifestyle pieces so if you have ideas in that direction, I would be interested to hear them.

With all good wishes.

Yours sincerely,
Bill Watts
Editor in Chief

POSTCARD

Date stamp: 22.07.84

Now then, Now then,

If this *Jim Could Fix It* for you, believe me boyo, you'd have a job for effort.

Keep at it. Persistence is one of the qualities I most admire in you.

Thank you for agreeing to proof the book. £50 quid is £50 quid, I suppose.

The publishers reckon it will sell 1,000 or so copies and have asked me to do a *Hiker's guide to Somerset.* Which should sell 1,500!

Bucket list item: #21 Swim with manatees. Dolphins are so yesterday. Manatees on the other hand/flipper…

Chin up,

Jim
PS: NORWICH?

LETTER

Good Housekeeping
22 July 1984

Dear Mr Milner,

Thank you for your letter of 18 July 1984. I found your piece interesting and useful, but I feel the subject is more appropriate for our Consumer Affairs Department rather than for Family Matters.

I have therefore passed it to Cassandra Kent, the Consumer Affairs Editor, to see if it may be of some use to her.

Yours sincerely,
Sandra Lane
Senior Commissioning Editor, Family Matters/Health and Beauty

POSTCARD

Date stamp: 26.07.84
My dear Jim,
Thanks for your card.
Life would have been simpler if I wanted to be an accountant, or a nurse a lawyer. Oh, hang on, I did!
Send my love to Jenny. Is she going to Somerset/Nepal with you?
(K)Nickers Off Ready When I Come Home ('NORWICH')

Olly

Wednesday, August 1, Haberdashery and Gussets

Inevitably the one application I didn't care for came good. BHS confirmed my role as a Graduate Management Trainee on a salary of £3,800. On successful completion of the six months' training, my salary as an assistant store manager would double.

BHS Norwich was ready to welcome me, and 17 other graduates, starting on August 14.

"A good plan violently executed right now is far better than a perfect plan executed next week."

– General George Paton

Sunday, September 9, Pants

If only it had been a good plan.

It's fair to say retail therapy wasn't my thing. I also hated working weekends on five days on two days off shift pattern. Nothing about the trainee scheme lived up to my expectations. We all felt like M&S rejects.

The store staff were suspicious of graduates with no experience being over promoted, and they were right to be.

The store manager was a kindly soul, presumably selected to lead the first cohort of graduate trainees because of his own 30-year experience, which would soon end presumably in his own retirement.

Compared to the quality of training, we received in the OTC, the Royal Corps of Signals and the Intelligence Corps, BHS was a joke.

Almost a month in, I decided to speak to the store manager today on my 24th birthday.

He didn't believe me when I ask him to accept my resignation. Making me work for the past two weeks on Department 15 had broken me.

I had measured up Norfolk turkey farmers' wives for the last time. Someone better qualified could help them select their bras and under wired scaffolding. I'm off to London to earn my living in publishing.

Or so I thought.

How wrong was I. I felt just like rambler in *The Road Not Taken* by Robert Frost:

> Two roads diverged in a yellow wood,
> And sorry I could not travel both
> And be one traveller, long I stood
> And looked down one as far as I could
> To where it bent in the undergrowth;

Then took the other, as just as fair,
And having perhaps the better claim,
Because it was grassy and wanted wear;
Though as for that the passing there
Had worn them really about the same,

And both that morning equally lay
In leaves no step had trodden black.
Oh, I kept the first for another day!
Yet knowing how way leads on to way,
I doubted if I should ever come back.

I shall be telling this with a sigh
Somewhere ages and ages hence:
Two roads diverged in a wood, and I –
I took the one less travelled by,
And that has made all the difference.[114]

My interviews to get into advertising copywriting didn't go too well, either.

POSTCARD

Date stamp: 10.09.84

My dear Jim,
Well that's a wasted month of my life, over.
BHS was every bit as bad as you feared it would be. What with that and the squealing pigs going into the slaughterhouse at dusk. I've seen enough of East Anglia for a lifetime.

How's Jenny? Did you enjoy yomping across Somerset together with notebook in hand?

Was she Dorothy, to your Wordsworth, nudge, nudge, wink, wink?
Say. No. More.

---

[114] Selected from *Poem for the Day* Book One (ISBN 185619499X).

Bucket list item: #21 Go to an Olympic Games. Eh? Wink? Wink?

Olly

During an interview at Benton & Bowles, a leading advertising agency of the day, my folding travel alarm clock suddenly went off inside my briefcase, which I had beside me.

In my panic, I couldn't find the right numbers on the combination lock (it should have been 134/134), so demonstrating what I thought was out-of-the-box-creative thinking, I threw the briefcase out of the open window. Luckily, it fell into an empty skip below.

How they could overlook my resourcefulness under pressure, I failed to fathom. I didn't get the traineeship.

But I do still admire a well-turned advertising strapline.

For years, the *Economist* competed with the *Financial Times'* clever "No FT, No Comment" with:

"Don't believe all you read."

Years later, they brilliantly turned that phrase around, and it's even more effective:

"Don't read all you believe."

For years, I used this on my Twitter descriptor: "One day, or day one."

Then I took it down in case it was a breach of copyright. Now I'm wondering if I wrote it?

POSTCARD

Date stamp: 14.09.84

My dear Olly,

Yes, I've finished the Somerset book and am off to Kathmandu at the end of the month.
Jenny and I have split up. Largely because she's going out with someone else. Perhaps I'll meet a lonely shepherdess in the mountains.

You could do worse than helping out Dobbo and crew in Cardiff whilst something better comes along. Remember Winston's words: "If you're going through hell, keep going."

Bucket list item: #20 Pass grade 1 in every orchestral instrument.

Bye for now,
Jim

Saturday, September 15, Back in Wales

Still without a full-time job salvation in part came via the OTC. Could I go back and help out during the first term with the new undergraduates?

Whilst back in Cardiff, I carried on going out with Sally, now in her final year. When she didn't want to be disturbed, I chewed that fat in the OTC mess and learned more about our Clansman kit. I was one of the first in uniform to fire the new SA80 assault rifle, which replaced the bulky SLR.

The problems with the SA80 are well documented, but I was one of the first to learn, as a left hander, the early models couldn't be fired from the left shoulder.

I also went to Bulford, the HQ of the Royal Corps of Signals, for several TEWTS (Tactical Exercises Without Troops), but the decision to join the TA Intelligence Corps was rather taken for me.

By now, I'd decided, and it seemed obvious to all around me that a permanent job in the Army was probably what I was most suited for.

One evening after parade, a Junior Officer Cadet bolshily claimed that far from being the back bone of the command structure, the role of Warrant Officer was redundant. Two weeks at university had made him an expert.

Foolishly (but as Dad had so often showed us as children), I put the dweeb's little finger into a knuckle lock. Amidst cheers in the mess, his pint fell from his other hand and his screech of pain reached the ear of the Commanding Officer.

As "I had displayed ungentlemanly conduct unbecoming of an Acting Second Lieutenant", I was asked to leave the OTC immediately. However whilst handing in my kit next day, Dobbo asked if I'd be interested in joining the junior ranks mess? As luck would have it, his new TA Intelligence Corps squad needed recruits to support to assist with some reconnaissance.

POSTCARD

Date stamp: 20.09.84

My dear Olly,

To be honest, I think you'll make a better LCpl in the Int Corp anyway. I'm glad you liked the last Bucket List challenge. I forget you play the trumpet, double bass, drums, violin, spoons etc.
Bucket List item: #19 Paraglide along the Grand Canyon.

Pip, pip, (or not, in your case now LCpl...!)
Jim

As a Lance Corporal, I much preferred being able to assist in actual photo recognition reconnaissance. Much of the interpretation work is nowadays electronic. In Hampstead where we trained midweek after work, I struggled to see the relevance of teaching non-linguists like me rudimentary Russian.

The threat was mostly emerging from the Middle East, and or the IRA, in my view.

As autumn was drawing in one night after we had all fallen out and the mess had opened for an evening beer, I saw this on the noticeboard:

Situations Vacant
PRESS OFFICER

Soldiers' Sailors & Airmen's Families Association, London

It looked like a great job for me. And it was. I applied and was offered my first career job.

I started on October 1.

Don't count the days. Make the days count.

POSTCARD

Date stamp: 28.09.84

My dear Jim,

Lawks a-mercy, SSAFA has offered me a job as a Press Officer.

I'm sending this to your Ma's address, since "somewhere on the side of a yak, Himalayas", might not reach you.

Thanks for all your support. By the time you read this you might even be back for New Year?

Bucket list item: #19 Walk across the Abbey Road zebra crossing.

Best wishes,
Olly

Saturday, September 29, Ireland

Another TA weekend, in Ulster, again, but a somewhat peculiar one for me, as I'm a Lance Corporal now not a Junior Lieutenant like Ralph and Sally. Still it's a rare treat for us to be together again.

Ralph goes off on his own, leaving some time for Sally and me to be alone. And true to form, losing his wits whilst all around him retain theirs, he misses the ferry home again.

Monday, October 1, SSAFA

The Soldier's Sailors' and Airmen's Families Association (SSAFA) is a remarkable charity helping hundreds of Forces families who might otherwise slip through the welfare and social services net. Life in the Forces can be a great strain on the families left at home, waiting for news of loved one, which one day might be dreadful.

I settled quickly into my new tasks, writing feature articles and gathering news for their magazine *SSAFA News*.

Major General Charles Gray was our Controller. Which made him sound as if he worked on the railway, but he was in fact the Chief Executive for a very well-run and large organisation.

Joe Perdue was the director of the communications team and my boss, the PR manager was Laura Rowlands.

There were two extraordinary characters who sat on the desk either side of me.

Giles Bradley, another press officer, did absolutely nothing all day but read the financial pages of the heavyweight newspapers and occasionally rang his stockbroker. "Buy Polly Peck. Sell BP," was all he said on the phone. He rarely uttered sentences longer than two words.

"Coffee, now?" he asked. "I'm making."

He was a millionaire by 25, and I think Joe largely kept him on because very occasionally Giles had a tip that invariably climbed and climbed. His particular speciality were penny shares, i.e. publicly listed companies whose shares were worth a few pence each but had the capacity to grow exceptionally fast.

He never concealed what he did, and in the pub was very generous in his careful explanations why the Stock Exchange was both a gold mine and a minefield.

Giles's other love was heavy rock. Whenever he emerged from his headphones, the decibel levels could be heard across the office. He had gothic rings and tattoos on his hands to match.

He later went on to have a society wedding marrying the Deb of the Week he spotted one day in *Country Life*.

My favourite colleague was Geoff, our post-room manager. Geoff had Tourette's, which he magnificently kept under wraps at work, or whenever he was bored or calm, i.e. mostly at work.

If anything excited him – a Chelsea win for example – his language abruptly shoot off the sweary Richter scale.

"Nob cheese, fuck off."

"Oh, morning, Geoff," I said.

"I saw Leeds beat Leicester last, bitches. Do you reckon, twat, you'll stay up, bugger, shit, arsehole?"

"Not sure. Chelsea look good for a top three place, though."

"Fuck off, knobhead."

SSAFA gave Geoff a safe space. Everyone in the charity knew his swearing was involuntary. The genius of his role was that as our post-room manager, his work rarely required him to discuss too much about the detail of what we needed him to do. Not only was he really efficient, he was also very popular. We all loved him.

And he was very good.

In the pub, the agony of his predicament was acute. We ordered drinks for him to avoid the embarrassment of bellowing random obscenities at the bar staff, many of whom were temporary staff and didn't know him.

"Cheese and onion, or salt and vinegar, Geoff?"

"Bumcheeks."

Friday, October 12, Murder of a Prime Minister, Almost

The Provisional Irish Republican Army attempts to assassinate Prime Minister Margaret Thatcher and the British Cabinet in the Brighton Hotel bombing. The terror attack kills five people and injures 31.

Under the circumstances, perhaps the last article I submitted for *Combat and Survival* was unpublishable, ill timed, and breached the Official Secrets Act. [115]

Wednesday, October 31, Murder of a Prime Minister

The Prime Minister of India, Indira Gandhi, is assassinated by her two Sikh security guards in New Delhi. Anti-Sikh riots break out, leaving 10,000 to 20,000 Sikhs dead in Delhi and surrounding areas with majority populations of Hindus. Rajiv Gandhi becomes Prime Minister of India.

---

[115] October 23 – The world learns from moving BBC News television reports presented by Michael Buerk of the famine in Ethiopia, where thousands of people have already died of starvation due to a famine, and as many as 10,000,000 more lives are at risk.

October 25 – The European Economic Community makes £1.8 million available to help combat the famine in Ethiopia.

October 26 – *The Terminator* is released.

On the same day Galileo was forgiven by the Vatican 368 years after being condemned, for proving the Earth was not the centre of the universe, but orbits the Sun.

POSTCARD

Date stamp: 28.11.84

My dear Olly,

Got your card, chuffed to hear you're at SSAFA. Not much has happened here. We're still snowed in, in Kathmandu because the weather's been too evil to start trekking, even over the lowlands.

But you'll be pleased to know I can ride a yak AND a Bactrian camel (two humps). Of the two, yaks are the more conversational.

I love the people here. I have queues of them waiting to listen to me swear at them in different accents.

Bucket list item: #18 Ride a camel or a yak. Tick.

Here's a helpful Nepali phrase, as I know you enjoy it so: "*Hi umbata cuda*" or "Fuck off snow," in English!

Jim

POSTCARD[116]

Date stamp: 20.12.84

Dear Jim,

Thank you for your Nepali Christmas card. I sent one to you Ma, of course.

I'm assuming you will be away from Main Camp, which is where I'm sending this.

Bernard Cribbins' narration on *The Snowman* moved me so much last week that I wrote and thanked him. And today he's sent me a Christmas card back, with thanks. Class act.

Bucket list item: #17 Float in the Dead Sea. (How many bags of salt would that need to replicate it in the bath?)

Happy New 1985,

Olly

---

[116] December 3 – Bhopal disaster: A methyl isocyanate leak from a Union Carbide pesticide plant in Bhopal, Madhya Pradesh, India, kills more than 8,000 people outright and injures over half a million (with more later dying from their injuries, the death toll reaches 23,000+) in the worst industrial disaster in history.

British Telecom is privatised.

December 19 – The People's Republic of China and United Kingdom sign the Sino-British Joint Declaration on the future of Hong Kong.

1983–85 famine in Ethiopia intensifies with renewed drought by mid-year, killing a million people by the end of this year.

Crack cocaine, a smokeable form of the drug, is first introduced into Los Angeles and soon spreads across the United States in what becomes known as the crack epidemic.

I'd almost forgotten we did this. For one mad weekend I (seated left), and a Bohemian Rhapsody mad friend (right), decided to hire a VW golf and drive from Land's End (above) to John O'Groats via Holyhead and Great Yarmouth. Just because we could. In spite of playing Bohemian Rhapsody on repeat for 22 hours, I still like Queen. Btw, it's not a trip I'd recommend, it involves lots of motorways, service stations, smelly loos, and John O'Groats is miles and miles away from civilisation and a warm meal.

1985, Penge, South London

Sunday, January 13

Nightmare. I am absolutely spent and ready to give the TA up. We've been on exercises all weekend around Belfast and begun training on interrogation techniques. I find the instructors absolutely terrifying and can honestly say I'd last less than a minute at the hands of the IRA. Ralph seemed to know his stuff, and for once seemed in his element. I'm not sure I'm cut out for this.

Apparently, next time we come across to Lisburn, we're taking part in an escape and evasion exercise with the SAS. Those we capture we'll be expected to interrogate.

I am delighted to be back home.[117]

Thursday, January 17, Nightmare

British Telecom announces it is going to phase out its famous red telephone boxes.

Monday, January 28, Nightmare

The charity single record *We Are the World* is recorded by USA for Africa. (Well, it was an awful song. Worthy cause.)

---

[117] January 1 – The Internet's Domain Name System is created. Not something we were aware of at the time. But good to know.

Greenland is withdrawn from the European Economic Community. Nightmare.

First UK cellular mobile phone network is launched by Vodafone. Nightmare.

Thursday, February 28, Mortar Attack

The Provisional Irish Republican Army carries out a mortar attack on the Royal Ulster Constabulary police station at Newry in Northern Ireland, killing nine officers in the highest loss of life for the RUC on a single day.

By coincidence, this is very close to where we were training last week. The mood in the mess is very sombre after midweek training.

Monday, March 11, Glasnost

Mikhail Gorbachev becomes General Secretary of the Soviet Communist Party and de facto leader of the Soviet Union. This turns out to be great news for the world but passed most of us by without a murmur, at the time. Certainly, in Penge.

After a desperately poor start to 1985, there's some great news. Tim and Anne have an announcement.

They are to get married on September 9 – in Cleveland, Ohio. And even better news, would Ralph, Jim and I come as the ushers – at their expense – on Tim's side of the church, which will otherwise be full mostly of Anne's family.

There is one thing though. Anne's family are Mormons. Is that okay?

Okay? It's a free trip, what's not to like…

POSTCARD

Date stamp: 20.04.85

Dear Olly,

Yes, I'd be delighted to be an usher at Tim and Anne's nuptials. It's good of them to think of me but then I suppose there's a connection with Jenny via the school? Ralph seems a decent bloke too, so I'm really looking forward to it. How you doing at SSAFA? I've been promoted to No 2 in charge of the larger parties. So am staying on here, much to Ma's disappointment, but relief.

Quarter of a bath of salt, I think, is the answer to the last Bucket challenge.

Bucket list item: #16 Hug a sequoia. (Wishful thinking on my part, we're above the treeline here.)

Happy New 1985 to you too.

Jim

I missed my regular exchanges with Jim whenever he was in Nepal, but the summer months were their most active, taking advantage of the warmer weather.

One of our bucket list items had been: # Get a tattoo on the top of my left arm saying, "Made in Yorkshire."

"Actually, you weren't," my mother tells me, when I mention this to her.

"You were *conceived* – to put it politely – in a basement bedsit in Swiss Cottage, London. Shortly after we'd seen Peter O'Toole in *Lawrence of Arabia*. You were nearly called Lawrence. Or Melanie."

Why I might have been Melanie is now lost to history. But I did always like the name of my parents' first lodging, which I've never managed to locate. They called it *Wuthering Depths*.

Monday, September 9, Wedding Bells

Given the Jeromes were paying for our travel, board and lodgings in Ohio, all we three boys felt obliged to jump to attention whenever anyone in the groom's party had a request. It quickly became apparent that Anne's side of the family were strictly alcohol free. Something Tim's father Tony quickly remedied for the groom's party by buying an adjacent room to ours and filling it full of booze from the local store, which we smuggled in.

From memory for the rehearsals (there were lots of rehearsals) and ceremony, we were each provided with pure white suits and looked, and felt, like members of a Motown band.

No one objected to the two being locked in holy matrimony but Tim did faint at the reception. Possibly to avoid making a speech. It was hard to tell.

The weather was extraordinary. Jim, having just spent the past eight months in the foothills of Everest, admitted he had never seen such blizzards. Snow fell deep and crisp and even constantly for the four days we were there.

Against the snow, in our white suits, just like polecats, the three ushers were almost perfectly camouflaged.

After the reception as a thank you gift for having endured three alcohol free days – in public at least – Mary and Alan Jerome gave the three ushers tickets to the Cleveland Browns, who were playing at home that night against the Tampa Bay Buccaneers.

None of us had been to an open air, American football match before so excitement was high. Jim, Ralph and I soon got into the spirit of the occasion and the beers flowed. I don't remember the score. Possibly nobody does because our overriding memory was of the biting cold and of the blizzard that dumped nearly six inches of snow during the game. It was practically impossible to see where the ball was, but we had a great time. Then it all changed.

"D-d-d-did you see what I saw on the way here?" said Ralph. "B-b-b-big Brenda's Brothel. Sex is legal here in Cleveland."

Shame to say we all agreed to take a further look. Our flights back to Manchester weren't till tomorrow afternoon. What could possibly go wrong?

Big Brenda's it said on the neon sign, outside what looked like a regular two storey motel. After we'd paid 50 dollars each to a man behind a wire grill with a handgun on his desk, we were each led to separate rooms. As my door opened, all I could see was a full-scale rack and crucifix with ties and ropes in each corner. It was a dungeon straight out of a Hammer Horror movie. JoJo entered, weighing in at 500 lbs. Clad in a large piece of floss and a black studded neck collar and bracelets.

"You from England ain't cha? What do you fancy? You guys like it kinda' kinky don'tcha?"

"I don't know." I trembled.

"Yeah, you look kinda young for this kind of thing. See, this is a House of Correction. As you can see we're fully equipped. And seeing as I'm a dominatrix you can look, but you *cain't* touch. I do the touchin' and hittin' with this whip." Crack.

"Do you like whippin'?" Crack.

"Err, no." Crack.

"Do you like being tied up?"

"What?"

"Wid' chains?" Crack.

"No."

"So where we gonna start? Over here?" she asked pointing at the crucifix. "Or over here?"

263

It looked like a commode. Indeed that was exactly what it was. A chair with a toilet seat you could see through.

"I can pee on yer if y'like? But you *cain't* touch."

With that, I fled.

"I'm sorry, I think there's been some kind of misunderstanding."

In spite of the blizzard, I quickly found the car in the car park, except the doors were locked. Jim had the keys. So, I just had to wait in the snow till one of them let me in. Except my co-ushers' business appeared not to have finished as soon as mine.

Jim emerged first, and we got into the car. "What did you get up to? Well, nothing much, she wanted to whip and wrestle me. She looked stronger than a yak."

Ralph arrives. "Well, lads, how was that?" A sheepish look in his face.

We both explain nothing much had happened to either of us. "How did you get on?"

"I hadn't realised, it's called Big Brenda's for a reason. My Brenda was three times bigger than me and I'm afraid when I took my clothes off nothing I could do would persuade little Ralph to pay attention. She just laughed. It was all a bit humiliating and overwhelming[118], really."

"Anyone fancy something to eat and drink? We need to forget about this. How about Wendy's? They can't all be as big as Brenda's," said Jim.

Sunday, September 29, Birthday Cake

Today is Ralph's 30th birthday. Being several years older than Jim and myself he was already well on the way to what we might describe as a comfortable, conventional lifestyle.

In fact, he'd achieved more than that. He was one of London's most sought after horologists, or clock experts and he had money. And his late father had given him enough money to buy a house in Brighton. But he was still single. As were we.

As it was his birthday, and as there was no TA this weekend, Jim and I decided to drive down to Brighton with a birthday cake to surprise him and take him out for a pub lunch.

---

[118] Have you ever noticed that people are rarely just whelmed? Overwhelmed or underwhelmed, but rarely just content/whelmed?

The drive in Jim's open top MG was great fun. The weather was great and we navigated safely enough to Ralph's address.

There was clearly someone in when I banged on the door, but the curtains were closed.

Eventually, Ralph opened the door, naked, and beckoned us in.

"Hey, g-g-g-guys, it's great to see you. C'mon on in."

"Ralph, are you pissed? It's only 10 o'clock," I asked.

"No, guys. This weed's r-r-r-really good. Try it. Come in, come in, come in."

In the living room, clouds of smoke were rising to the ceiling and in middle of the room was a bed surrounded by bright lights. Possibly three cameramen, it was difficult to see in the shadows, were training their cameras on the bed and lying in the middle were two – beautiful – nude women and another naked man.

"Hi, guys," went the girls.

"We're filming *Naughty Stepdad II*. You're very welcome to join us. There's no script as such, we've just got to get it finished by tonight."

"Ralph, we just bought you this cake, as it's your birthday. We'd thought you might like to come to the pub? But I can see you're busy," I said.

"Is it my birthday? Today?" said Ralph. "Wow, guys. Thanks."

Turning to go I was struck that Ralph probably wouldn't remember we'd been there by tomorrow morning. I tried not to look him in the eye, or anywhere else, as we let ourselves out.

In the pub, Jim and I started giggling. Has he always been like that? Drugs? Hardcore porn? Fancy clocks and watches?

Clearly not that conventional, after all.

Thursday, October 3, *Per Adua Ad Astra*

The Space Shuttle *Atlantis* makes its maiden flight.

POSTCARD

Date stamp: 07.010.85

Dear Jim,

I hope you saw the Space Shuffle on TV?
It makes my heart sing when Man's ingenuity works as well as that.

My boss is acting a bit odd at work, but I'm about to go to Bielefeld again to get material for the next *SSAFA News,* so at least I'll be out of the way. I shall have a bratwurst for you.

Bucket list item: #15 Whistle with two fingers.

Auf wiedersehen,
Olly

Tuesday, October 8, Inhale

I make a rare visit to the doctors as my chest is wheezy.

One of the reasons I didn't feel I could commit to joining the Army full time was the dilemma I'd be in if ever I was forced to complete any NBC training. Nuclear, Biological and Chemical warfare training consisted of breathing through a mask and a respirator and wearing a special uniform that would prevent vapour touching the skin or being inhaled. To assess whether you had the mask on correctly, the annual test required you to go into a hut where a tear gas canister had been released. Then disorientated and choking, you then had to put on your mask, breathing normally through the mask, wait 30 seconds and then safely emerge at the other end of the test.

I always managed to ensure that not only was I on another training exercise whenever the OTC or TA were having an NBC assessment weekend but the one weekend NBC training was sprung on us I volunteered to be an assistant to the directing staff, and no one noticed I never completed my turn.

I'm not especially proud I cheated the system, but I compensated by ensuring I always passed my Basic Physical Fitness training assessment with flying : colours. I was a reasonable shot and my Intelligence Corps tradecraft was better than average.

Today I just need another prescription for my salbutamol spin haler. But the days of placing the powder encased in a capsule onto its little egg cup, putting on its lid, clicking down twice to puncture the sides of the capsule and then sharply inhaling the powder as if starting up a miniature turbo jet engine, are over.

"Salbutamol is in aerosol form now. Two puffs when you get up, two puffs before you go to bed. Two puffs before any exercise, and two puffs before sex," bellows Dr Day with a wink.

I think my doctor's deaf.

I ponder the white marks on my nails as he writes out a prescription form. The mysterious white marks appear as if from nowhere, completely unprompted and then take aeons to slide towards the tip of the nail, trapped, like a tiny prehistoric mosquito caught for millennia inside a globule of amber.

I ask Dr Day if he knows what they're called, and what causes them?

"Science has no name for them. It's a medical mystery," booms Dr Day.

"I called them prenums as a child," I murmur.

"Well, they're calcium deposits."

Now everyone sitting in reception knows I'm an idiot.

What if I'd come in with a genital wart? Does Monica on reception wear earmuffs? Presumably, she knows who's dying or who's pregnant almost as soon as they do, I muse.

In any case, Dr Day's clearly wrong. How could they be calcium deposits? I've not been pecking at a cuttlefish or grinding bones in my soup.

POSTCARD[119]

Date stamp: 25.010.85

Dear Olly,

I flew in via Dubai to Karachi with an amazing new airline today, called Emirates. That's the last luxury I'll see for 6 months.

I did see the Space Shuffle, thanks for asking, agree.

Against my better judgement I have accepted this tour or it would have been cancelled as my boss is unwell too. It can be really dangerous here in January, with whiteouts and avalanches.

Most of our Nepali crew won't work till Easter, when it's safer.

Don't wish to brag, but I can whistle with 2 fingers already, so here's 2 thoughts for the Bucket List, today:

Bucket list item: #14 Get *prenum* adopted as the official word for the white dots that appear on your fingernails.

---

[119] October 18 – The first Nintendo home video game console in the United States is released as the Nintendo Entertainment System.

October 25 – Emirates Airlines establishes in Dubai and performs its first flight to Karachi.

Bucket list item: #13 Spend a weekend at the Monaco Grand Prix.

Take care,
Jim

This is the last postcard card I have from Jim Roberts.

He and his team went to the aid of an inexperienced tour party and were lost in a white out, six miles north of Kathmandu, during which there were several avalanches. Just as he feared there might be. He was lost some time between 13 January, 1986.[120]

Friday, December 13, Noxious Gas

Back at SSAFA my boss, Joe, and his wife Jo Perdue nearly die of carbon monoxide poisoning. Joe's behaviour and attendance at work had become increasingly erratic, but the causes were a mystery, until one morning the controller, Major General Charles Grey, told us that it was their milkman who had called for an ambulance, realising something was wrong when neither came to the door.

Their lives were saved but recovering eventually at home, Joe and Jo were advised to take six months off work. As a result, Major Grey decided to appoint a PR agency for a different approach whilst Joe was away.

Sadly for us, the in-house team was due to be slimmed down in size as much of our work was to be outsourced, and as a result, we were all offered redundancy but very generously offered a year's salary in lieu notice, payable at the end of the month, until then we could take paid leave and were free to go whenever we chose.

The windfall was amazing, but I needed to find something else to do.

The smallest job ad in the back of *PR Week* caught my eye:

Account Executive wanted
Poole, Dorset
I year's minimum public relations experience required.
Send CV to Box No. 134

---

[120] His remains have not yet been found.

Box No. 134 was a lucky omen.

On my last day at SSAFA, my desk phone, which never rings, rang.

"Hi, is that Olive Milner? My PA's given me your CV. My name's Harrison Barber, I'm the MD of Associated Promotions."

"Actually, it's Oliver Milner."

There was a slight pause. "Yeah, sorry about that, can't read my own writing."

"Anyway, I like your CV. What's your notice period?"

"Err, well today's my last day, but I was thinking of taking two weeks off and then start looking for something starting in January."

"Well, that would be a shame as we have lots of candidates and the role will be filled by then."

"Okay. When were you thinking I should start?"

"Tomorrow?"

"Okay."

"Excellent. We have a meeting with a new client at 9:00 am. Iron your shirt, wear a tie and for God's sake brush your shoes. You'll know him; the guy's a Major General for some forces charity or other."

And that was it. I left SSAFA on Wednesday. And on Thursday, SSAFA was my first client at Associated Promotions Marketing & Public Relations Limited.[121]

Thursday, December 19, Public Relations

I subsequently learned that Harrison had hoped to recruit a female Account Executive. And of course, there was no PA when I arrived at Associated. Harrison worked with his brother Jonathan, the Head of the Graphics department, who was utterly useless and didn't actually seem to do any designing, graphics, writing or pick up a phone. And Sophie, Harrison's cousin, who was our part-time bookkeeper and very cross when I told her Harrison had introduced her as his PA.

"The cheeky bugger, he knows full well I'm the only one holding down two part-time jobs. Three if you include keeping a home going."

---

[121] Having left SSAFA one weekend some three years later, the social isolation of Geoff's Tourette's pressed down on him so much that he took his own life. Geoff hung himself. He was 26.

In the weeks and months that followed, Harrison taught me all he knew about public relations consultancy. Turned out, it wasn't much but once we both realised it's a bit like selling, so long as you're not embarrassed to *sell* an idea to a client, or a story to a journalist, on behalf of your client, it's plain sailing.

Even Jonathan got it in the end.

1986, The Sidings, Poole, Dorset, England

Wednesday, January 1

In Northern Ireland, as part of The Troubles, police officers James McCandless and Michael Williams are killed by a Provisional Irish Republican Army remote controlled bomb hidden in a litter bin and detonated when their foot patrol passes at Thomas Street, Armagh.

Tragedies like this were intensifying. The IRA was beginning to dominate the news.

Tuesday, January 28, Challenger

It's a tragedy. The Space Shuttle *Challenger* disintegrates 73 seconds after launch from the United States, killing the crew of seven astronauts, including schoolteacher Christa McAuliffe.

Unfortunately, we have another problem.

I'm at work when the phone rings, and it's my dad. I wasn't expecting a call as I was planning on going to Harrogate to see him at the weekend.

He'd had enough of life in a trailer park encampment in the middle of the Saudi Arabian desert where he had worked for the last three years and had decided it was time to come home for good. The tax-free salary had been fabulous but expatriates were worked liked slaves, and he'd had enough at 50 of enduring the boredom as well.

As he was travelling home for good, he had some suitcases this time, carrying a rug, too valuable to pack, under his arm. And when he left through customs at Yeadon airport with Nothing to Declare, that's when he was arrested for smuggling.

"You wouldn't happen to have £1,000 on you, Olly, would you? They won't let me out unless we pay the tax on the carpet."

I didn't have £1,000, of course. But Harrison did and the company leant me the money immediately.

That weekend I was furious with my father. "'Made 'round to go 'round,' you always tell us. Surely you had £1,000? You're minted?"

"Yes, well. I knew you'd come good. Besides I didn't have much sterling in my wallet because it was in here." He took off his belt. On the inside, along the length of the belt was a zip, and inside the belt was crammed tight with crisply folded £50 notes.

"My God, how much is there?"

"£100,000, exactly. If I'd taken off my belt to pay the fine, they'd have really thrown the book at me. This is ten times more than you can bring into the country at the moment.

"The rug was a decoy."

First company portrait – and full of PR knowledge – or soon to be, thanks to Harrison at Associated Promotions Ltd. I can tell you how to get into the papers, or more valuably, how to stay out.

Monday, February 3, What Makes News?

As well as being a generous and thoughtful boss, Harrison was also a great teacher.

A good PR person goes out of their way to make journalists your friend. A great PR person even remembers their name.

Remember, our client's news may be of interest to them, but for a journalist it must be local, timely and ideally something no one has heard before.

NEWS is not really an acronym for North, East, West and South. But if it works for you, fine.

There are essentially only two types of journalism: news or features.

– news is short.

– features are longer (easier to get in to because the writer needs more information).

Take any front-page story on a newspaper or on a TV bulletin. There are ONLY EVER five elements to news. It is either about:

1. Conflict
2. Hardship
3. Celebrity
4. Scandal
5. Oddity

In that order of importance. If it's about more than one of these, chances are it's a front-page lead and will run and run.

(Try it out, it's failsafe).

Tuesday, March 18, Hand Bagged[122]

It's Mum and Dad's 25th wedding anniversary. Dad invests a small fortune on buying Mum a handbag. Unfortunately in spite of the cost, he's gone for one that would have made Margaret Thatcher proud.

Talk about disappointment. We felt for them both: he was disappointed he'd broken the bank for nothing; she was disappointed he seemed to be channelling Margaret Thatcher when he bought her a present.

Sadly, he didn't quite live long enough to have bought her the bag of her dreams for their golden wedding anniversary.

Thursday, March 22, Ballroom[123]

---

[122] February 9 – Halley's Comet reaches its perihelion, the closest point to the Sun, during its second visit to the solar system in the twentieth century (the first was in 1910).

February 25 – The 27th Congress of the Communist Party of the Soviet Union opens in Moscow. General Secretary Mikhail Gorbachev introduces the keywords of his mandate to the audience: Glasnost and Perestroika.

March 9 – United States Navy divers find the largely intact but heavily damaged crew compartment of the Space Shuttle Challenger; the bodies of all seven astronauts are still inside. An article in *The New York Times* charges that Kurt Waldheim, former United Nations Secretary-General and candidate for president of Austria, may have been involved in Nazi war crimes during World War II.

[123] Twelve More Bucket List Challenges

Bucket list item #12: Create the Oliver Milner club and invite everyone called Oliver Milner to meet in a restaurant.

Bucket list item #11: Get an MSc.

Bucket list item #10: Drive a Lamborghini. A motoring correspondent once gave me a spin in his Countach. Possibly, the most exciting 30 minutes of my life. Certainly on tarmac. Tick.

Bucket list item #9: Cuddle a Koala.

Bucket list item #8: Record a song.

Bucket list item #7: Be a member of a TV studio audience. This actually came about, twice. *The Wright Stuff* was a daytime TV programme in which Matthew Wright would challenge panellists and studio audience in a particularly hostile way. My work colleagues challenged me to say the phrase "Rhinoceros Jamboree" without him picking me up on it or it appearing forced. (Tick)

I was an audience member on BBC's *Question Time* following Margaret Thatcher's outburst when she applauded the arrests of Liverpool fans and their lifetime bans. I asked

Our key client, the marketing manager of a tyre manufacturer was also the three time World Competitive Origami champion.

"Here they come, Laurel and Hardy," said Steve Blakeney. It was a cruel sobriquet, which quickly stuck since Harrison invariably looked dishevelled like Stanley, and my name was Olly. I hated him.

Steve and Harrison mysteriously disappeared every third Thursday of the month. I used to think it was to play a sneaky round of golf during working hours. It was the one meeting of the month that Harrison never wanted me to attend. That and when he played golf with a potential client. Quoting Churchill's clever dick quip about golf to Steve probably did little to endear me to him either. "Golf is an ineffectual attempt to direct an uncontrollable sphere into an inaccessible hole with instruments ill adapted to the purpose."

I am beyond bad on the links to the extent that Harrison couldn't play whenever I accompanied him on the course, he laughed so hard he could barely stand. Plus I tend to agree with Robert Townsend: "If you don't do it excellently,

---

what did she knew about football? To applause from the audience. The Heysel Stadium disaster occurred on 29 May 1985 when mostly Juventus fans escaping from a breach by Liverpool fans were pressed against a collapsing wall in the Heysel Stadium in Brussels, Belgium, before the start of the 1985 European Cup Final between the Italian and English clubs. There was no criminality or malicious intent, other than from the mad cow who said the Liverpool fans deserved to be punished. Sadly, she served another five years before she was kicked out of office on November 29, 1990.

Bucket list item #6: Become an MP. In descending order, I have been a paid up member of each of the following parties. But never at the same time: Greens; Liberals; Social Democrats; Liberal Democrats; Conservatives; LibDems and now none. I'm nothing if not inconsistent. Actually, I've not changed. The parties did. I ran for Parliament in 2005 and lost.

Bucket list item #5: Find a four-leaf clover. Daisy, a lovely party activist, gave me hers before she died, to bring me luck in that general election. It's still in my wallet. (Tick)

Bucket list item #4: Why not save a species. Butterflies? Release millions into the wild. Chicken farmers barn rear chickens whose bodies must surely create conditions at the tops of the barn suitable to rear pupae? Why not use all that space and heat to grow butterflies? Simple.

Bucket list item #4: Indoor skydive – always looks such fun.

Bucket list item #3: Send a message in a bottle. On my honeymoon, I put a cheque for £100 in a bottle and threw it into the Indian Ocean. It's never been cashed. (Tick)

Bucket list item #2: Visit all 195 countries in the world. (134 visited. Tick)

don't do it at all. Because if it's not excellent, it won't be profitable or fun, and if you're not in business for fun or profit, what the hell are you doing there?"

One day, I asked Sophie where Steve and Harrison went to.

"Oh, it's a scam they've been playing for years. Steve gets a budget of £20,000 a month to spend on *marketing*, which he splits 50/50 with Harrison. In return for invoicing us £10,000 and scratching his back, Steve invited Harrison to be a Freemason. They go to the Grand Lodge in Holborn every month, on the third Thursday.

"But don't say anything, it's supposed to be a secret. We none of us know why Harrison keeps going – he thinks it's all a bit silly – but that £10K a month has kept us going every now and then when things get tough."

Whilst Harrison kept me away from Steve Blakeney suspecting that I didn't really approve of him, and that was before I learned about the sharp practice and the Freemasonry, Jonathan's lack of any financial contribution to the firm began to gnaw away at me.

Wednesday, March 26, The Drinks Trolley

As the most junior member of the team at Associated Promotions, it was my job to go to the cash and carry and top up the trolley every Tuesday. Harrison's favourite tipple was Guinness and champagne. Jonathan thought Snowballs were more upmarket. Sophie was partial to a Babycham and I chased after whatever popular beverage was being promoted on TV. Leonard Rossiter and Joan Collin's campaign for Cinzano must have been financed largely by yours truly.

The drinks trolley only ever came out if a) one of us – invariably me – scored a media hit with a story; b) one of us – invariably Harrison – secured a new PR client (new projects were worth a whole bottle, a 12 months' retainer was worth the afternoon off); c) if Sophie – poor woman – farted loud enough for all three of us to hear her, or if she swore as she slammed the phone down; d) if we were all still working in the office past 6:30 pm and d) after 4:00 pm on a Friday when we downed tools for the week.

As you can imagine, there were very few days we didn't go home drunk.

Now I dwell on it, Jonathan and Harrison's propensity to write off their latest company cars – always a soft top – probably has a causal link back to the drinks trolley.

Whilst my salary was even less than it had been at SSAFA, Harrison was generous to a fault. Every time we won new work, I would get a bonus equal to 20% of the new account's fees.

Sunday, April 13, Lucky Jim

Pope John Paul II officially visits the Great Synagogue of Rome, the first time a modern Pope has visited a synagogue.

The next evening at Associated Promotions, I learned what Sophie's other job was.

The phone rang. Harrison and I were pulling a late one, trying to get a presentation finished for a pitch in the morning. The drinks trolley was in fully deployed mode.

"Hello, is that Sophie?"

"No."

"Can you take a message then. It's Jackie here. I think she must have taken my strap-on. Because I've got one here, and it doesn't fit. I think it's hers.

"Could you let her know tonight I need mine back as I'm seeing Little Jim in the morning, tell her. Tarraa."

Synthesising what I had just heard I rushed in to Harrison to tell him what I'd heard.

"Well, I suppose you were bound to hear it sooner or later. She's a hooker.

"Although she likes to call it a sex worker.

"Most of the men in Poole have seen her *at work* at some time or other. We met at a Swingers party arranged through the golf club. When she said she was a part-qualified accountant, I jumped at the chance to ask if she'd look after my books. Don't look at me like that. It was the sixties, and besides, that's all she looks after for me now. She'll be embarrassed if she thinks you know."

"But she, she's nearly sixty," I stammered.

"I think you'll find – young man – there's a market for experience."

"I'd better tell her to call Jackie. It would be a shame if Little Jim missed his fun. Lucky Jim more like."

Saturday, April 26, Fallout

A mishandled safety test at the Chernobyl Nuclear Power Plant in Pripyat, in the Ukrainian Soviet Union, killed at least 4,056 people and damaged almost $7 billion of property. Radioactive fallout from the accident is concentrated near

Belarus and Russia, and at least 350,000 people are forcibly resettled away from these areas. After the accident, traces of radioactive deposits unique to Chernobyl were found in nearly every country in the northern hemisphere.[124]

Wednesday, July 23, Keys

In London, Prince Andrew, Duke of York, marries Sarah Ferguson at Westminster Abbey.

I'd been at AP, as we called Associated Promotions, for about six months when one summer lunchtime Harrison stood by my desk.

"Here, Olly, it's been another great month. Why don't you take the rest of the day off?"

"You'll be needing these." And he threw me some keys.

"It's outside."

Outside was a brand-new Rover 200 cabriolet, in gleaming hairdresser white, with personalised number plate OM 134 CC. I called her Millie.

That afternoon, with the lid down, riding along the country lanes of Dorset in the sunshine was one of the happiest of my life.

Later that evening, I decided I had to show Millie off to my dad, so off to Harrogate I zoomed. As I expected, he was just about to give the dog it's last walk before bedtime.

"Wow, that looks like it goes like shit off a shovel."

"Well done, lad!" I knew he'd be pleased.

And then I drove back to Dorset. A round trip of 706 miles. Well, petrol was 42p a litre in 1986.

I loved that car.[125]

---

[124] Chernobyl reminds us of Churchill's advice, "The best defence against the atom bomb is not to be there when it goes off."

[125] September 7 – Desmond Tutu becomes the first black Anglican Church bishop in South Africa.

October 9 – *The Phantom of the Opera*, the longest running Broadway show in history, opens at Her Majesty's Theatre in London.

October 11 – Ronald Reagan and Soviet leader Mikhail Gorbachev meet in Reykjavík, Iceland, to continue discussions about scaling back their intermediate missile arsenals in Europe, which end in failure. It is clear to all, however, that Gorbachev is a brilliant man and that the Cold War is thawing rapidly to an end.

Saturday, December 13, Ten Tonner

All the while, life at AP contrasts sharply with the Territorial Army. Harrison took little interest in my TA existence other than to let me go early on a Wednesday so as never to be late for training, and he took great pride in always mentioning that "Olly is in the TA Intelligence Corps, you know. Of course he is." I often wondered if he thought I was making it up.

Tonight it's another long night in the 10 tonner to the ferry, then to Lisburn, another recce, and another long weekend. The countryside around Armagh is so beautiful, just like parts of the Dales, but I wouldn't die for it. Working alongside the RUC is interesting, they're really up against it at the moment.

I do admire anyone prepared to wear a policeman's uniform in this situation. The IRA could take you out at any moment. Theirs is a very dangerous work. I'm just pleased to be working in the fresh air.

Ralph remembers spending summer holidays here with his grandma and grandad.

Regular soldiers often sneer at those of us in the (part-timers) Territorial Army, but in Intelligence Corps uniform, it's impossible to tell who's full time, and who's not. Next month, we're doing a Conduct After Capture training course in Ashford, which should be interesting.

At the end of the weekend, I can barely keep my eyes open in the pub. The fresh air's worn me out. Ralph finds his second wind and goes off to say hello briefly to Granny before the journey back to London.

Monday, December 23, Cigars

As we prepared to wind down for Christmas full of office party lunch in The Feathers, Harrison and I were once again in his office making a post-prandial attack on the drinks trolley.

The other two had left for Christmas.

October 27 – The Big Bang in the London Stock Exchange abolishes fixed commission charges, paving the way for an electronic trading platform.

October 29 – Prime Minister Margaret Thatcher officially opens the M25 Motorway, which encircles Greater London, in a ceremony on the carriageway near Potters Bar. It became Europe's second longest orbital road upon completion, and provides the first and only full bypass of London.

"Harrison, do you mind my asking, why on earth do you still keep Jonathan on? Is it because he's your brother?"

Harrison relit a cigar. "I did it as a bet."

"My father bet me £10,000 last Christmas that Jonathan couldn't hold down a job with me – or anyone else for that matter – for twelve months. And since Jonathan earns £3,500 a year, I'm bloody determined to pocket the £6,500 myself.

"Anyway, here's a toast. I collect my bet-on Christmas Day because we've broken up for the year now and even my father can't claim the bet's not won.

"So, I can decide – sorry, *we* can decide – what to do with him when we come back after the holidays. Hopefully, Sophie will have also done the pay run by 31st of December, so you'll see I've given you a little present. I'm doubling your salary.

"You and me share the work fifty-fifty, so it seems only fair that from January 2nd when we come back, we should both be Joint Managing Directors. I'll do the paperwork over Christmas."

"I don't know what to say," I said. My eyes were pricked with tears.

"Well, we've both worked bloody hard and had a fantastic year."

"I'll drink to that," I replied.

"And *you* can deal with my useless brother instead when we get back. You know what they say, 'A problem shared, is a problem doubled…'!"

Tuesday, December 31, Harrison

As you might imagine, Christmas 1986 was one of my best yet and I spent it in Harrogate with my parents. Just after breakfast on New Year's Eve, the phone rang. My father answered it.

"Olly, it's for you. A woman, says she's Sophie?" I wasn't aware I had given anyone my parents' number at work but didn't mind the call.

"Hi, Sophie, is that you? Happy New Year for tomorrow!"

"Olly, I'm afraid I've some sad news."

"Harrison died of a heart attack on Boxing Day. He was dancing at a party and just keeled over. The ambulance people tried to revive him for nearly two hours, but they reckon the combination of the cigars and the stress killed him. You didn't know this as he asked me not to say anything, but for the last six months, we've not had any money from Steve and Harrison hasn't been drawing a salary.

"I'm just here now in the office with the accountants winding things up. I'm ever so sorry, but there's no money in the business to pay us."

Harrison was 42.

I miss him every day.

The year wasn't done with us yet either. You'll remember Gaddo – Musa's eldest son – and I had been pen pals for years. This year was no exception. In fact, completely on trend I think Gaddo's Christmas card had three new children's names on it (remember he had two wives). This year he'd had twins as well.

Sadly, Musa's last years were not completely spent in the peaceful retirement he had so selflessly earned. Several of the women in his family came under the spell of Boko Haram in the early 80s, leaving the army, the only dependable career for all his boys, Gaddo included.

Nonetheless we were delighted – my father especially – when out of the blue, just after tea who should call from Lagos but Gaddo.

My father called us all to the phone at the bottom of the stairs excited. We all crowded excited, delighted to hear his voice. But Gaddo was calling with sad news.

Musa had been tending his goats on their small holding, as per usual. Totally blind now, he tended not to stray off the land which my father had bought for him when we left Nigeria.

But Gaddo, crying now down the phone, said, "Masta, I must tell you. I call to ring with bad announcement. Musa was bitten by a mamba at the weekend. And he has died.

"I am very sorry for your loss, sah."

1987, Southwark Bridge, London

Monday, February 2, Hangovers[126]

What a gig. I have somehow wangled my way onto the tasting panels at *Wine* magazine. All we have to do is swish, swirl and slurp 48 bottles of wine each separately concealed in their silver sleeping bags to protect their identity and then write up our notes.

Presumably because I wrote longer descriptions than other members of the public who just put *delicious*, I was invited back.

The sweet wines evening is especially delicious. As a special treat, we are offered a thimble full of Chateau d'Yquem, easily the world's greatest sweet white wine, and at £75 per sip, easily the most expensive beverage I'll ever taste.

However, who doesn't love a freebie. The expensive jewellery world that Ralph inhabited occasionally produced red carpet, red letter day invitations. He took me to a vintage car auction at Sotheby's and for a brief moment at least, I was one of the lead bidders for a British racing green Bentley 4½ litre Supercharger that had won at Le Mans. Until Ralph shook his head and took my numbered paddle.

Not put off, Ralph took me to the pre-auction reception of fine art at Christies. Champagne and canopies just appeared at our elbows, and our glasses were replenished with every swig. This went on for nearly an hour before the chairman on Christies, Lord Gowrie himself drifted over to Ralph.

"Good evening, Ralph, it's good to see you here. I didn't know you ever put down your horologist's eye piece to look at Fine Art? Are you buying?"

"Oh, n-n-n-no, Lord Gowrie, but Olly here is especially interested in that Lucio Fontana canvas, aren't you, Olly?"

---

[126] January 20 – Terry Waite, the special envoy of the Archbishop of Canterbury in Lebanon, is kidnapped in Beirut (he was finally released in November 1991).

"What? Are you kidding me? He's just slashed a piece of canvass! Look at that one. It isn't even painted. Any idiot could do that."

"Yes, I know a lot of people feel that way, but we're expecting it could fetch as much as $10,000,000 this evening."

"Care to bid?" And with that Lord Gowrie drifted on his way to the sensible people.

I certainly had every best intention of being sensible, at all times, with one of our most important clients. Richard Wakefield was an overseas property developer who hugely appreciated the media coverage we achieved for him.

As a thank you, once a quarter, our monthly meeting would take place over lunch in a restaurant instead of in the boardroom. As his business expanded and our success for him grew, the lunches became ever more extravagant affairs often merging into dinner and in my case a champagne stupor.

On one such occasion returning to Paddington station from a particularly long lunch in a very famous Berkshire restaurant, I realised to my dismay I was locked in the toilet and couldn't open the door.

As the train pulled into the station, I did the only sensible thing I could think of. And went to sleep.

Sometime later, I woke up surrounded by engineers in Hi-Viz jackets carefully manoeuvring me out of the toilet, through the window that they had had to remove. The door being wedged shut by my briefcase they'd had no option.

Somewhat worse for wear, I managed to weave my way back to Penge and put all my clothes, suit and shoes included, into the washing machine on a hot wash.

I sheepishly avoided Paddington station as much as possible for several years after that. Not surprisingly, I've never managed to reserve a table at the famous restaurant either, which is a shame, as I can't remember having been taken there.

Tuesday, February 3, ABCDEFT

I still needed a full time job though and thanks to one of Jim's many girlfriends, he tells me the *Financial Times* is recruiting so I applied. After a series of bizarre group exercises, I was offered a job.

Still slightly hung over from last night's *Wine* magazine tasting, one of the interview exercises we had to do was to sell sand to a sheikh. With my sales skills sharply honed at Associated Promotions, I found it a doddle.

Without any evidence of any direct expertise, I was set the task of building up the property section of the yet to be launched *Weekend FT*. At least I'd proved I could sell a desert.

Now that Tim and Anne were married, it is was time to move out of Poole and I found a bedsit in Muswell Hill, north London, which seemed ideal. It was also extremely inexpensive, and immediately available. Overlooking the centre of Muswell Hill opposite the 7/11, the mansion block was a bit antiquated and musty, but my attic room had a magnificent view across London if I stood on the bed. However, the rat standing on the breadbin might have been a concern.

I turned my back, but when I turned around, he'd gone.

So that was all right.[127]

Saturday, February 14, Penguin Suit

As neither of us had a better offer on Valentine's Day, Ralph rang to ask if I'd like to go to a TV awards dinner that night. His boss was having to take his wife out, so Ralph had a spare ticket.

It was a black tie affair, being televised live, so we had to be at the address in Piccadilly promptly at 8 pm. In between the awards, the TV channel cut to an advertising break and to keep the audience warmed up, entertainers were circulating the tables, doing magic tricks or on this occasion letting us stroke some of the animals that had featured in an award nominated TV advertisement.

At our table, a man appeared with a penguin.

Most of the women[128] at the table recoiled in horror in case it was greasy and would spoil their outfits, but I was fascinated. It was a baby Emperor Penguin, which had been rescued as it had broken its leg. It was about 18" inches high and when the keeper handed it to me, didn't smell of fish, as I was expecting.

Suddenly, all hell broke loose. At the table next door, the python had slithered out of its keeper's grasp and was heading for the toilets. Leaving me stood up, holding our penguin, our keeper darted off with his colleagues after the snake. Then the lights went back up for the live TV show to continue.

---

[127] 11 February – Cynthia Payne is acquitted of controlling prostitutes in her London home.

12 February – Edwina Currie MP sparks controversy by stating that "good Christians won't get AIDS".

[128] 26 February – Church of England's General Synod votes to allow the ordination of women.

Our table, not having any celebrities on it, was some distance from the stage, but it was obvious that I couldn't just stand still through the whole of the next sequence, so as soon as the first TV clip was showing, I asked an attendant to lead me backstage so I could return the penguin.

It was all fine and I was ushered into a room where other people were waiting to go on stage.

"Oh, hello," said a voice. "Is that a Magellanic penguin? I understand there are several types."

"Actually, this is a baby Emperor penguin. He's totally tame because he damaged his foot and can't be released back into the sea."

"Your job must be fascinating," said the woman.

"Oh, actually I've just come backstage to hand him back to his keeper. But you can stroke him, look. He's totally tame. What do you do? Do you have an interesting job?"

"I'm Madonna."

Wednesday, March 4, Monte Carlo

The *Financial Times* sent me to interview one of the British lions of the boardroom, Sir John Harvey-Jones. Regarded by many people as one of the best businessmen of any age. The chairman of ICI was speaking at a conference in Monaco, and if I flew to Nice, I should just about have time to meet him after his speech before he flew home.

It was great to be traveling abroad again so soon for work. Whilst at SSAFA I had flown to and from the Forces' families' accommodation blocks in Germany, but they were fairly austere trips compared to travelling business class to the south of France.

But it got better. On my arrival at Nice airport, the *FT*'s France correspondent had arranged for me to arrive in Monaco in the best way possible.

"Mr Milner?" said the man in uniform as I left the arrivals hall. "Your helicopter's over here."

It's only a six-minute flight from Nice airport, but if you've never arrived by helicopter into Monte Carlo skimming across the waves, you're in for a treat when you do.

In case all this seemed recklessly extravagant, it got worse. Unbeknownst to us, Sir John had changed his plans, and by the time I'd arrived, he'd gone.

My boss was very apologetic. Would I mind staying in Monte Carlo for 48 hours until my return flight was due? Meanwhile I'd meet Sir John later in London, or in ICI's HQ in Hull.

I would have played roulette in the famous casino, but a dinner jacket and black tie was required for all men to play at a table. But I was able to watch for an hour or so. At my table alone, I reckoned the casino was up £1 million compared to the mugs in black tie.

Saturday, March 7, Drivers

From Monaco back to the bedsit in Muswell Hill, via the 134 bus, hardly the style to which I had all too briefly become accustomed. Still I was in my safe in my new nest.

Unlike Mum, who years earlier when arriving with the three children for the summer holidays in Kaduna, Nigeria, was picked up by the bank's driver. He was to take us to the Excelsior Hotel, where we would stay overnight because Dad was waiting for the keys for the new house, which we would move into the next day.

The Nigerian Airways flight from Heathrow was delayed by six hours, but Dad wasn't worried, knowing the driver would wait for us at the airport. He had dinner in the hotel.

When we cleared customs and baggage reclaim at the airport, the driver, dutifully waiting for us, carried our luggage, loaded the car and took us to the Excelsior. It wasn't until we checked in to find there were only curtains on the rooms of the doors that Mum started to get really worried. We appeared to be in a back street somewhere too, with no streetlights and no phone.

Concern turned to horror when Mum realised that there was a queue of impatient men waiting outside her room. The Excelsior was a brothel in downtown Kaduna. The Excelsior Hotel was on the other side of town in the diplomatic quarter.

London 1987: Have you seen this man: last seen travelling by helicopter to Monte Carlo and the 134 Bus to Muswell Hill?

Back in the room, I helped her drag the bed across the room and propped it up against the door. And there we huddled, my young sister who was a toddler, and my brother who was still a baby, in the semi dark listening to the grunts and moans until the small hours.

Reporting us missing to the police when we hadn't shown up after dinner, Dad's first thought was that we must have been kidnapped. Sometime after midnight, the police went to the driver's house and the mistake was revealed.

History doesn't record what Mum said to Dad when we finally arrived at the correct Excelsior, nor what the bank said to the driver in the morning.

Back in Muswell Hill, the rat had eaten most of the bread in the breadbin. But he was the least of my troubles.

A new lodger had taken up residence in the room next to mine whilst I'd been away. In the kitchen we introduced ourselves, and then tired from the journey back from Monaco I said to Jack I was going to call it a day and get some sleep.

Just after midnight, there was a tap, tap, tap at the door. It was Jack.

"Can I come in?" he asked.

"Are you okay? It's a bit late."

But Jack wasn't to be deterred. By now the whole flat was awake. There were three other bedsits in the flat and the lodgers were all in a grumpy mood. The collective mood seemed to cow Jack into submission and we all went to bed again.

An hour later, there was another tap, tap, tap at the door. It was Jack. "Let me in."

"No. Please, go to sleep."

And that was the last sleep any of us got that night. This went on for another hour, and then Jack went berserk. First punching a hole through the partition wall between our rooms, which grew steadily larger and larger as he kept ripping at the hole.

I dragged the wardrobe over the hole in the hope he'd just give up.

Then he attacked the door of my bedsit. And kept at it.

I managed to muffle the assault by propping my mattress and bed up against the door. But that was all I had by way of furniture. Mercifully, the exertion seemed to tire him out. Then after another hour, he started on the door again.

This time soon after, I was aware of blue lights flashing in the street below and in moments, I heard the police in the corridor outside shouting at Jack to stand back or be tased.

There was a few more moments shouting, then silence.

Cuffed, his hands behind his back, Jack was taken away in the back of a police van.

The police took witness statements from us all in the kitchen. Evidently, Jack had caused trouble each night whilst I'd been away. A rapist on the sex offenders' register, he'd recently left jail and was currently on probation. Now he was back in prison.

I should have done more to listen to him.

Perhaps he'd just wanted someone to talk to?

Monday, March 9, Brillig

Seeing the mess, the landlord agreed to waive my rent for the rest of the month. I didn't want to stay in Muswell Hill anymore.

Jim offered me a floor in the house he rented with his friend Richard, in Pimlico, and I lived behind their settee for the next nine months.

We had lots of fun, lots of parties and were always in *The Tipsy Lintel* (obviously more usually called The Lentil or The Pisshed). One of my pub party pieces that impressed Richard and Jim the first two or three times at least was being able to recite Jabberwocky from *Through the Looking-Glass* by Lewis Carroll:

'Twas brillig, and the slithy toves
Did gyre and gimble in the wabe:
All mimsy were the borogoves,
And the mome raths outgrabe.
"Beware the Jabberwock, my son!
The jaws that bite, the claws that catch!
Beware the Jubjub bird, and shun
The frumious Bandersnatch!"
He took his vorpal sword in hand;
Long time the manxome foe he sought –
So rested he by the Tumtum tree
And stood awhile in thought.

And, as in uffish thought he stood,

The Jabberwock, with eyes of flame,

Came whiffling through the tulgey wood,

And burbled as it came!

One, two! One, two! And through and through

The vorpal blade went snicker-snack!

He left it dead, and with its head

He went galumphing back.

"And hast thou slain the Jabberwock?

Come to my arms, my beamish boy!

O frabjous day! Callooh! Callay!"

He chortled in his joy.

'Twas brillig, and the slithy toves[129]

Did gyre and gimble in the wabe:

All mimsy were the borogoves,

And the mome raths outgrabe.[130]

Tuesday, April 1, Beamish Boy

Unusually, the whole section is called to assemble in Handel Street by 18:00 hrs. This has happened once or twice before but more often than not when our Wednesday training sessions have to be moved, possibly because the staff are away being trained themselves.

Tonight is different. An Intelligence Corps Officer, who doesn't introduce himself, introduces us to a plain clothes officer from Special Branch, who doesn't give us his name either.

The Bulgarian Embassy has called for UK Security Services' assistance to apprehend one of their military attachés who is understood to be seeking asylum to an unknown government, probably Russia.

Each of us are given different instructions, ostensibly fanning out across the south east to potential ports of exit. Ralph and I are to travel on the 19:09 hrs rail

---

[129] 23 March – 31 people are injured when a suspected Provisional Irish Republican Army (IRA) bomb explodes at a British army barracks in Rheindahlen, West Germany. 1 April – MPs vote against the restoration of the death penalty by 342–230.

[130] Selected from *Poem for the Day* (*Book* One) (ISBN 185619499X).

service from Victoria to Portsmouth Harbour and if we see a man fitting this description, or acting particularly suspiciously on the train, call this number.

At Portsmouth Harbour, we get out not having seen anything out of the ordinary but at the station see a man in a coat carrying a briefcase who *might* be our target.

As we follow the man, I'm aware that we too are possibly being followed.

Opposite HMS Warrior, the man enters The Ship and Castle, a nice-looking pub on the quayside.

"Should we go in or call to say we have a suspect?" I mention to Ralph.

"L-l-let's just see if this really is our man. We haven't seen his f-f-f-face yet," said Ralph.

Hanging back a little, so our man can get himself settled down, we go in and order two pints at the bar. Our man gets up from his table and goes to the gents, with his green leather briefcase.

Ralph follows.

Just then the two men, who were of course tracking us, enter and come over to me. One of them is my CO. "Hello, Milner, where's Atkinson?"

"He's followed the suspect into the gents, sir." With that another three men immediately spring from their beers and rush into the gents.

"This may come as a surprise, Olly, but this guy's been under surveillance now for nearly a year. He's one of the IRA's top bomb makers. Unusually, his fingerprints were found all over the detonator that went off in Armagh in January. It's always as if he wanted to get caught."

It seemed as if I was the only person in the pub who didn't know what was going on.

Two policemen in full riot gear with assault rifles led two plain clothes policemen through the pub. They held Ralph tightly, one on either side, his hands cuffed behind his back.

As he passed, he avoided looking me in the eye.

"Tell me this isn't an elaborate April Fool's joke? We're not on an exercise?" I asked the CO.

"He was about to be promoted, so we were doing further background checks. Ralph hasn't ever met his grandmother.

"She was a staunch Republican, a Catholic, who was killed in a shootout with the police before he was born.

"He's been seeking revenge ever since."

Clearly, not that conventional after all.

Ralph's double life still mystifies me. How did he balance his friendship alongside us in the TA with his furtive life as a bomb maker for the IRA? Which side did he like best?

Evidently, his skill as a horologist was eminently useful, and clearly as our trip on his birthday had shown, there were darker sides to his personality. Ralph and I often chatted about Chapman Pincher's 1981 book *Their trade is treachery*. How he must have smiled inside knowing I suspected nothing, and just thought of him as a good, if sometimes shambolic friend.

We've not met again since that day in Portsmouth.

Monday, May 4, Back Up Plans

Fortunately, I had a new focus, a new job to master.

One of my favourite roles at the *Financial Times* was acting as a host to guests interested in seeing the newspaper being printed. This might include executives who were advertising extensively through the paper, or it could just be curious readers.

The only difficulty was that the presses didn't start rolling – in those days – much before 1 am, so not everyone was keen to volunteer to be an East India Docks tour guide.

However, it paid triple time, and that included the journey to and from your home to the presses, so it was a way of earning quite a lot more money if you volunteered once a week.

The only drawback was having to do a full day's work the next day. If I'd also been away on a TA exercise the weekend before, it was all I could do to drag myself into work the next day.

So the next day, after a tour of the presses, travelling up to Hull on the first train north to interview Sir John Harvey Jones was a challenge. But I slept most of the three hours on the train and was soon in the presence of the great man. He was very sorry for having stood me up in Monte Carlo and was utterly charming through the interview.

He'd been chairman of ICI, then one of the UK's biggest companies for five years and was about to retire from leading the business. I was collecting information for a feature about his illustrious career. I didn't take written notes, as I had a small tape recorder but read my pre-prepared questions out to him.

After about an hour, we were winding up. I reached for my tape recorder.

To my horror, I realised I was so sleepy I'd forgotten to switch it on.

"Here, young man," said Sir John, reaching into the drawer at the top of his desk.

"One of the things I've learned in my career is to always have a backup plan. It's one of the threats in a job like mine that you'll be misquoted by the press. So I always tape my media interviews.

"You can have my tape."

Thursday, May 7, Faithful Hounds

As we're running out of pages, there's just space to mention that none of this history occurred in an animal vacuum. Of course the most famous dog in a vacuum – i.e. space – was Laika the Soviet space dog who became the first animal to orbit the Earth. Laika, a stray mongrel from the streets of Moscow, was selected to be the occupant of the Soviet spacecraft Sputnik 2 that was launched into outer space on 3 November 1957, so technically out with this biography. However, dogs who shaped this history deserve more than a mention; firstly, they break your heart. Can you spot the common feature in these lists?

Faithful Hounds List

1. Toby (deceased), short, long, and slightly rude.
2. Cindy (deceased), Nigerian, ran across the road and lost a leg.
3. Bracken (deceased), Mum's Lhasa Apso.
4. Hobbit (deceased), Dad's bearded collie, best dog ever, cuddly and loyal.
5. Saffron (deceased), Mum's second Lhasa Apso.
6. Pepper (deceased), Saffron's best mate, also a Lhasa Apso.
7. Gucci (deceased), Tibetan terrier.
8. Dior (still barking), smiley, Giant Labradoodle, charity fundraiser, cuddly and loyal. Bought behind my back, by which time it was too late to ask for a refund. (Next time can we not get a dog that weighs 32 kg.)

1. Taffeta (deceased), grey, almost purple, Persian.
2. Smudge (deceased), brown and ginger. With a smudge on her forehead.
3. Tinkerbell (deceased), brown Persian, cutie.
4. Tory (deceased), RSPCA rescue. Best cat of all time.
5. Fluffyribbons (deceased), huge ginger Persian.
6. Elgar (deceased), gnarly RSPCA rescue, smelly, sans teeth and one eye. Adorable.
7. Wolfie (Wolfgang Amadeus Mozart) (deceased). Nemesis of Smudge, so sadly rehomed.
8. Einstein (deceased), clever, obviously. Died of cat flu.
9. Hercules (still clawing the furniture), £350 for a ball of fluff. Ninja.
10. Caesar (still shitting just outside the litter tray), 8.5 kg Norwegian Forest Cat.

Indeed, they all cost a small fortune. But much worse, they all become your friends, steal your heart, and then die. Far too soon.

Friday, May 8, Ambushed[131]

A 24-man unit of the British Army Special Air Service (SAS) ambushed eight members of the Provisional Irish Republican Army (IRA) as they mounted an attack on a Royal Ulster Constabulary (RUC) barracks.

All IRA members were killed as well as one civilian.

---

[131] February 11 – British Airways is privatised and listed on the London Stock Exchange.
March 6 – Zeebrugge disaster: Roll-on/roll-off cross-channel ferry MS Herald of Free Enterprise capsizes off Zeebrugge harbour in Belgium; 193 people die.
March 30 – The 59th Academy Awards take place in Los Angeles, with Platoon winning Best Picture.
March 31 – Margaret Thatcher conducts a 45-minute interview on Soviet television.
April 19 – *The Simpsons* cartoon first appears as a series of shorts on The Tracey Ullman Show.

Friday, May 15, Property Ladder

Today, I also bought my first house, 51 Woodhouse Road, Leytonstone in east London, with Jim Roberts and his friend Richard Dawson. One of the advantages of having lived rent free behind the settee was that I'd saved some money.

It's a house on five floors, including the basement and two attic rooms and before long, three of the spare rooms are let out to three other people we work with who are still life-long friends.

I'm a lucky lad. I've travelled abroad. I have an excellent job, with prospects. I'm on the property ladder.

I'm absolutely indebted to all those years at Malsis, Bootham, UWIST and my first jobs for giving me a love of current affairs, journalism, writing, and the stage.

Perhaps I should give drama one last try. How many times did our English teachers tell us to *write what you know*?

Here goes.

Friday, May 22
A play for radio: *Cleopatra's Needle*
By Oliver Milner
[*Scene 1: In a lift at the Financial Times, 1 Southwark Bridge, London SE1 9HL.*]

Narrator: It is the end of the working day, 17:35 to be precise. The lift is descending and Oliver enters at the fourth floor.

[*Doors swish closed. The lift descends and opens at the third floor.*]

Woman 1: Excuse me. Going down?

Oliver: Sure, yes.

[*Swish. The lift descends and opens at the second floor. A slight, dark haired, gypsy-eyed woman enters*].

Woman 2: Hi, hello again.

Oliver: Oh, hello?

Woman 2: You remember? You came down to Classified Ads to give me a fax, last week.

Oliver: I did, and I came back to invite all of you to our house last Sunday. We had a barbeque yesterday. But you didn't come?

[*Swish. The doors open and the three passengers exit the lift and head for the street via the revolving doors. Woman 1 leaves and turns left, for the underground. Woman 2 leaves and turns right towards Southwark Bridge.*]

[*Scene 2: A few paces behind, Oliver catches up with Woman 2.*]

Oliver: I was really hoping you'd come last week. Everyone was pretty well paired off by the end, but it was you I wanted to see.

Woman 2: Really? Well, I didn't get an invitation. I was out when you came into the office to tell us, and no one thought to tell me Editorial wanted to meet Classified, until this morning.

Oliver: I live in Leytonstone. Where are you heading?

Woman 2: Morden. The opposite end of the Tube, from you.

Oliver: Come to my club. It's on the way to the Northern Line, and we can have dinner there.

Woman 2: Really, a club? Aren't you a bit young for a smoking jacket and a cigar?

Oliver: It's the East India Club, I went to a school that's affiliated to it, so it doesn't cost thousands.

Woman 2: It sounds posh, and I don't have a better offer. Why not? Taffeta can wait for her tea.

Oliver: Who's Taffeta?

Woman 2: My Persian. The love of my life. She's a grey, but in some lights she's almost purple.

Oliver: You know, we've been chatting but I'm so sorry, I don't even know your name. I'm Oliver Milner.

Woman 2: I know.

[*They walk on in silence for a few moments. The constant noise of the commuter traffic building behind them.*]

Woman 2: I'm Catherine Hogg.

Oliver: Well, you're very beautiful. Has anyone ever told you, you look like Kate Bush?

Catherine: No. But it's the nicest thing anyone has said in a long time.

[*She takes his arm, and they walk slowly over the bridge together, almost in slow motion compared to the other commuters who are hurrying home, heads down.*]

Oliver: Pardon?

Catherine: I didn't say anything?

Oliver: No, I didn't either.

Catherine: How long have you been at the *FT*?

Oliver: Coming up to six months now.

Catherine: Same.

Oliver: Where are you from? You sound Scottish?

Catherine: I was born in Edinburgh, but my parents are English. So I'm English really. Where are you from?

Oliver: Yorkshire.

Catherine: You don't sound like a Yorkshireman?

Oliver: No one born in Harrogate ever does. It's like the Cheltenham of the North. A bit posh.

Catherine: Do you like it there?

Oliver: I love the Dales and the Moors, hate Harrogate. In my family, it's where people go to give birth or die. Uh oh, have you got a brolly? It's going to pour down.

[Sound of heavy rain falling, and umbrella opening.]

That was lucky, or we'd be soaked. Here, let's get off the bridge it'll be more sheltered on the Embankment.

Catherine: I love the Thames, don't you?

Oliver: Absolutely. I love it here. I couldn't think of anywhere else I'd rather be.

Catherine: Me too. The girls in the office were telling me the three of you boys have bought your place in Leytonstone?

Oliver: Yeah. Just last week. The barbeque was just a way of showing off really. *[They both laugh]*. Look, the rain's stopped we can take the brolly down.

Catherine: Not, yet. It's cosy. And the rain's still dripping off the trees.

[They walk on in silence. Sound of traffic.]

Oliver: Here's Cleopatra's Needle. We're quite close to the club. Still hungry?

Catherine: Dinner would be nice.

Oliver: You know, I feel very comfortable around you.

Catherine: Likewise.

Oliver: What's your favourite colour? Mine's green. I've been saving up for years to buy an MG in British Racing Green.

Can I ask you a question?

Catherine: Please.

Oliver: If I didn't buy my car but bought an emerald engagement ring instead, if I asked you to marry me. What would you say?

Catherine: Yes.

Oliver: Catherine Hogg, will you marry me?

Catherine: Yes!

[*It is 6:15 pm. Fade out.*] [*Scene: 3. Sometime later.*]

Narrator: What happens next is his (and her) story.[132]

---

[132] Saturday, October 29, 1988 – Oliver Milner and Catherine Hogg were married.

[133] Bucket list item #1: Write this book

[134] Get it published. Tick.

Keep on the lookout for *Memory Stick II*. If you liked this, you'll love that.